ROLAND BARTHES

The Rustle of Language

Translated by Richard Howard

University of California Press
Berkeley and Los Angeles

University of California Press
Berkeley and Los Angeles, California
First California Paperback Printing 1989
Published by Agreement with Farrar, Straus and Giroux, Inc.

Printed in the United States of America
Designed by Jack Harrison

6 7 8 9 10

Library of Congress Cataloging-in-Publication Data

Barthes, Roland.
The rustle of language.

Translation of: Le bruissement de la langue.
1. Philology. 2. Discourse analysis. 3. Semiotics.
I. Title.
P49.B3513 1989 401'.41 88-29579
ISBN 978-0-520-06629-8

The paper used in this publication meets the minimum requirements of American National Standard for Information Sciences—Permanence of Paper for Printed Library Materials, ANSI Z39.48–1984. ♾

THE RUSTLE OF LANGUAGE

OTHER BOOKS BY ROLAND BARTHES

A Barthes Reader
Camera Lucida
Critical Essays
The Eiffel Tower and Other Mythologies
Elements of Semiology
The Empire of Signs
The Fashion System
The Grain of the Voice
Image-Music-Text
Incidents
A Lover's Discourse
Michelet
Mythologies
New Critical Essays
On Racine
The Pleasure of the Text
The Responsibility of Forms
Roland Barthes
Sade / Fourier / Loyola
S / Z
Writing Degree Zero

A Note from the French Editor

The number of texts (the notion of counting would have amused him) written by Roland Barthes since 1964 (when *Critical Essays* appeared in France) is remarkable: 152 articles, 55 prefaces and contributions to miscellanies, 11 books. Throughout, as in the texts already published in *New Critical Essays* and *The Responsibility of Forms* (those in the latter devoted to photography, cinema, painting, and music), R.B.'s work was articulated around writing and the sign.

It can be specified on three levels. The semiologist's research, which has oriented several generations: texts still to be collected under the title *The Semiological Adventure*. At the other extreme, a number of writings which no longer interrogate texts but (according to the title R.B. gave one of them) *incidents* of everyday life; these pages will constitute another—brief—book.

Between these two types of textuality, *The Rustle of Language*: almost all the essays in this collection deal with language and with literary writing, or, better still, with the pleasure owed to the text. It is easy enough to recognize, in the course of these pages, the shifts in concept and procedure which over fifteen years lead to this term *text* and perhaps transcend it, with R.B.'s accession to the method of the fragment and to a project of joining writing ever more emphatically to the body.

François Wahl

Contents

4 / FROM HISTORY TO REALITY

5 / THE LOVER OF SIGNS

6 / READINGS

1
FROM SCIENCE TO LITERATURE

From Science to Literature

"Man cannot speak his thought without thinking his speech."
—BONALD

French university faculties possess an official list of the social and human sciences which constitute the object of a recognized instruction, thereby necessarily limiting the specialty of the diplomas they confer: you can be a doctor of aesthetics, of psychology, of sociology—not of heraldry, of semantics, of victimology. Thereby the institution directly determines the nature of human knowledge, imposing its modes of division and of classification, just as a language, by its "obligatory rubrics" (and not only by its exclusions), compels us to think in a certain way. In other words, what defines *science* (the word will henceforth be used, in this text, to refer to all the social and human sciences) is neither its content (which is often ill defined and labile) nor its method (which varies from one science to the next: what do the science of history and that of experimental psychology have in common?), nor its morality (neither seriousness nor rigor is the property of science), nor its mode of communication (science is printed in books, like everything else), but only its *status*, i.e., its social determination: the object of science is any material society deems worthy of being transmitted. In a word, science is what is taught.

Literature has all the secondary characteristics of science, i.e., all the attributes which do not define it. Its contents are precisely those of science: there is certainly not a single scientific matter which has not at some moment been treated by universal literature: the world of the work is a total world, in which all (social, psychological, historical) knowledge takes place, so that for us literature has that grand cosmogonic unity which so delighted the ancient Greeks but which the compartmentalized state of our sciences denies us today. Further, like science, literature is methodical: it has its programs of research, which vary according to schools and periods (like those of science, moreover), its rules of investigation, sometimes even its experimental pretensions. Like science, literature has its morality, a certain way of extracting its rules of procedure from the image it assumes of its being, and consequently of submitting its enterprises to a certain absolute spirit.

One last feature unites science and literature, but this feature is also the one which divides them more certainly than any other difference: both are discourses (which was well expressed by the idea of the ancient *logos*), but science and literature do not assume—do not profess—the language which constitutes them in the same way. For science, language is merely an instrument, which it chooses to make as transparent, as neutral as possible, subjugated to scientific matters (operations, hypotheses, results), which are said to exist outside it and to precede it: on one side and *first of all,* the contents of the scientific message, which are everything; and on the other and *afterwards*, the verbal form entrusted with expressing these contents, which is nothing. It is no coincidence if, since the sixteenth century, the combined rise of empiricism, of rationalism, and of religious evidence (with the Reformation), i.e., of the scientific spirit (in the very broad sense of the term), has been accompanied by a regression of the automy of language, henceforth relegated to the status of "instrument" or of "fine style," whereas in the Middle Ages human culture, as interpreted by the *Septenium*, shared almost equally the secrets of language and those of nature.

For literature, on the contrary—at least for that literature which has issued from classicism and from humanism—language can no longer be the convenient instrument or the sumptuous decor of a social, emotional, or poetic "reality" which preexists it and which it is responsible, in a subsidiary way, for expressing, provided it abides by a few rules of style: no, language is the *being* of literature, its very world: all literature is contained in the act of writing, and no longer in that of "thinking," of "painting," of "recounting," of "feeling." Technically, according to Roman Jakobson's definition, the "poetic" (i.e., the literary) designates that type of message which takes for object its own form, and not its contents. Ethically, it is solely by its passage through language that literature pursues the disturbance of the essential concepts of our culture, "reality" chief among them. Politically, it is by professing (and illustrating) that no language is innocent, it is by employing what might be called an "integral language" that literature is revolutionary. Literature thus is alone today in bearing the entire responsibility for language; for though science needs language, it is not, like literature, *within* language; science is taught, i.e., it makes itself known; literature fulfills more than it transmits itself (only its history is taught). Science speaks itself; literature writes itself; science is led by the voice, literature follows the hand; it is not the same body, and hence the same desire, which is behind the one and the other.

Bearing essentially on a certain way of taking language—in the former case dodged and in the latter assumed—the opposition between science and literature is of particular importance to structuralism. Of course this word, generally imposed from outside, actually overlaps very diverse, sometimes divergent, sometimes even hostile enterprises, and no one can claim the privilege of speaking in its name; the author of these lines makes no such claim; he merely retains the most particular and consequently the most pertinent version of contemporary structuralism, meaning by that name a certain mode of analysis of cultural works, insofar as this mode is inspired by the methods of contemporary linguistics. Thus, itself resulting from a linguistic model, structuralism finds in literature, the work of language, an object much more than affinitary: homogeneous to itself. This coincidence does not exclude a certain embarrassment, even a certain laceration, depending on whether structuralism means to keep the distance of a science in relation to its object, or whether, on the contrary, it is willing to compromise and to spoil the analysis it wields in that infinitude of language of which literature is today the conduit—in a word, depending on whether it seeks to be science or writing.

As science, structuralism "finds itself," one might say, on every level of the literary work. First of all, on the level of contents, or more exactly, on the level of the form of contents, since structuralism seeks to establish the "language" of the stories told, their articulations, their units, the logic which links some to others—in short, the general mythology in which each literary work participates. Next, on the level of the forms of discourse: structuralism, by virtue of its method, pays special attention to classifications, orders, arrangements; its essential object is taxonomy, or the distributive model inevitably established by any human work, institution, or book, for there is no culture without classification; now discourse, or ensemble of words superior to the sentence, has its forms of organization; it too is a classification, and a signifying one; on this point, literary structuralism has a glamorous ancestor, one whose historical role is in general underestimated or discredited for ideological reasons: Rhetoric, grandiose effort of an entire culture to analyze and classify the forms of speech, to render the world of language intelligible. Finally, on the level of words: the sentence has not only a literal or denoted meaning; it is crammed with supplementary significations: since it is at once a cultural reference, a rhetorical model, a deliberate ambiguity of the speech-act, and a simple unit of denotation, the "literary" word has the depth of a space, and this space is the field of structural analysis itself, whose project is much greater than that of the old stylistics, entirely based as it was on an erroneous idea of "expressivity." On all its levels—that of the argument, that of discourse, that of the words—the literary work thereby offers structuralism the image of a structure perfectly homological (present-day investigations tend to prove this) to the structure of language itself; derived from linguistics, structuralism encounters in literature an object which is itself derived from language. Henceforth, it will be understood that structuralism may attempt to found a science of literature, or more exactly a linguistics of discourse, whose object is the "language" of literary forms, apprehended on many levels: a new project, for hitherto literature has been approached "scientifically" only in a very marginal fashion—by the history of works, or of authors, or of schools, or of texts (philology).

New as it may be, this project is nonetheless not satisfactory—or at least not sufficient. It leaves untouched the dilemma I mentioned at the beginning, one that is allegorically suggested by the opposition between science and literature, insofar as literature assumes its own language—under the name of writing—and science avoids it, feigning to regard it as purely instrumental. In a word, structuralism will never be anything but one more "science" (several of these are born every century, some quite ephemeral), if it cannot make its central enterprise the very subversion of scientific language, i.e., cannot "write itself": how can it fail to call into question the very language by which it knows language? Structuralism's logical extension can only be to join literature no longer as "object" of analysis but as activity of writing, to abolish the distinction, born of logic, which makes the work into a language-object and science into a meta-language, and thereby to risk the illusory privilege attached by science to the ownership of a slave language.

It remains therefore for the structuralist to transform himself into a "writer," not in order to profess or to practice "style," but in order to recognize the crucial problems of any speech-act, once it is no longer swathed in the kindly cloud of strictly *realist* illusions which make language the simple medium of thought. This transformation—still rather theoretical, it must be admitted—requires a certain number of clarifications—or acknowledgments. First of all, the relations of subjectivity and objectivity—or, to put it another way, the subject's place in his work—can no longer be conceived as in the palmy days of positivist science. Objectivity and rigor, attributes of the scholar which we still hear so much about, are essentially preparatory virtues, necessary to the work's moment, and as such there is no reason to mistrust them or to abandon them; but these virtues cannot be transferred to discourse, except by a kind of hocus-pocus, a purely metonymic procedure which identifies *precaution* with its discursive effect. Every speech-act supposes its own subject, whether this subject expresses himself in an apparently direct fashion, by saying *I*, or indirect, by designating himself as *he*, or in no fashion at all, by resorting to impersonal turns of speech; what is in question here are purely grammatical stratagems, simply varying how the subject constitutes himself in discourse, i.e., gives himself, theatrically or fantasmatically, to others; hence they all designate forms of the image-repertoire. Of these forms, the most specious is the privative form, precisely the one usually employed in scientific discourse, from which the scholar excludes himself in a concern for objectivity; yet what is excluded is never anything but the "person" (psychological, emotional, biographical), not the subject; moreover, this subject is filled, so to speak, with the very exclusion it so spectacularly imposes upon its person, so that objectivity, on the level of discourse—an inevitable level, we must not forget—is an image-repertoire like any other. In truth, only an integral formalization of scientific discourse (that of the human sciences, of course, for in the case of the other sciences this has already been largely achieved) could spare science the risks of the image-repertoire—unless, of course, it consents to employ this image-repertoire *with full knowledge*, a knowledge which can be achieved only in writing: only writing has occasion to dispel the bad faith attached to every language unaware of its own existence.

Again, only writing—and this is a first approach to its definition—effectuates language in its totality. To resort to scientific discourse as to an instrument of thought is to postulate that a neutral state of language exists, from which would branch off, like so many gaps and ornaments, a certain number of special languages, such as the literary language or the poetic language; this neutral state would be, it is assumed, the code of reference for all the "eccentric" languages which would be only so many sub-codes; by identifying itself with this referential code, basis of all normality, scientific discourse arrogates to itself the very authority which writing must contest; the notion of "writing" implies in effect the idea that language is a vast system of which no single code is privileged—or, one may say, central—and of which the departments are in a relation of "fluctuating hierarchy." Scientific discourse believes it is a superior code; writing seeks to be a total code, including its own forces of destruction. It follows that only writing can break the theological image imposed by science, can reject the paternal terror spread by the abusive "truth" of contents and reasonings, can open to research the complete space of language, with its logical subversions, the mixing of its codes, with its slippages, its dialogues, its parodies; only writing can set in opposition to the savant's assurance—insofar as he "expresses" his science—what Lautréamont called the writer's "modesty."

Last, between science and writing, there is a third margin, which science must reconquer: that of *pleasure*. In a civilization inured by monotheism to the idea of Transgression, where every value is the product of a punishment, this word has an unfortunate resonance: there is something light, trivial, partial about it. Coleridge said: "A poem is that species of composition which is opposed to works by science, by purposing, for its immediate object, pleasure, not truth"—an ambiguous declaration, for if it assumes the "erotic" nature of the poem (of literature), it continues to assign it a special and guarded canton, distinct from the major territory of truth. "Pleasure," however—we admit this more readily nowadays—implies an experience much wider, more significant than the simple satisfaction of "taste." Now, the pleasure of language has never been seriously considered; the old Rhetoric had, in its fashion, some idea of it when it set up a special genre of discourse dedicated to spectacle and to admiration, the *epidictic*; but classical art wrapped the *pleasing* which it claimed as its law (Racine: "The first rule is to please . . .") in all the constraints of the "natural"; only the baroque, a literary experiment which has never been more than tolerated by our societies, at least by French society, dared some exploration of what might be called the Eros of language. Scientific discourse is remote from this; for if it accepted the notion, it would have to renounce all the privileges with which the social institution surrounds it and agree to return to that "literary life" Baudelaire calls, apropos of Poe, "the sole element in which certain *déclassés* can breathe."

Mutation of consciousness, of structure, and of the purposes of scientific discourse—that is what must be demanded today, precisely where the flourishing, constituted human sciences seem to leave less and less room for a literature commonly accused of unreality and inhumanity. But precisely: the role of literature is to *represent* actively to the scientific institution just what it rejects, i.e., the sovereignty of language. And structuralism should be in a good position to provoke this scandal; for, intensely conscious of the linguistic nature of human works, only structuralism today can reopen the problem of the linguistic status of science; having language—all languages—for object, it has very quickly come to define itself as our culture's meta-language. This stage, however, must be transcended, for the opposition of language-objects and their meta-language remains ultimately subject to the paternal model of a science without language. The task facing structural discourse is to make itself entirely homogeneous to its object; this task can be accomplished by only two methods, each as radical as the other: either by an exhaustive formalization, or else by an integral writing. In this second hypothesis (which we are defending here), science will become literature, insofar as literature—subject, moreover, to a growing collapse of traditional genres (poem, narrative, criticism, essay)—is already, has always been, science; for what the human sciences are discovering today, in whatever realm: sociological, psychological, psychiatric, linguistic, etc., literature has always known; the only difference is that literature has not *said* what it knows, it has *written* it. Confronting this integral truth of writing, the "human sciences," belatedly constituted in the wake of bourgeois positivism, appear as the technical alibis our society uses to maintain the fiction of a theological truth, superbly—abusively—disengaged from language.

The Times Literary Supplement, 1967

To Write: An Intransitive Verb?

1. Literature and linguistics

For centuries, Western culture conceived of literature not as we do today, through a study of works, authors, and schools, but through a veritable theory of language. This theory had a name, *Rhetoric*, and it triumphed in the West from Gorgias to the Renaissance, i.e., for over two thousand years. Threatened since the sixteenth century by the advent of modern rationalism, rhetoric was altogether ruined when rationalism was transformed into positivism, at the end of the nineteenth. By then, there was no longer any common zone of reflection between literature and language: literature no longer regarded itself as language, except in the work of a few precursor writers, such as Mallarmé, and linguistics claimed only very limited rights over literature, these being enclosed within a secondary philological discipline of uncertain status: stylistics.

As we know, this situation is changing, and it seems to me that it is in part to take cognizance of this change that our colloquium has been assembled: literature and language are in the process of recognizing each other. The factors of this rapprochement are various and complex; I shall cite the most obvious: on the one hand, the action of certain writers who since Mallarmé have undertaken a radical exploration of writing and who have made their work a search for the total Book, such as Proust and Joyce; on the other, the development of linguistics itself, which henceforth includes within its scope *poetics*, or the order of effects linked to the message and not to its referent. Hence, there exists today a new perspective of reflection—common, I insist, to literature and to linguistics, to the creator and the critic, whose tasks, hitherto absolutely self-contained, are beginning to communicate, perhaps even to converge, at least on the level of the writer, whose action can increasingly be defined as a critique of language. It is in this perspective that I want to indicate by a few brief observations, of a prospective and not conclusive nature, how the activity of writing can today be expressed [*énoncée*] with the help of certain linguistic categories.

2. Language

This new conjunction of literature and linguistics, which I have just mentioned, might provisionally be called, for lack of a better name, *semio-criticism,* since it implies that writing is a system of signs. Now, semio-criticism cannot be identified with stylistics, even in a new form, or in any case, stylistics is far from exhausting it. It involves a perspective of an altogether different scope, whose object cannot be constituted by simple accidents of form, but by the very relations between the *scriptor* and language. This perspective does not imply a lack of interest in language, but, on the contrary, a continual return to the "truths," however provisional, of linguistic anthropology. Certain of these truths still have a power of provocation, in respect to a certain current idea of literature and of language, and for this reason, we must not fail to consider them.

1. One of the teachings of contemporary linguistics is that there is no archaic language, or that, at least, there is no relation between a language's simplicity and its age: ancient languages can be as complete and as complex as the recent ones; there is no "progressive" history of languages. Hence, when we try to recognize in modern writing certain fundamental categories of language, we make no claim to reveal a certain archaism of the "psyche"; we are not saying that the writer harks back to the origin of language, but that language is for him the origin.

2. A second principle, especially important with regard to literature, is that language cannot be considered as a simple

instrument—utilitarian or decorative—of thought. Man does not exist prior to language, either as a species or as an individual. We never encounter a state where man is separated from language, which he then elaborates in order to "express" what is happening within him: it is language which teaches the definition of man, not the contrary.

3. Moreover, from a methodological view, linguistics accustoms us to a new type of objectivity. The objectivity hitherto required in the human sciences is an objectivity of the given, which must be accepted totally. Linguistics suggests, on the one hand, that we distinguish levels of analysis and describe the distinctive elements of each of these levels, in short, that we establish the distinctness of the fact and not the fact itself; and on the other, it asks us to recognize that, unlike physical and biological facts, cultural facts are twofold, that they refer to something else: as Benveniste has observed, it is the discovery of language's "duplicity" which gives Saussure's reflection all its value.

4. These few preliminaries are contained in a final proposition which justifies all semio-critical research. Culture increasingly appears to us as a general system of symbols, governed by the same operations: there is a unity of the symbolic field, and culture, in all its aspects, is a language. Hence, it is possible today to foresee the constitution of a unique science of culture, which will certainly be based on various disciplines, but all devoted to analyzing, at different levels of description, culture as language. Semio-criticism will obviously be only a part of this science, which will always remain a discourse on culture. This unity of the human symbolic field authorizes us to elaborate a postulate which I shall call a postulate of homology: the structure of the sentence, object of linguistics, can be recognized homologically in the structure of works: discourse is not only a sum of sentences, it is, itself, one great sentence. It is in terms of this working hypothesis that I would like to confront certain categories of language with the writer's situation in relation to his writing. I am not concealing the fact that this confrontation

does not have a demonstrative force and that for the moment its value remains essentially metaphorical: but perhaps, too, in the order of objects which concerns us, metaphor has—more than we suppose—a methodological existence and a heuristic force.

3. Temporality

As we know, there is a linguistic temporality, equally different from physical time and from what Benveniste calls "chronicle" time, or the time of calendars and computations. This linguistic time receives extremely various contours and expressions in various languages—for example, certain languages like Chinook employ several pasts, including a mythic one—but one thing seems certain: the generating center of linguistic time is always the present of the speech-act [*énonciation*]. This leads us to ask whether there is, homologous to linguistic time, a time specific to discourse. On this point, Benveniste offers an initial clarification: in many languages, specifically Indo-European ones, the system is twofold: (1) a first system, or system of discourse proper, adapted to the temporality of the speaker, whose speech-act is always the point of origin; (2) a second system, or system of history, of narrative, appropriate to the recounting of past events, without the speaker's intervention and consequently deprived of present and future (except periphrastically), its specific tense the aorist (or its equivalents, like the French *passé simple*), precisely the one tense missing from the system of discourse. The existence of this a-personal system does not contradict the essentially logocentric nature of linguistic time we have just asserted: the second system merely lacks the characteristics of the first: one is linked to the other by the opposition *marked / unmarked*: consequently, they participate in the same field of pertinence.

The distinction between the two systems is not at all the same as the one traditionally made between objective discourse and subjective discourse, for we cannot identify the relation of the speaker and the referent on one hand with the relation of this same speaker and the speech-act on the other, and it is only this second relation which determines the temporal system of the discourse. These linguistic phenomena were difficult to perceive so long as literature was regarded as the docile and "transparent" expression of either so-called objective (or chronicle) time, or of psychological subjectivity, i.e., so long as literature was placed within a totalitarian ideology of the referent. Today, however, literature discovers in the unfolding of discourse what I call certain fundamental subtleties: for example, what is told in the aorist does not appear immersed in the past, in "what has taken place," but only in the non-personal, which is neither history nor science nor even the *one* of so-called anonymous writing, for what prevails in this *one* is the indefinite, not the absence of person: *one* is marked; *he*, paradoxically, is not. At the other extreme of the experience of discourse, the writer today, it seems to me, can no longer be content to express his own present according to a lyrical project: he must learn to distinguish the speaker's present, which remains grounded in psychological plenitude, from the present of the locution, which is as flexible as that locution and in which event and writing are absolutely coincidental. Thus literature, at least in its explorations, is taking the same path as linguistics when, with Gustave Guillaume, it concerns itself with operative time, or the time of the speech-act itself.

4. Person

This leads to a second grammatical category, quite as important in linguistics as in literature: that of *person*. First of all, we are reminded by the linguists that person (in the grammatical sense of the term) seems to be universal, linked to the very anthropology of language. Every language, as Benveniste has shown, organizes person into two oppositions: a correlation of personality, which sets person (*I* or *you*) in opposition to the non-person (*he* or *it*), sign of what is absent, of absence itself; and, within this first great opposition, a correlation of subjectivity sets two persons in opposition, the *I* and the *non-I* (i.e., *you*). For our purposes, we must make three oppositions, following Benveniste's lead. First of all, the polarity of persons, a basic condition of language, is nonetheless very special, for this polarity involves neither equality nor symmetry: *ego* always has a position of transcendence with regard to *you*, *I* being interior to what is stated and *you* remaining exterior to it; and yet *I* and *you* are reversible, *I* can always become *you*, and vice versa; this is not the case for the non-person (*he* or *it*), which can never reverse itself into person or vice versa. Second, the linguistic *I* can and must be defined in an entirely a-psychological fashion: *I* is nothing but "the person who utters the present instance of discourse containing the linguistic instance *I*" (Benveniste). Last, the non-person never reflects the instance of discourse, being situated outside of it; we must give its full weight to Benveniste's recommendation that *he* or *it* is not to be represented as a more or less diminished or distanced person: *he* or *it* is absolutely non-person, marked by the absence of what specifically (i.e., linguistically) constitutes *I* and *you*.

From this linguistic explanation we shall draw several suggestions for an analysis of literary discourse. First of all, we note that whatever the varied and often cunning forms (marks) person may take when we proceed from sentence to discourse, just as in the case of temporality, the work's discourse is subject to a double system, that of person and that of non-person. What produces an illusion, here, is that our classical discourse (in the broad sense) is a mixed one, which frequently alternates—at a rapid rate (for example, within the same sentence)—the personal speech-act and the a-personal one, by a complex interplay of pronouns and descriptive verbs. This mixed system of person and non-person produces an ambiguous consciousness which manages to keep the personal quality of what is stated, yet periodically breaking off the speaker's participation in the statement.

Second, if we return to the linguistic definition of the first person (*I* is the one who says *I* in the present instance of discourse), we may better understand the effort of certain writers today (I am thinking of Sollers's *Drame*) when they try to distinguish, on the level of the narrative itself, psychological person from the author of the writing: contrary to the current illusion of autobiographies and traditional novels, the subject of the speech-act can never be the same as the one who acted yesterday: the *I* of the discourse can no longer be the site where a previously stored-up person is innocently restored. Absolute recourse to the instance of discourse in order to determine person, which with Damourette and Pichon we might call *nyn-egocentrism* (consider the exemplary beginning of Robbe-Grillet's novel *In the Labyrinth*: "I am alone here now")—this recourse, imperfect as its practice may still be, thus seems a weapon against the general bad faith of a discourse which makes or would make literary form merely the expression of an interiority constituted previous to and outside of language.

Last, let us recall this detail of linguistic analysis: in the process of communication, the course of the *I* is not homogenous: when I liberate the sign *I,* I refer to myself insofar as I am speaking, and here there is an act which is always new, even if repeated, an act whose "meaning" is always unprecedented; but upon reaching its destination, this *I* is received by my interlocutor as a stable sign, product of a complete code, whose contents are recurrent. In other words, the *I* of the one who writes *I* is not the same as the *I* which is read by *you.* This basic dissymmetry of language, explained by Jespersen and Jakobson by the notion of *shifter* or an overlapping of code and message, is finally beginning to disturb literature by showing it that intersubjectivity, or rather interlocution, cannot be accomplished simply by a pious wish about the merits of "dialogue," but only by a deep, patient, and often circuitous descent into the labyrinth of meaning.

5. Diathesis

There remains to be discussed one last grammatical notion which may illuminate the activity of writing at its very center, since it concerns the verb *to write* itself. It would be interesting to know at what moment this verb began to be used intransitively, the writer no longer being the one who writes something, but the one who writes—absolutely: this shift is certainly the sign of an important change in mentality. But does it really involve intransivity? No writer, of whatever period, can be unaware that he always writes something; we might even say that it is paradoxically at the moment when *to write* seems to become intransitive that its object, under the name *book* or *text*, assumes a special importance. Hence, it is not, at least primarily, on the side of intransivity that we must look for the definition of the modern verb *to write*. Another linguistic notion may give us the key: that of diathesis or, as the grammar books put it, "voice" (active, passive, middle). Diathesis designates the way in which the subject of the verb is affected by the action; this is obvious for the passive; and yet linguists tell us that, in Indo-European at least, the diathetical opposition is not between active and passive but between active and middle. According to the classic example given by Meillet and Benveniste, the verb *to sacrifice* (ritually) is active if the priest sacrifices the victim in my place and for me, and it is middle voice if, taking the knife from the priest's hands, I make the sacrifice for my own sake; in the case of the active voice, the action is performed outside the subject, for although the priest makes the sacrifice, he is not affected by it; in the case of the middle voice, on the contrary, by acting, the subject affects himself, he always remains inside the action, even if that action involves an object. Hence, the middle voice does not exclude transitivity. Thus defined, the middle voice corresponds exactly to the modern state of the verb *to write*: to write is today to make oneself the center of the action of speech, it is to effect writing by affecting oneself, to make action and affection coincide, to leave the *scriptor* inside the writing—not as a psychological subject (the Indo-European priest could perfectly well be overflowing with subjectivity while actively sacrificing for his client), but as agent of the action. We can even take the diathetic analysis of the verb *to write* a little further. We know that in French certain verbs have an active meaning in their simple form (*aller*—to go, *arriver*—to arrive, *rentrer*—to return, *sortir*—to leave) but take the passive auxiliary (*être*—to be) in forming the perfect tense (*je suis allé, je suis arrivé*); in order to explain this bifurcation peculiar to the middle voice, Guillaume distinguishes between what he calls a *diriment* perfect (with the auxiliary *avoir*—to have), which supposes an interruption of the action due to the speaker's initiative (*je marche, je m'arrête de marcher, j'ai marché*—I walk, I stop walking, I have walked), and an *integrant* perfect (with the auxiliary *être*—to be), peculiar to the verbs which designate a semantic whole, which cannot be delivered by the subject's simple initiative (*je suis sorti, il est mort*—I have left, he has died—do not refer to a *diriment* interruption of leaving or dying). *To write* is traditionally an active verb, whose past is *diriment*; but in our literature the verb is changing status (if not form): *to write* is becoming a middle verb with an *integrant* past, precisely insofar as *to write* is becoming an indivisible semantic whole; so that the true past, the "right" past of this new verb is not *j'ai écrit* but *je suis écrit*—as one says *je suis né, il est mort,* etc., expressions in which, despite the verb *être,* there is no notion of the passive, since without forcing matters we cannot transform *je suis écrit*—I am written—into *on m'a écrit*—someone has written me.

Thus, in the middle voice of *to write,* the distance between *scriptor* and language diminishes asymptotically. We could even say that it is the writings of subjectivity, such as romantic writing, which are active, for in them the agent is not interior but *anterior* to the process of writing: here the one who writes does not write for himself, but as if by proxy, for an exterior and antecedent person (even if both bear the same name), while, in the modern verb of middle voice *to write,* the subject is constituted as immediately contemporary with the writing, being effected and affected by it: this is the exemplary case of the Proustian narrator, who exists only by writing, despite the reference to a pseudo-memory.

6. The instance of discourse

These observations suggest that the central problem of modern writing exactly coincides with what we might call the problematics of the verb in linguistics: just as temporality, person, and diathesis define the positional field of the subject, so modern literature is trying, by various experiments, to establish a new position for the agent of writing in writing itself. The meaning or the goal of this effort is to substitute the instance of discourse for the instance of reality (or of the referent), that mythic alibi which has dominated—still dominates—the idea of literature. The field of the writer is only writing itself, not as pure "form," conceived by an aesthetic of art for art's sake, but much more radically as the only possible space of *the one who writes.*

It seems to me necessary to remind those who accuse such investigations of solipsism, formalism, or scientism that by returning to the fundamental categories of language, such as person, tense, and voice, we place ourselves at the heart of a problematics of interlocution, for such categories are precisely the ones where we may examine the relations of *I* and of what is deprived of the mark of *I*. Inasmuch as person, tense, and voice (so properly named) imply these remarkable linguistic beings known as shifters, they compel us to conceive language and discourse no longer in terms of an instrumental and consequently reified nomenclature, but as the very exercise of discourse: for example, the pronoun, which is doubtless the most dizzying of the shifters, belongs structurally (I insist) to discourse; this is, one might say, its scandal, and it is on this scandal that we must work today, in linguistics and in literature; we are trying to sound the depths of the "pact of speech" which unites the writer and the other, so that each moment of discourse is both absolutely new and absolutely understood. We can even, with a certain temerity, give this research a historical dimension. We know that the medieval *Septenium*, in its grandiose classification of the universe, prescribed two great sites of exploration: on the one hand the secrets of nature (*quadrivium*), on the other the secrets of discourse (*trivium: grammatica, rhetorica, dialectica*); this opposition was lost between the end of the Middle Ages and our own time, language being considered only as an instrument in the service of either reason or the heart. Today, however, something of that ancient opposition is reviving: to the exploration of the cosmos corresponds, once again, the exploration of language, conducted by linguistics, psychoanalysis, and literature. For literature itself is a science—no longer of the "human heart," but of human discourse; its investigation, however, is no longer addressed to the secondary forms and figures which constituted the object of rhetoric, but to the fundamental categories of language: just as, in our Western culture, grammar was born only long after rhetoric, so it is only after having made its way for centuries through *le beau littéraire* that literature can raise the fundamental problems of language without which it would not exist.

Colloquium at Johns Hopkins University, 1966

Reflections on a Manual

I should like to offer some simple, even simplistic observations suggested by a recent reading or rereading of a manual of French literary history. While rereading or reading this manual, which closely resembles those I remember from the *lycée*, I asked myself this question: Can literature be anything else for us than a childhood memory? I mean, what is it that continues, what is it that persists, what is it that speaks of literature after the *lycée*?

If we were to make an objective inventory, we would answer that what abides (from literature) in adult, current life is: certain crossword puzzles, some televised quiz shows, the posters of the centenaries of some writer's birth, some writer's death, a few paperback titles, some critical allusions in the newspaper we're reading for altogether different reasons—looking for something altogether different from these allusions to literature. All of which has a lot to do, I believe, with the fact that we French have always been accustomed to identify literature with the history of literature. The history of literature is an essentially academic object which in fact exists only because it is taught; so that the title of our conference, "The Teaching of Literature," is for me almost tautological. Literature is what is taught, period. It is an object of teaching. It is generally agreed that at least in France no major synthesis—say of the Hegelian type—has been produced on the history of our literature. If this French literature is a childhood memory—and that is how I am taking it—I should like to see—this will be the object of a very limited and quite banal inventory—what elements this memory consists of.

First of all, this memory consists of certain objects which recur, which continually repeat themselves, and which we might almost call monemes of the meta-literary language or the language of literary history; these objects are of course the authors, the schools, the movements, the genres, and the centuries. And then, around these objects, there is a certain—actually very limited—number of features or predicates which find a place and combine with each other. If we were to read the manuals of literary history, we should have no difficulty in determining the paradigmatics, the elementary structure of these features, which appears to be that of couples in opposition with an occasional mixed term; this is an extremely simple structure: for instance, there is the archetypal paradigm of our whole literature, *romanticism-classicism* (though French romanticism, on the international scale, seems a relatively poor thing), occasionally amplified into *romanticism-realism-symbolism* (for the nineteenth century). As you know, the law of combinative operations permits, with very few elements, the immediate production of an apparent proliferation: by applying certain of these features to certain of the objects I have mentioned, we produce certain individualities, or certain literary individuals. This is how the manuals always present the centuries themselves: in a paradigmatic fashion. Actually, it's odd how a century comes to have a kind of individual existence, but it is precisely our childhood memories which accustom us to make the centuries into individuals of a sort. The four great centuries of our literature are strongly individuated by our literary history: the sixteenth is overflowing life; the seventeenth is unity; the eighteenth is movement; and the nineteenth is complexity.

Other features are added which again can very nicely be set in opposition, paradigmatized. Here is a random sampling of these oppositions, these predicates which are fastened onto literary objects: there is "exuberant" opposed to "restrained"; there is "lofty art" or "deliberate obscurity" opposed to "expansiveness"; "rhetorical coldness" to "sensibility"—which overlaps the familiar romantic paradigm of *cold* and *warm*—or again the opposition between "sources" and "originality," between "labor" and "inspiration." What we have here are the rudiments of a little roster of this mythology of our literary history, one which would begin by establishing those mythic paradigms of which French textbooks have always been so fond, perhaps because this was a good method of memorization or perhaps, on the contrary, because a mental structure that functions by contraries has a high ideological yield (we need an ideological analysis to tell us). It is this same opposition that we encounter, for instance, between *Condé* and *Turenne*, the great archetypes of two French temperaments: if you put them together in a single writer (Jakobson has taught that the poetic act consists in extending a paradigm into a syntagm), you produce an author who reconciles, for example, "formal art and extreme sensibility" or who manifests "a witty nature concealing a tragic sense" (such as Villon). What I am saying here is simply the sketch of what we might imagine as a kind of little *grammar* of our literature, a grammar which would produce stereotyped individuations: authors, movements, schools.

Second element of this memory: French literary history consists of dismissals we need to explore. There is—as we know, as has already been said—a whole *other* history which would be precisely the history of such dismissals. What are these "censorships"? First of all, the social classes; the social structure which underlies this literature is rarely found in manuals of literary history, we must turn to more emancipated, more highly developed critical works in order to find it; when we read these manuals, references to class structure may sometimes exist, but only in passing and as aesthetic oppositions. Actually, what the manual sets in opposition are class *atmospheres*, not realities; when the aristocratic "spirit" is opposed to the bourgeois and folk spirit, at least for previous centuries, it is the distinction of a refined taste which is opposed to good humor and realism. We also find, even in recent textbooks, sentences of this sort: "A plebeian, Diderot lacks tact and delicacy; he commits faults of taste which affect the sentiments themselves with a certain vulgarity . . ." Thus, class exists, but as an aesthetic or ethical atmosphere; on the level of the instruments of knowledge, these manuals betray the flagrant absence of any economics or sociology of our literature. The second "censorship" would obviously be that of sexuality, but I shall not discuss it here, because it overlaps the much more general censorship which our entire society brings to bear upon sex. A third "censorship"—for my part, I regard it as a censorship—would be that of the very concept of literature, which is never defined as a concept, literature in these manuals being an object which is self-understood and never interrogated in order to define, if not its being, at least its social, symbolic, or anthropological functions; whereas in fact we might reverse this omission and say—in any case, I personally should be glad to say—that the history of literature ought to be conceived as a history of the idea of literature, and that such a history does not seem to exist, for the moment. Finally, a fourth "censorship," and not the least important, bears on "languages," as always. A language is a much more important object of censorship, perhaps, than all the rest. By which I mean a manifest censorship, the kind these manuals bring to bear on states of language remote from the classical norm. This is a well-known phenomenon: there is a vast censorship of preciosity, which notably in the seventeenth century is described as a sort of classical inferno: every French person, through the teaching of our school system, has the same judgment and the same view of preciosity as Boileau, Molière, or La Bruyère. This one-way indictment is repeated for centuries—and this despite what a real history of literature would readily make clear, i.e., the enormous and persistent success of preciosity throughout the seventeenth century, since even in 1663 a voluminous collection of *poésies galantes* by the Comtesse de Suze went into fifteen printings. Hence, there is a point to clarify here—a point of censorship. There is also the case of sixteenth-century French, what is called Middle French, which is rejected from our language, on the pretext that it consists of ridiculous novelties, Italianisms, jargon, baroque audacities, etc., without ever raising the question of what it is we have lost today in the great traumatism of classical purity. We have lost not only means of expression, as they are called, but mental structures as well, for language is a mental structure. Here again, there is perhaps an indictment to be brought, one which should obviously begin with a condemnation of "classico-centrism," which in my opinion still marks our whole literature, specifically in regard to language. Once again, we must include these problems of language in the problems of literature; we must raise the great questions: When does a language begin? What does *to begin* mean for a language? When does a genre begin? What does it mean when we are told of the first French novel, for instance? It is evident that there is always, behind the classical idea of the language, a political idea: the language's very being, i.e., its perfection and even its name, is linked to a culmination of power: the Latin classic is Latin or Roman power; the French classic is monarchic power. This is why it must be said that, in our teaching, we cultivate, or we promote, what I should call the paternal language and not the mother tongue—particularly since, let me say in passing, we do not know what spoken French is; we know what written French is because there are grammars of good usage; but no one knows what spoken French is; and in order to know, we should have to begin by escaping our classico-centrism.

Third element of this childhood memory: this memory is centered, and its center is—as I have just said—classicism. This classico-centrism seems anachronistic to us; yet we are still living with it. Even now, we pass doctoral theses in the Salle Louis-Liard, at the Sorbonne, and we must inventory the portraits in that hall; they are the divinities which preside over French knowledge in its entirety: Corneille, Molière, Pascal, Bossuet, Descartes, Racine under the protection—this is an admission—of Richelieu. This classico-centrism goes far, then, since it always identifies literature—and this even in the discussions of the manuals—with the king. Literature *is* the monarchy, and invincibly the academic image of literature is constructed around the name of certain kings: Louis XIV, of course, but also François I, St. Louis, so that, ultimately, we are presented with a kind of shiny image in which king and literature reflect each other. There is also, in this centered structure of our literary history, a *national* identification; these manuals of history perpetually advance what are called typically French values or typically French temperaments; we are told, for instance, that Joinville is typically French; what is French—General de Gaulle has provided one definition—is what is *"regular, normal, national."* This is obviously the range of our literature's norms and values. From the moment that this history of our literature has a center, it is obvious that it is constructed in relation to this center; what comes after or before in the structure is presented as harbinger or desertion. What is before classicism heralds classicism—Montaigne is a precursor of the classics; what comes after classicism revives or betrays it.

A last remark: the childhood memory I invoke borrows its permanent structuration, down through these centuries, from a grid which is no longer a rhetorical grid in our teaching, for that was abandoned around the middle of the nineteenth century (as Gérard Genette has shown in a splendid article on the problem); it is now a psychological grid. All academic judgments rest on the conception of form as the subject's "expression." Personality is translated into style: this postulate nourishes all judgments and all analyses concerning authors; whence, ultimately, the key value, the one most often invoked to judge authors: *sincerity*. For instance, du Bellay will be praised for having produced certain sincere and personal cries; Ronsard had a sincere and profound Catholic faith; Villon, a cry from the heart, etc.

These remarks are simplistic, and I am uncertain as to their value in a discussion, but I should like to conclude them with a last observation. To my sense, there is a profound and irreducible antinomy between literature as practice and literature as teaching. This antinomy is serious because it is attached to what is perhaps the most serious problem we face today, the problem of the transmission of knowledge; this is doubtless, now, the fundamental problem of alienation, for if the great structures of economic alienation have been more or less revealed, the structures of the alienation of knowledge have not; I believe that in this regard a political conceptual apparatus is not enough and that there must be, precisely, one of psychoanalytic analysis.

Hence, it is for this that we must work, and this will have many subsequent repercussions on literature and on what can be done with it in teaching, supposing that literature can subsist in teaching, that it is compatible with teaching.

Meanwhile, we can indicate certain points of provisional correction; within a teaching system which retains literature on its program, I see three immediate ones. The first would be to reverse classico-centrism and to "do" literary history *backwards*: instead of envisioning the history of literature from a pseudo-genetic point of view, we should make *ourselves* the center of this history, and if we really want to "do" literary history, organize this history starting from the great modern break; thus, past literature would be dealt with through present-day disciplines, and even in present-day language: we should no longer see first-year *lycée* students obliged to study a sixteenth century whose language they scarcely understand, on the pretext that it comes *before* the seventeenth century, itself beset by religious disputes unrelated to their present situation. Second principle: to substitute *text* for author, school, and movement. The text, in our schools, is treated as an object of explication, but an explication of the text is itself always attached to a history of literature; the text must be treated not as a sacred object (object of a philology), but essentially as a space of language, as the site of an infinite number of digressions, thereby tracing, from a certain number of texts, a certain number of codes of knowledge invested in them. Finally, a third principle: at every opportunity and at every moment to develop the polysemic reading of the text, to recognize finally the rights of polysemy, to construct a sort of polysemic criticism, to open the text to symbolism. This would produce, I believe, a considerable decompression in the teaching of our literature—not, I repeat, as teaching is practiced—that depends on the teachers—but as it seems to me to be codified still.

Colloquium at the Centre culturel
international de Cerisy-la-Salle, 1969

Writing Reading

Has it never happened, as you were reading a book, that you kept stopping as you read, not because you weren't interested, but because you were: because of a flow of ideas, stimuli, associations? In a word, haven't you ever happened *to read while looking up from your book?*

It is such reading, at once insolent in that it interrupts the text, and smitten in that it keeps returning to it and feeding on it, which I tried to describe. In order to write it, in order for my reading to become in its turn the object of a new reading (that of the readers of *S/Z*), I obviously had to try to systematize all those moments when one *looks up*. In other words, to interrogate my own reading was to try to grasp the *form* of all readings (form: sole site of science), or again: to devise a theory of reading.

I therefore took a short text (this was essential to the detailed scope of the enterprise), Balzac's *Sarrasine*, a little-known tale (but isn't Balzac defined precisely as Inexhaustible, the author no one ever reads all of, except by some exegetic vocation?), and I kept *stopping* as I read this text. Criticism ordinarily functions (this is not a reproach) either by microscope (patiently illuminating the work's philological, autobiographical, or psychological details) or by telescope (scrutinizing the great historical space surrounding the author). I denied myself these two instruments: I spoke neither of Balzac nor of his time, I explored neither the psychology of his characters nor the thematics of the text nor the sociology of the anecdote. Recalling the camera's first feats in decomposing a horse's trot, I too attempted to "film" the reading of *Sarrasine* in slow motion: the result, I suspect, is neither quite an analysis (I have not tried to grasp the *secret* of this strange text) nor quite an image (I don't think I have projected myself into my reading; or if I have, it is from an unconscious site which falls far short of "myself"). Then what is *S/Z*? Simply a text, that text which we write in our head *when we look up*.

Such a text, which we should be able to call by a single word, text-as-reading, is little known because for centuries we have been overly interested in the author and insufficiently in the reader; most critical theories try to explain why the author has written his work, according to which pulsions, which constraints, which limits . . . This exorbitant privilege granted to the site the work comes from (person or Story), this censorship applied to the site it seeks and where it is dispersed (reading) determine a very special (though an old) economy: the author is regarded as the eternal owner of his work, and the rest of us, his readers, as simple usufructuaries. This economy obviously implies a theme of *authority*: the author, it is believed, has certain rights over the reader, he constrains him to a certain *meaning* of the work, and this meaning is of course the right one, the real meaning: whence a critical morality of the right meaning (and of its defect, "misreading"): we try to establish *what the author meant,* and not at all *what the reader understands.*

Though certain authors have themselves notified us that we are free to read their text as we choose and that they are not really interested in our choice (Valéry), we still find it hard to perceive how the logic of reading differs from the rules of composition. These, inherited from rhetoric, are still taken as referring to a deductive, i.e., rational model: as in the case of the syllogism, it is a matter of compelling the reader to a meaning or an issue: composition *channels*; reading, on the contrary (that text we write in ourselves when we read), *disperses,* disseminates; or at least, dealing with a story (like that of the sculptor Sarrasine), we see clearly that a certain constraint of our progress (of "suspense") constantly struggles within us against the text's explosive force, its digressive energy: with the logic of reason (which makes this story readable) mingles a logic of the symbol. This latter logic is not deductive but associative: it associates with the material text (with each of its sentences) *other* ideas, *other* images, *other* significations. "The text, only the text," we are told, but "only the text" does not exist: there is *immediately* in this tale, this novel, this poem I am reading, a supplement of meaning for which neither dictionary nor grammar can account. It is this supplement whose space I wanted to explore in writing my reading of Balzac's *Sarrasine.*

I have not reconstituted a reader (you or myself) but reading. I mean that every reading derives from trans-individual forms: the associations engendered by the letter (but where is that letter?) are never, whatever we do, anarchic; they are always caught up (sampled and inserted) by certain codes, certain languages, certain lists of stereotypes. The most subjective reading imaginable is never anything but a game played according to certain rules. Where do these rules come from? Certainly not from the author, who does nothing but apply them in his own way (this can be inspired, as in Balzac's case); visible apart from him, these rules come from an age-old logic of narrative, from a symbolic form which constitutes us even before we are born—in a word, from that vast cultural space through which our person (whether author or reader) is only one passage. To open the text, to posit the system of its reading, is therefore not only to ask and to show that it can be interpreted freely; it is especially, and much more radically, to gain acknowledgment that there is no objective or subjective truth of reading, but only a *ludic* truth; again, "game" must not be understood here as a distraction, but as a piece of work—from which, however, all labor has evaporated: to read is to make our *body* work (psychoanalysis has taught us that this body greatly exceeds our memory and our consciousness) at the invitation of the text's signs, of all the languages which traverse it and form something like the shimmering depth of the sentence.

I can easily imagine readable narrative (the one we can read without declaring it "unreadable": who does not understand Balzac?). As one of those articulated lay figures that painters use (or used to use) in order to "catch" the various postures of the human body; reading, we too imprint on the text a certain posture, and it is for this reason that it is alive; but this posture, which is our invention, is possible only because there is a governed relation among the elements of the text, in short a *proportion*: I have tried to analyze that proportion, to describe the topological disposition which gives the reading of a classical text both its contour and its freedom.

Le Figaro littéraire, 1970

On Reading

I should like, first of all, to thank the Writing Conference of Luchon for welcoming me here. Many things unite us, beginning with that shared question which each of us asks from his own position: *What is reading? How does one read? Why does one read?* One thing, however, separates us, which I shall not attempt to disguise: I have, for a long while, ceased to engage in any pedagogical practice: school, *lycée,* and college are today unknown to me, and my own teaching practice—which counts for a great deal in my life—at the Ecole des Hautes Etudes, is very marginal, very anomic, even within university teaching. Now, since this is a congress, it seems to me that each of us should make his own voice heard—the voice of his practice; hence, I shall not compel myself to join, to mimic, a pedagogical competence which is not my own: I shall abide by a particular reading (as any reading is?)—the reading of the subject I am, whom I believe myself to be.

I am, with regard to reading, in a great doctrinal confusion: as for a doctrine of reading, I have none; on the other hand, a doctrine of writing is gradually taking shape. This confusion sometimes goes so far as to become a doubt: I do not even know if one must have a *doctrine* of reading; I do not know if reading is not, constitutively, a plural field of scattered practices, of irreducible effects, and if, consequently, the reading of reading, meta-reading, is not itself merely a burst of ideas, of fears, of desires, of delights, of oppressions about which we should speak in fits and starts, blow by blow, in the plural image of the many and various workshops which constitute this congress.

I shall not attempt to reduce this confusion (moreover, I have no means of doing so), but only to situate it, to comprehend the *excess* of which the notion of reading is evidently the object in myself. Where to start? Well, perhaps with what has permitted modern linguistics to get under way: with the notion of *pertinence*.

1. Pertinence

Pertinence is—or at least was—in linguistics the point of view from which one chooses to consider, to question, to analyze an ensemble as heteroclite, as disparate as language: it was only when he had made up his mind to regard language from the point of view of meaning, and from that point of view alone, that Saussure stopped fumbling, left panic behind, and was able to establish a new linguistics; it was by deciding to consider sounds alone within the pertinence of meaning alone that Trubetskoy and Jakobson launched the development of phonology; it was by consenting, at the expense of many other possible considerations, to see in hundreds of folk tales only situations and stable, recurrent roles—in short, forms—that Propp founded the structural analysis of narrative.

If, then, we could determine a *pertinence* within which to interrogate reading, we might hope to develop, gradually, a linguistics, a semiology, or simply an analysis of reading—from *anagnosis*: an anagnosology: why not?

Unfortunately, reading has not yet encountered its Propp or its Saussure; that desired pertinence, image of the scholar's alleviation, has not been found—at least not yet: the old pertinences do not suit reading, or at least reading overflows them.

1. In the field of reading, there is no pertinence of objects: the verb *to read*, apparently much more transitive than the verb *to speak*, can be saturated, catalyzed by a thousand complements of objects: I read texts, images, cities, faces, gestures, scenes, etc. These objects are so varied that I cannot unify them within any substantial nor even formal category; I can find only one intentional unity for them: the object I read is founded by my *intention* to read: it is simply *legendum*, to be read, issuing from a phenomenology, not from a semiology.

2. In the field of reading—and this is more serious—there is not only no pertinence of *levels*, there is no possibility of describing *levels* of reading, because there is no possibility of closing the list of these levels. Of course, there is an *origin* of graphic reading: this is the apprenticeship to letters, to written words; but, on the one hand, there are readings without apprenticeship (images)—at least without technical, if not cultural apprenticeship—and on the other hand, once this *technè* is acquired, we do not know where to halt the depth and the dispersion of reading: at the apprehension of a meaning? Which meaning? Denoted? Connoted? These are artifacts, I shall call them *ethical* artifacts, since denoted meaning tends to pass for the simple, true meaning and to found a law (how many men have died for *a* meaning?), while connotation permits (this is its *moral* advantage) positing a law with multiple meanings and thereby liberating reading: but how far? To infinity: there is no *structural* obligation to close my reading: I can just as well extend the limits of the readable to infinity, decide that *everything* is finally readable (unreadable as this seems), but also, conversely, I can decide that in the depths of every text, however readable its conception, there is, there remains a certain measure of the unreadable. Our knowing *how to read* can be determined, verified at its inaugural stage, but it very quickly becomes a knowledge without basis, without rules, without degrees, and without end.

This difficulty in finding a *pertinence*, from which to establish a coherent analysis of reading, we must assume we are responsible for simply because we lack genius. But we can also suppose that *non-pertinence* is somehow congenital to reading: something, statutorily, comes to blur the analysis of the objects and levels of reading, and thereby checkmates not only any search for a pertinence in the analysis of reading, but even, perhaps, the very concept of pertinence (for the same thing seems to be happening in the realm of linguistics and narratology). This something I believe I can name (in a quite banal fashion, moreover): it is Desire. It is because every reading is steeped in Desire (or Disgust) that anagnosology is difficult, perhaps impossible—in any case, that it is likely to be achieved just where we do not expect it, or at least not *exactly* where we expect it: by—recent—tradition, we expect it in the realm of structure; and no doubt we are partly right: every reading occurs within a structure (however multiple, however open), and not in the allegedly free space of an alleged spontaneity: there is no "natural," "wild" reading: reading does not *overflow* structure; it is subject to it: it needs structure, it respects structure; but reading *perverts* structure. Reading is the gesture of the body (for of course one reads with one's body) which by one and the same movement posits and perverts its order: an interior supplement of perversion.

2. Repression

I am not inquiring, strictly speaking, about the avatars of the desire to read; notably, I cannot answer this irritating question: Why don't Frenchmen today want to read? Why, it appears, do fifty percent of them not read? What we might consider is the trace of desire—or of non-desire—that there is *within* a reading, supposing that the will-to-read has already been assumed. And first of all, the *repressions* of reading. Two of which come to mind.

The first results from all the constraints—social or interiorized by a thousand relays—which make reading a *duty*, in which the very act of reading is determined by a law: the act of reading, or better still, the act of *having read*, the almost ritual trace of an initiation. Hence, I am not speaking of the "instrumental" readings necessary to the acquisition of a specific kind of knowledge, of a technique, and according to which the gesture of reading vanishes beneath the act of learning: I am talking about "free" readings, which you "must" nonetheless have performed: *you "must" have read (The Princess of Clèves, Anti-Oedipus).* Where does the law come from? From various instances, each of which is instituted as a value, as ideology: for the avant-garde militant, *you "must" have read* Bataille, Artaud. For a long time, when reading was narrowly elitist, there were duties of universal reading; I suppose that the collapse of humanist values has put an end to these duties of reading: for them have been substituted certain private duties, linked to the "role" the subject acknowledges he has in today's society; the law of reading no longer comes from an eternity of culture, but from a bizarre, or at least enigmatic, instance located between History and Fashion. What I mean is that there are group laws, micro-laws, from which one must be entitled to liberate oneself. Or again: freedom to read, whatever its price, is *also* freedom not to read. Who knows if certain things are not transformed, who knows if certain important things do not happen (in work, in the history of the historical subject) not only by the effect of readings but also by the effect of reading's omissions (forgettings): by what we might call the *unconstraints* of reading? Or again: in reading, Desire cannot be detached, whatever the cost to our institutions, from its own pulsional negativity.

A second repression is perhaps that of the Library. No question, of course, of contesting the institution, or of ignoring its necessary development; but a question of acknowledging the trace of repression in this fundamental and inevitable feature of the public (or simply: collective) Library: its *facticity*. Facticity in itself is not a road to repression (Nature has nothing particularly liberating about it); if the Library's facticity produces a failure in the Desire to read, it is for two reasons.

1. By status, whatever its dimension, the Library is infinite, insofar as it is always (however well-conceived it may be) both short of and in excess of demand: tendentially, the book you want is never there, while another book is offered to you: the Library is the space of substitutes for desire; confronting the adventure of reading, it is reality, in that it calls Desire to order: to derive pleasure, satisfaction, gratification from a Library, the subject must renounce the effusion of his own image-repertoire; he must have *done his Oedipus*—that Oedipus I must not only "do" at the age of four, but every day of my life that I desire. Here in the Library, it is the very profusion of books which is the law, castration.

2. The Library is a space one visits, but not that one inhabits.

We should have in our language, versatile as it is said to be, two different words: one for the Library book, the other for the book-at-home (let us use hyphens, producing an autonomous syntagm whose referent is a specific object); one for the book "borrowed"—usually through a bureaucratic or magistral mediation—the other for the book grasped, held, taken up as if it were already a fetish; one for the book-as-object of a debt (it must be returned), the other for the book-as-object of a desire or an immediate (without mediation) demand. Domestic (and not public) space deprives the book of any function of social, cultural, institutional *appearance*. Of course the book-at-home is not a pure fragment of desire: it is (generally) traversed by a mediation which has nothing particularly clean about it: money; we have had to buy it, which means not having bought others; but things being what they are, money is itself a liberation—which the Institution is not: in the Fourierist utopia, books are worth virtually nothing, but they nonetheless experience the mediation of a few pennies: they are covered by an *Expense*, whereupon Desire functions: something is released.

3. Desire

What is there of Desire in reading? Desire cannot be named, not even (unlike Demand) expressed. Yet it is certain that there is an eroticism of reading (in reading, desire is there with its object, which is the definition of eroticism). Of this eroticism of reading, there is perhaps no purer apologue than that episode in Proust's novel where the young Narrator shuts himself up in the Combray bathroom in order to read, so as not to see his grandmother suffer when she has been told, as a joke, that her husband is going to drink cognac . . .): "I went up sobbing to the very top of the house, to the room next to the schoolroom, under the roof, a little room smelling of iris, and also perfumed by a wild currant bush sprouting between the stones of the wall outside and which thrust a flowering branch through the open window. Intended for a more particular and vulgar use, this room, from which one had a view, during the day, all the way to the donjon of Roussainville-le-Pin, long served me as a refuge, doubtless because it was the only place I was allowed to lock myself in, for all those occupations of mine which required an inviolable solitude: reading, reverie, tears, and pleasure."

Thus, a *desiring* reading appears, marked with two institutive features. By shutting himself up to read, by making reading into an absolutely separated, clandestine state in which the whole world is abolished, the reader is identified with two other human subjects—actually quite close to each other—whose state also requires a violent separation: the amorous subject and the mystic subject; Theresa of Avila specified reading as a substitute for mental prayer; and the amorous subject, as we know, is marked by a retreat from reality, he releases himself from the outer world. This certainly confirms that the reader-subject is a subject entirely transposed into the register of the image-repertoire; his whole economy of pleasure consists in nursing his dual relation with the book (i.e., with the Image), by shutting himself up alone with it, fastened to it, like the child fastened to the mother and the Lover poring over the beloved face. The iris-smelling bathroom is the very closure of the Mirror, the site of the paradisiac coalescence of subject and Image—of the book.

The second feature from which a desiring reading is constituted—as we are told explicitly by the bathroom episode—is this: in reading, all the body's emotions are present, mingled, coiled up: fascination, emptiness, pain, voluptuousness; reading produces an overwhelmed body, but *not parceled out* (otherwise, reading would not issue from the image-repertoire). Yet something more enigmatic is presented for us to read, to interpret in the Proustian episode: reading—the delight of reading—has some relation with anality; one and the same metonymy connects reading, excrement, and—as we have seen—money.

And now—without leaving the reading room—this question: Are there different pleasures of reading? Is there a possible typology of these pleasures? It seems to me that there are, in any case, at least three types of pleasure of reading or, to be more specific, three ways by which the Image of reading can capture the reading subject. According to the first mode, the reader has a fetishist relation with the text being read: he takes pleasure in the words, in certain words, in certain arrangements of words; in the texts, certain areas, certain isolates are formed and in their fascination the reader-subject is lost, ruined; this would be a kind of metaphoric or poetic reading; to enjoy this pleasure, is there any need of an extended linguistic culture? This is not certain: even the very young child, at the stage of prattle, knows the eroticism of the word, an oral and aural practice available to pulsion. According to the second mode, which is just the contrary, the reader is drawn onward *through* the book's length by a force always more or less disguised, belonging to the order of suspense: the book is gradually abolished, and it is in this impatient, impassioned erosion that the delectation lies; a matter, chiefly, of the metonymic pleasure of all narration, without forgetting that knowledge itself can be recounted, subjected to a movement of suspense; and because this pleasure is visibly linked to the observation of what is unfolding and to the revelation of what is hidden, we can suppose there is some relation to the discovery of the primal scene; I want to *surprise*, I am about to faint from expectation: a pure image of delectation, in that it does not belong to the order of satisfaction; we should also question, conversely, the blockages, the distastes of reading: Why don't we go on with a book? Why cannot Bouvard, deciding to take up the Philosophy of History, "finish Bossuet's celebrated *Discours*"? Is this Bouvard's fault, or Bossuet's? Are there universal mechanisms of attraction? Is there an erotic logic of Narration? Here the structural analysis of narrative should raise the problem of Pleasure: it seems to me that it now has the means to do so. Then there is a third adventure of reading (I am calling *adventure* the way in which pleasure comes to the reader): that of Writing; reading is a conductor of the Desire to write (we are now sure that there is a delectation of writing, although it is still very enigmatic for us); not that we necessarily wanted to write *like* the author we enjoy reading; what we desire is only the desire the *scriptor* has in writing, or again: we desire the desire the author had for the reader when he was writing, we desire the *love-me* which is in all writing. This has been very clearly put by the writer Roger Laporte: "A *pure* reading which does not call for *another writing* is incomprehensible to me . . . Reading Proust, Blanchot, Kafka, Artaud gave me no desire to write *on* these authors (not even, I might add, *like* them), but to *write*." In this perspective, reading is a veritable production: no longer of interior images, of projections, of hallucinations, but literally of *work*: the (consumed) product is reversed into production, into promise, into desire for production, and the chain of desires begins to unroll, each reading being worth the writing it engenders, to infinity. Is this pleasure of production an elitist pleasure, reserved only to potential writers? In our society, a society of consumption and not of production, a society of reading, seeing, and hearing, and not a society of writing, looking, and listening, everything is done to block the answer: lovers of writing are scattered, clandestine, crushed by a thousand—even internal—constraints.

This is a problem of civilization: but, for me, my profound and constant conviction is that it will never be possible to liberate reading if, in the same impulse, we do not liberate writing.

4. Subject

There has been a great deal of discussion, and long before the advent of Structural Analysis, of the different points of view an author can adopt to tell a story—or simply to produce a text. A way of connecting the reader to a theory of Narration, or more broadly to a Poetics, would be to consider him as *himself* occupying a point of view (or several in succession); in other words, to treat the reader *as a character*, to make him into one of the characters (not even necessarily a privileged one) of the fiction and/or the Text. Greek tragedy affords an example: the reader is that character who is on stage (even if clandestinely) and who hears what each of the partners of the dialogue does not hear; his hearing is double (and therefore virtually multiple). In other words, the reader's specific site is the *paragram*, as it obsessed Saussure (did he not feel he was going mad, this scholar, from being *solely* and *completely* the reader?): a "true" reading, a reading which would assume its affirmation, would be a mad reading, not because it would invent improbable meanings (misconstructions), not because it would be "delirious," but because it would perceive the simultaneous multiplicity of meanings, of points of view, of structures, a space extended outside the laws which proscribe contradiction ("Text" is the very postulation of such a space).

This imagination of a total—i.e., totally multiple, paragrammatic—reader may be useful in that it permits us to glimpse the Paradox of the reader: it is commonly admitted that to read is to decode: letters, words, meanings, structures, and this is incontestable; but by accumulating decodings (since reading is by rights infinite), by removing the safety catch of meaning, by putting reading into freewheeling (which is its structural vocation), the reader is caught up in a dialectical reversal: finally, he does not decode, he *overcodes*; he does not decipher, he produces, he accumulates languages, he lets himself be infinitely and tirelessly traversed by them: he is that traversal.

Now, this is the very situation of the human subject, at least as psychoanalytic epistemology tries to understand him: a subject who is no longer the *thinking subject* of idealistic philosophy, but rather devoid of all unity, lost in the double misreading of his unconscious and of his ideology, and remembering only a whirligig of languages. I mean by this that the reader is the complete subject, that the field of reading is that of absolute subjectivity (in the materialistic sense which this old idealistic word can now have): every reading proceeds from a subject, and it is separated from this subject only by rare and tenuous mediations, the apprenticeship of letters, a few rhetorical protocols, beyond which (very quickly) it is the subject who rediscovers himself in his own, individual structure: either desiring, or perverse, or paranoiac, or imaginary, or neurotic—and of course in his historical structure as well: alienated by ideology, by the routines of codes.

This is to indicate that we cannot reasonably hope for a Science of reading, a Semiology of reading, unless we conceive the possibility, some day, of—a contradiction in terms—a Science of the Inexhaustible, of infinite Displacement: reading is *precisely* that energy, that action which will seize—in *this* text, in *this* book—the very thing "which refuses to be exhausted by the categories of Poetics";* reading, in short, is the permanent hemorrhage by which structure—patiently and usefully described by Structural Analysis—collapses, opens, is lost, thereby consonant with any logical system which *ultimately* nothing can close—leaving intact what we must call the movement of the subject and of history: reading is the site where structure is made hysterical.

Le Français aujourd'hui, 1976

* Oswald Ducrot and Tzvetan Todorov, *Dictionnaire encyclopédique des sciences du langage* (Paris, 1972), p. 107.

Freedom to Write

Flaubert's last novel is missing a chapter on orthography. In it we would find Bouvard and Pécuchet ordering from Dumouchel a whole little library of spelling manuals, at first delighted, then astounded by the comminatory and contradictory character of the rules prescribed, finally working each other up and endlessly arguing: Why this *particular* written form? Why write *Caen, Paon, Lampe, Vent, Rang* when the vowel sound is the same in each case? Why *Quatre* and *Caille*, since these two words have the same initial consonant? Whereupon Pécuchet would inevitably conclude, bowing his head: "Spelling might be a hoax!"

This hoax, as we know, is not an innocent one. Of course, for a historian of the language, these accidents of French orthography are explicable: each one has its reason, analogical, etymological, or functional; but the sum of these reasons is unreasonable, and when this unreason is imposed, by means of education, upon an entire nation, it becomes culpable. It is not the arbitrary character of our orthography which is shocking, it is the fact that this arbitrariness is statutory. Since 1835, the official orthography of the Academie Française has had the value of law in the eyes of the State; from the very first classes of the young French citizen, "spelling mistakes" are punished: how many lives spoiled for a few spelling errors!

The first effect of spelling is discriminatory; but it also has secondary effects of a psychological order. If orthography were free—free to be simplified or not, according to the subject's desire—it might constitute a very positive practice of expression; the written physiognomy of the word might acquire a properly poetic value, insofar as it emerged from the *scriptor*'s phantasmatics, and not from a uniform and reductive law; just think of the kind of intoxication, of baroque jubilation which explodes in the orthographic "aberrations" of old manuscripts, of texts by children and the letters of foreigners: might one not say that in such efflorescences as these the subject seeks his freedom: to trace, to dream, to remember, to understand? Are there not occasions when we encounter particularly "happy" spelling mistakes—as if the *scriptor* were obeying not academic law but a mysterious commandment that comes to him from his own history—perhaps even from his own body?

Conversely, once spelling is made uniform, legalized, sanctioned by state means, in its very complication and its irrationality, it is obsessional neurosis which is instated: the spelling mistake becomes Transgression. I have just sent off a letter of application for a job which can change my life. But have I remembered to put an *s* on that plural? Was I careful to put two *p*'s and just one *l* in *appeler*? I worry, I am in agony, like the vacationer who can't remember if he turned off the gas and the water back home, and if a fire or a flood will be the result. And just as such worry keeps our vacationer from enjoying his vacation, legalized spelling keeps the *scriptor* from enjoying writing, that euphoric gesture which permits putting into the tracing of a word *a little more* than its mere intention to communicate.

Reform spelling? It has been tried several times, it is tried periodically. But what is the use of remaking a code, even an improved one, if it is once again in order to impose it, to legalize it, to make it a specifically arbitrary instrument of selection? It is not spelling which should be reformed, but the law which prescribes its minutiae. What *can* be asked is this: a certain "laxism" of the Institution. If I enjoy writing "correctly", i.e., "in conformity," I am quite free to do so, as I am to enjoy reading Racine or Gide today: statutory spelling is not without its charm, it is not without perversity; but let "ignorances" and "blunders" be penalized no longer; let them cease to be perceived as aberrations or debilities; let society agree at last (or once again) to release writing from the state apparatus to which it belongs today; in short, let us stop excluding "for reasons of spelling."

Le Monde de l'éducation, 1976

2
FROM WORK TO TEXT

The Death of the Author

In his tale *Sarrasine*, Balzac, speaking of a castrato disguised as a woman, writes this sentence: "She was Woman, with her sudden fears, her inexplicable whims, her instinctive fears, her meaningless bravado, her defiance, and her delicious delicacy of feeling." Who speaks in this way? Is it the hero of the tale, who would prefer not to recognize the castrato hidden beneath the "woman"? Is it Balzac the man, whose personal experience has provided him with a philosophy of Woman? Is it Balzac the author, professing certain "literary" ideas about femininity? Is it universal wisdom? Romantic psychology? We can never know, for the good reason that writing is the destruction of every voice, every origin. Writing is that neuter, that composite, that obliquity into which our subject flees, the black-and-white where all identity is lost, beginning with the very identity of the body that writes.

No doubt it has always been so: once a fact is *recounted*—for intransitive purposes, and no longer to act directly upon reality, i.e., exclusive of any function except that exercise of the symbol itself—this gap appears, the voice loses its origin, the author enters into his own death, writing begins. However, the affect of this phenomenon has been variable; in ethnographic societies, narrative is never assumed by a person but by a mediator, shaman, or reciter, whose "performance" (i.e., his mastery of the narrative code) can be admired, but never his "genius." The *author* is a modern character, no doubt produced by our society as it emerged from the Middle Ages, inflected by English empiricism, French rationalism, and the personal faith of the Reformation, thereby discovering the prestige of the individual, or, as we say more nobly, of the "human person." Hence, it is logical that in literary matters it should be positivism, crown and conclusion of capitalist ideology, which has granted the greatest importance to the author's "person." The *author* still reigns in manuals of literary history, in biographies of writers, magazine interviews, and in the very consciousness of litterateurs eager to unite, by means of private journals, their person and their work; the image of literature to be found in contemporary culture is tyrannically centered on the author, his person, his history, his tastes, his passions; criticism still largely consists in saying that Baudelaire's oeuvre is the failure of the man Baudelaire, Van Gogh's is his madness, Tchaikovsky's his vice: *explanation* of the work is still sought in the person of its producer, as if, through the more or less transparent allegory of fiction, it was always, ultimately, the voice of one and the same person, the *author*, which was transmitting his "confidences."

Though the Author's empire is still very powerful (the new criticism has quite often merely consolidated it), we know that certain writers have already tried to subvert it. In France, Mallarmé, no doubt the first, saw and foresaw in all its scope the necessity to substitute language itself for the subject hitherto supposed to be its owner; for Mallarmé, as for us, it is language which speaks, not the author; to write is to reach, through a preliminary impersonality—which we can at no moment identify with the realistic novelist's castrating "objectivity"—that point where not "I" but only language functions, "performs": Mallarmé's whole poetics consists in suppressing the author in favor of writing (and thereby restoring, as we shall see, the reader's place). Valéry, entangled in a psychology of the ego, greatly edulcorated Mallarmean theory, but led by a preference for classicism to conform to the lessons of Rhetoric, he continued to cast the Author into doubt and derision, emphasized the linguistic and "accidental" nature of his activity, and throughout his prose works championed the essentially verbal condition of literature, as opposed to which any resort to the writer's interiority seemed to him pure superstition. Proust himself, despite the apparently psychological character of what is called his *analyses*, visibly undertook to blur by an extreme subtilization the relation of the writer and his characters: by making the narrator not the one who has seen or felt, or even the one who writes, but the one who *is going to write* (the young man of the novel—but, as a matter of fact, how old is he and *who* is he?—wants to write but cannot, and the novel ends when writing finally becomes possible), Proust has given modern writing its epic: by a radical reversal, instead of putting his life into his novel, as is so often said, he made his life itself a work of which his own book was the model, so that it is quite clear to us that it is not Charlus who imitates Montesquiou, but Montesquiou, in his anecdotal, historical reality, who is only a secondary, derived fragment of Charlus. Finally Surrealism, to keep to this prehistory of modernity, could doubtless not attribute a sovereign place to language, since language is system, and what this movement sought was, romantically, a direct subversion of the codes—an illusory subversion, moreover, for a code cannot be destroyed, only "flouted"; yet, by constantly striving to disappoint expected meanings (this was the famous surrealist "shock"), by urging the hand to write as fast as possible what the head was unaware of (this was automatic writing), by accepting the principle and the experiment of collective writing, Surrealism helped desacralize the image of the Author. Last, outside literature itself (in fact, such distinctions are becoming quite dated), linguistics furnishes the destruction of the Author with a precious analytic instrument, showing that the speech-act in its entirety is an "empty" process, which functions perfectly without its being necessary to "fill" it with the person of the interlocutors: linguistically, the author is nothing but the one who writes, just as *I* is nothing but the one who says *I*: language knows a "subject," not a "person," and this subject, empty outside of the very speech-act which defines it, suffices to "hold" language, i.e., to exhaust it.

The removal of the Author (with Brecht, we might speak here of a veritable *distancing*, the Author diminishing like a figure at the far end of the literary stage) is not only a historical fact or an act of writing: it utterly transforms the modern text (or—which is the same thing—the text is henceforth produced and read so that the author absents himself from it at every level). Time, first of all, is no longer the same. The Author, when we believe in him, is always conceived as the past of his own book: book and author are voluntarily placed on one and the same line, distributed as a *before* and an *after*: the Author is supposed to *feed* the book, i.e., he lives before it, thinks, suffers, lives for it; he has the same relation of antecedence with his work that a father sustains with his child. Quite the contrary, the modern *scriptor* is born *at the same time* as his text; he is not furnished with a being which precedes or exceeds his writing, he is not the subject of which his book would be the predicate; there is no time other than that of the speech-act, and every text is written eternally *here* and *now*. This is because (or it follows that) *writing* can no longer designate an operation of recording, of observation, of representation, of "painting" (as the Classics used to say), but instead what the linguists, following Oxfordian philosophy, call a performative, a rare verbal form (exclusively found in the first person and in the present), in which the speech-act has no other content (no other statement) than the act by which it is uttered: something like the *I declare* of kings or the *I sing* of the earliest poets; the modern *scriptor*, having buried the Author, can therefore no longer believe, according to the pathos of his predecessors, that his hand is slower than his passion and that in consequence, making a law of necessity, he must emphasize this delay and endlessly "elaborate" his form; for him, on the contrary, his hand, detached from any voice, borne by a pure gesture of inscription (and not of expression), traces a field without origin—or at least with no origin but language itself, i.e., the very thing which ceaselessly calls any origin into question.

We know now that a text consists not of a line of words, releasing a single "theological" meaning (the "message" of the

Author-God), but of a multi-dimensional space in which are married and contested several writings, none of which is original: the text is a fabric of quotations, resulting from a thousand sources of culture. Like Bouvard and Pécuchet, those eternal copyists, at once sublime and comical, whose profound absurdity *precisely* designates the truth of writing, the writer can only imitate an ever anterior, never original gesture; his sole power is to mingle writings, to counter some by others, so as never to rely on just one; if he seeks to *express himself,* at least he knows that the interior "thing" he claims to "translate" is itself no more than a ready-made lexicon, whose words can be explained only through other words, and this ad infinitum: an adventure which exemplarily befell young Thomas De Quincey, so versed in his Greek that in order to translate certain absolutely modern ideas and images into this dead language, Baudelaire tells us, "he had a dictionary made for himself, one much more complex and extensive than the kind produced by the vulgar patience of purely literary themes" (*Les Paradis artificiels*); succeeding the Author, the *scriptor* no longer contains passions, moods, sentiments, impressions, but that immense dictionary from which he draws a writing which will be incessant: life merely imitates the book, and this book itself is but a tissue of signs, endless imitation, infinitely postponed.

Once the Author is distanced, the claim to "decipher" a text becomes entirely futile. To assign an Author to a text is to impose a brake on it, to furnish it with a final signified, to close writing. This conception is quite suited to criticism, which then undertakes the important task of discovering the Author (or his hypostases: society, history, the psyche, freedom) beneath the work: once the Author is found, the text is "explained," the critic has won; hence, it is hardly surprising that historically the Author's empire has been the Critic's as well, and also that (even new) criticism is today unsettled at the same time as the Author. In multiple writing, in effect, everything is to be *disentangled,* but nothing *deciphered,* structure can be followed, "threaded" (as we say of a run in a stocking) in all its reprises, all its stages, but there is no end to it, no bottom; the space of writing is to be traversed, not pierced; writing constantly posits meaning, but always in order to evaporate it: writing seeks a systematic exemption of meaning. Thereby, literature (it would be better, from now on, to say *writing*), by refusing to assign to the text (and to the world-as-text) a "secret," i.e., an ultimate meaning, liberates an activity we may call countertheological, properly revolutionary, for to refuse to halt meaning is finally to refuse God and his hypostases, reason, science, the law.

To return to Balzac's sentence. No one (i.e., no "person") says it: its source, its voice is not the true site of writing, it is reading. Another very specific example will help us here: recent investigations (J.-P. Vernant) have shed some light on the constitutively ambiguous nature of Greek tragedy, whose text is "woven" of words with double meanings, words which each character understands unilaterally (this perpetual misunderstanding is precisely what we call the "tragic"); there is, however, someone who understands each word in its duplicity, and further understands, one may say, the very deafness of the characters speaking in his presence: this "someone" is precisely the reader (or here the listener). Here we discern the total being of writing: a text consists of multiple writings, proceeding from several cultures and entering into dialogue, into parody, into contestation; but there is a site where this multiplicity is collected, and this site is not the author, as has hitherto been claimed, but the reader: the reader is the very space in which are inscribed, without any of them being lost, all the citations out of which a writing is made; the unity of a text is not in its origin but in its destination, but this destination can no longer be personal: the reader is a man without history, without biography, without psychology; he is only that *someone* who holds collected into one and the same field all of the traces from which writing is constituted. That is why it is absurd to hear the new writing condemned in the name of a humanism which hypocritically claims to champion the reader's rights. Classical criticism has never been concerned with the reader; for that criticism, there is no other man in literature than the one who writes. We are no longer so willing to be the dupes of such antiphrases, by which a society proudly recriminates in favor of precisely what it discards, ignores, muffles, or destroys; we know that in order to restore writing to its future, we must reverse the myth: the birth of the reader must be requited by the death of the Author.

Manteia, 1968

From Work to Text

A change has lately occurred, or is occurring, in our idea of language and consequently of the (literary) work which owes to that language at least its phenomenal existence. This change is obviously linked to the present development of (among other disciplines) linguistics, anthropology, Marxism, psychoanalysis (the word *link* is used here in a deliberately neutral manner: no determination is being invoked, however multiple and dialectical). The transformation of the notion of the work does not necessarily derive from the internal renewal of each of these disciplines, but rather from their intersection at the level of an object which traditionally proceeds from none of them. We might say, as a matter of fact, that *interdisciplinary* activity, today so highly valued in research, cannot be achieved by the simple confrontation of specialized branches of knowledge; the interdisciplinary is not a comfortable affair: it begins *effectively* (and not by the simple utterance of a pious hope) when the solidarity of the old disciplines breaks down—perhaps even violently, through the shocks of fashion—to the advantage of a new object, a new language, neither of which is precisely this discomfort of classification which permits diagnosing a certain mutation. The mutation which seems to be affecting the notion of the work must not, however, be overestimated; it is part of an epistemological shift, more than of a real break of the kind which in fact occurred in the last century upon the appearance of Marxism and Freudianism; no new break has occurred since, and we might say that for the last hundred years we have been involved in a repetition. What History, our History, allows us today is merely to displace, to vary, to transcend, to repudiate. Just as Einsteinian science compels us to include within the object studied the *relativity of reference points*, so the combined action of Marxism, Freudianism, and structuralism compels us, in literature, to relativize the relations of *scriptor*, reader, and observer (critic). Confronting the *work*—a traditional notion, long since, and still today, conceived in what we might call a Newtonian fashion—there now occurs the demand for a new object, obtained by a shift or a reversal of previous categories. This object is the *Text*. I know that this word is fashionable (I myself am compelled to use it frequently), hence suspect in some quarters; but this is precisely why I should like to review the main propositions at whose intersection the Text is located, as I see it; the word *proposition* must here be understood more grammatically than logically: these are speech-acts, not arguments, "hints," approaches which agree to remain metaphorical. Here are these propositions: they concern method, genres, the sign, the plural, filiation, reading, pleasure.

1. The text must not be understood as a computable object. It would be futile to attempt a material separation of works from texts. In particular, we must not permit ourselves to say: the work is classical, the text is avant-garde; there is no question of establishing a trophy in modernity's name and declaring certain literary productions *in* and *out* by reason of their chronological situation: there can be "Text" in a very old work, and many products of contemporary literature are not texts at all. The difference is as follows: the work is a fragment of substance, it occupies a portion of the spaces of books (for example, in a library). The Text is a methodological field. The opposition may recall (though not reproduce term for term) a distinction proposed by Lacan: "reality" is shown [*se montre*], the "real" is proved [*se démontre*]; in the same way, the work is seen (in bookstores, in card catalogues, on examination syllabuses), the text is demonstrated, is spoken according to certain rules (or against certain rules); the work is held in the hand, the text is held in language: it exists only when caught up in a discourse (or rather it is Text for the very reason that it knows itself to

be so); the Text is not the decomposition of the work, it is the work which is the Text's imaginary tail. Or again: *the Text is experienced only in an activity, in a production.* It follows that the Text cannot stop (for example, at a library shelf); its constitutive moment is *traversal* (notably, it can traverse the work, several works).

2. Similarly, the Text does not stop at (good) literature; it cannot be caught up in a hierarchy, or even in a simple distribution of genres. What constitutes it is on the contrary (or precisely) its force of subversion with regard to the old classifications. How to classify Georges Bataille? Is this writer a novelist, a poet, an essayist, an economist, a philosopher, a mystic? The answer is so uncertain that handbooks of literature generally prefer to leave Bataille out; as a matter of fact, Bataille has written texts, or even, perhaps, always one and the same text. If the Text raises problems of classification (moreover, this is one of its "social" functions), it is because it always implies a certain experience of limits. Thibaudet used to speak (but in a very restricted sense) of limit-works (such as Chateaubriand's *Life of Rancé*, a work which indeed seems to us to be a "text"): the Text is what is situated at the limit of the rules of the speech-act (rationality, readability, etc.). This notion is not rhetorical, we do not resort to it for "heroic" postures: the Text attempts to locate itself very specifically *behind* the limit of the *doxa* (is not public opinion, constitutive of our democratic societies, powerfully aided by mass communications—is not public opinion defined by its limits, its energy of exclusion, its *censorship*?); taking the word literally, we might say that the Text is always *paradoxical.*

3. The text is approached and experienced in relation to the sign. The work closes upon a signified. We can attribute two modes of signification to this signified: either it is claimed to be apparent, and the work is then the object of a science of the letter, which is philology; or else this signified is said to be secret

and final, and must be sought for, and then the work depends upon a hermeneutics, an interpretation (Marxist, psychoanalytic, thematic, etc.); in short, the work itself functions as a general sign, and it is natural that it should represent an institutional category of the civilization of the Sign. The Text, on the contrary, practices the infinite postponement of the signified, the Text is dilatory; its field is that of the signifier; the signifier must not be imagined as "the first part of the meaning," its material vestibule, but rather, on the contrary, as its *aftermath*; similarly, the signifier's *infinitude* does not refer to some notion of the ineffable (of an unnamable signified) but to a notion of *play*; the engendering of the perpetual signifier (in the fashion of a perpetual calendar) in the field of the Text is not achieved by some organic process of maturation, or a hermeneutic process of "delving deeper," but rather by a serial movement of dislocations, overlappings, variations; the logic governing the Text is not comprehensive (trying to define what the work "means") but metonymic; the activity of associations, contiguities, cross-references coincides with a liberation of symbolic energy (if it failed him, man would die). The work (in the best of cases) is *moderately* symbolic (its symbolics runs short, i.e., stops); the Text is *radically* symbolic: *a work whose integrally symbolic nature one conceives, perceives, and receives is a text.* The Text is thus restored to language; like language, it is structured but decentered, without closure (let us note, to answer the scornful suspicion of "fashion" sometimes lodged against structuralism, that the epistemological privilege nowadays granted to language derives precisely from the fact that in it [language] we have discovered a paradoxical idea of structure: a system without end or center).

4. The Text is plural. This does not mean only that it has several meanings but that it fulfills the very plurality of meaning: an *irreducible* (and not just acceptable) plurality. The Text is not coexistence of meaning, but passage, traversal; hence, it depends not on an interpretation, however liberal, but on an explosion, on dissemination. The plurality of the Text depends, as a matter

of fact, not on the ambiguity of its contents, but on what we might call the stereographic plurality of the signifiers which weave it (etymologically, the text is a fabric): the reader of the Text might be compared to an idle subject (who has relaxed his image-repertoire): this fairly empty subject strolls (this has happened to the author of these lines, and it is for this reason that he has come to an intense awareness of the Text) along a hillside at the bottom of which flows a wadi (I use the word to attest to a certain alienation); what he perceives is multiple, irreducible, issuing from heterogeneous, detached substances and levels: lights, colors, vegetation, heat, air, tenuous explosions of sound, tiny cries of birds, children's voices from the other side of the valley, paths, gestures, garments of inhabitants close by or very far away; all these incidents are half identifiable: they issue from known codes, but their combinative operation is unique, it grounds the stroll in a difference which cannot be repeated except *as difference*. This is what happens in the Text: it can be Text only in its difference (which does not mean its individuality); its reading is semelfactive (which renders any inductive-deductive science of texts illusory: no "grammar" of the text) and yet entirely woven of quotations, references, echoes: cultural languages (what language is not cultural?), antecedent or contemporary, which traverse it through and through, in a vast stereophony. The intertextuality in which any text is apprehended, since it is itself the intertext of another text, cannot be identified with some *origin* of the text: to seek out the "sources," the "influences" of a work is to satisfy the myth of filiation; the quotations a text is made of are anonymous, irrecoverable, and yet *already read*: they are quotations without quotation marks. The work disturbs no monistic philosophy (there are antagonistic ones, as we know); for such a philosophy, plurality is Evil. Hence, confronting the work, the Text might indeed take for its motto the words of the man possessed by devils: "My name is legion, for we are many" (Mark 5:9). The plural or demonic texture which sets the Text in opposition to the work may involve profound modifications of reading, precisely where monologism seems to be the law: certain "texts" of Scripture, traditionally adopted by theological (historical or anagogical) monism, may lend themselves to a diffraction of meanings (i.e., finally, to a materialist reading), while the Marxist interpretation of the work, hitherto resolutely monistic, may become more materialist by pluralizing itself (if, of course, Marxist "institutions" permit this).

5. The work is caught up in a process of filiation. What is postulated are a *determination* of the world (of the race, then of History) over the work, a *consecution* of works among themselves, and an *appropriation* of the work to its author. The author is reputed to be the father and the owner of his work; literary science thus teaches us to *respect* the manuscript and the author's declared intentions, and society postulates a legality of the author's relation to his work (this is the "author's rights," actually a recent affair, not legalized in France until the time of the Revolution). The Text, on the other hand, is read without the Father's inscription. The metaphor of the Text is here again detached from the metaphor of the work; the latter refers to the image of an *organism* which grows by vital expansion, by "development" (a significantly ambiguous word: biological and rhetorical); the metaphor of the Text is that of the *network*; if the Text expands, it is by the effect of a combinative operation, of a systematics (an image, moreover, close to the views of contemporary biology concerning the living being); no vital "respect" is therefore due to the Text: it can be *broken* (moreover, this is what the Middle Ages did with two nonetheless authoritarian texts: Scripture and Aristotle); the Text can be read without its father's guarantee; the restoration of the intertext paradoxically abolishes inheritance. It is not that the Author cannot "return" in the Text, in his text, but he does so, one might say, as a guest; if he is a novelist, he inscribes himself there as one of his characters, drawn as a figure in the carpet; his inscription is no longer privileged, paternal, alethic, but ludic: he becomes, one can say, a paper author; his life is no

longer the origin of his fables, but a fable concurrent with his life; there is a reversion of the work upon life (and no longer the contrary); the work of Proust and Genet permits us to read their lives as a text: the word *bio-graphy* regains a strong, etymological meaning; and thereby the sincerity of the speech-act, a veritable "cross" of literary ethics, becomes a false problem: the *I* that writes the text is never anything but a paper *I*.

6. The work is ordinarily the object of consumption; I intend no demagoguery by referring to what is called a consumer culture, but we must recognize that today it is the work's "quality" (which ultimately implies an appreciation of "taste") and not the actual operation of reading which can make differences between books: "cultivated" reading is not structurally different from reading on trains. The Text (if only by its frequent "unreadability") decants the work (if it permits it at all) from its consumption and recuperates it as play, task, production, practice. This means that the Text requires an attempt to abolish (or at least to diminish) the distance between writing and reading, not by intensifying the reader's projection into the work, but by linking the two together into one and the same signifying practice. The distance that separates reading from writing is historical. In the period of strongest social division (before the instauration of democratic cultures), reading and writing were *equally* class privileges: Rhetoric, the great literary code of that time, taught *writing* (even if what was ordinarily produced were discourses, not texts); it is significant that the advent of democracy reversed the watchword: the (secondary) school prides itself on teaching *reading* and no longer writing. In fact, *reading*, in the sense of *consuming*, is not *playing* with the text. "Playing" must be taken here in all the polysemy of the term: the text itself "plays" (like a door that "plays" back and forth on its hinges; like a fishing rod in which there is some "play"); and the reader plays twice over: he *plays at* the Text (ludic meaning), he seeks a practice which reproduces it; but, so that this practice is not reduced to a passive, interior *mimesis* (the Text being

precisely what resists this reduction), he *plays* the Text; we must not forget that *play* is also a musical term; the history of music (as practice, not as "art") is, moreover, quite parallel to that of the Text; there was a time when, active amateurs being numerous (at least within a certain class), "to play" and "to listen" constituted a virtually undifferentiated activity; then two roles successively appeared: first of all, that of the *interpreter*, to which the bourgeois public (though it could still play a little itself: this is the entire history of the piano) delegated its playing; then that of the (passive) amateur who listens to music without being able to play it (the piano has effectively been replaced by the record); we know that today post-serial music has disrupted the role of the "interpreter," who is asked to be in a sense the co-author of the score which he completes rather than "expresses." The Text is a little like a score of this new kind: it solicits from the reader a practical collaboration. A great novation this, for who *executes* the work? (Mallarmé raised this question: he wanted the audience to *produce* the book.) Today only the critic executes the work (pun intended). The reduction of reading to consumption is obviously responsible for the "boredom" many feel in the presence of the modern ("unreadable") text, the avant-garde film or painting: to be bored means one cannot produce the text, play it, release it, *make it go.*

7. This suggests one final approach to the Text: that of pleasure. I do not know if a hedonist aesthetic ever existed (eudaemonist philosophies are certainly rare). Of course, a pleasure of the work (of certain works) exists; I can enjoy reading and rereading Proust, Flaubert, Balzac, and even—why not?—Alexandre Dumas; but this pleasure, however intense, and even when it is released from any prejudice, remains partly (unless there has been an exceptional critical effort) a pleasure of consumption: for, if I can read these authors, I also know that I cannot *rewrite* them (that one cannot, today, write "like that"); and this rather depressing knowledge suffices to separate me from the production of these works, at the very moment

when their distancing founds my modernity (to be modern—is this not really to know that one cannot begin again?). The Text is linked to delectation, i.e., to pleasure without separation. Order of the signifier, the Text participates in its way in a social utopia; before History (supposing that History does not choose barbarism), the Text fulfills if not the transparency of social relations, at least the transparency of language relations: it is the space in which no language prevails over any other, where the languages circulate (retaining the *circular* meaning of the word).

These few propositions do not necessarily constitute the articulation of a Theory of the Text. This is not merely the consequence of the presenter's inadequacies (moreover, in many points he has merely recapitulated what is being investigated and developed around him). This is a consequence of the fact that a Theory of the Text cannot be satisfied with a meta-linguistic exposition: the destruction of meta-language, or at least (for it may be necessary to resort to it provisionally) calling it into question, is part of the theory itself: discourse on the Text should itself be only text, research, textual activity, since the Text is that *social* space which leaves no language safe, outside, and no subject of the speech-act in a situation of judge, master, analyst, confessor, decoder: the theory of the Text can coincide only with a practice of writing.

Revue d'esthétique, 1971

Mythology Today

Some fifteen years ago, a certain idea of contemporary myth was proposed. This idea, which on its first appearance was hardly developed at all (the word retained an openly metaphoric value), nonetheless included several theoretical articulations. 1. Myth, close to what Durkheimian sociology calls a "collective representation," can be read in anonymous statements of the press, advertising, mass consumption; it is a social determinate, a "reflection." 2. This reflection, however, in accord with Marx's famous dictum, is *inverted*: myth consists in turning culture into nature, or at least turning the social, the cultural, the ideological, the historical into the "natural": what is merely a product of class division and its moral, cultural, aesthetic consequences is presented (stated) as a natural consequence; the quite contingent grounds of the statement become, under the effect of mythic inversion, Common Sense, Right Reason, the Norm, Public Opinion, in a word, the *Endoxa* (the secular figure of the Origin). 3. Contemporary myth is discontinuous: it is no longer stated in extended, constituted narratives, but only in "discourse"; at most, it is a *phraseology*, a corpus of phrases (of stereotypes); myth disappears, but the *mythic* remains, all the more insidious. 4. As speech (this was, after all, the meaning of *muthos*), contemporary myth issues from a semiology which permits the "correction" of mythic inversion by decomposing the message into two semantic systems: a connoted system whose signified is ideological (and consequently "straight," "non-inverted," or, to be clearer, even by speaking a moral jargon, *cynical*), and a denoted system (the apparent literalness of the image, of the object, of the sentence), whose function is to "naturalize" the class proposition by giving it the guarantee of the most "innocent" of natures: that of language (age-old, maternal, academic, etc.).

This was how myth today appeared, or at least appeared to me. Has anything changed? Not French society, at least on this level, for mythic history is on a different time scale from political history; nor the myths, nor even the analysis; there is still a great deal of *the mythic* in our society: equally anonymous, slippery, fragmented, garrulous, available both to an ideological criticism and to a semiological dismantling. No, what has changed in the last fifteen years is the *science of reading*, under whose scrutiny myth, like an animal long since captured and observed, nonetheless becomes a *different object.*

A science of the signifier (even if it is still being elaborated) has in fact taken its place in the work of the period; its goal is not so much the analysis of the sign as its dislocation. With regard to myth, and though this is still a task which remains to be accomplished, the new semiology—or the new mythology—can no longer (or will no longer be able to) separate so easily the signifier from the signified, the ideological from the phraseological. Not that this distinction is false or ineffectual, but it has become mythic itself: any student can denounce the bourgeois or petit-bourgeois character of a form (of life, of thought, of consumption); in other words, a mythological *endoxa* has been created: demystification (or demythification) has itself become a discourse, a corpus of phrases, a catechistic statement; confronting which a science of the signifier can only be displaced and stop (provisionally) farther on: no longer at the (analytic) dissociation of the sign, but at its vacillation: it is no longer the myths which must be unmasked (the *endoxa* now undertakes that), but the sign itself which must be perturbed: not to reveal the (latent) meaning of a statement, of a feature, of a narrative, but to fissure the very representation of meaning; not to change or to purify symbols, but to contest the symbolic itself. What is happening to (mythological) semiology is a little like what happened to psychoanalysis: it began, necessarily, by establishing lists of symbols (a loosened tooth = the castrated subject, etc.), but today, much more than interrogating this lexicon which, without being false, is no longer of much interest (except to amateurs of the psychoanalytic vulgate), it examines the very dialectics of the signifier; semiology began in the same way by establishing a mythological lexicon, but the task facing it today is rather of a syntactical order (which articulations, which displacements constitute the mythic fabric of a mass-consumption society?); initially, we sought the destruction of the (ideological) signified; now we seek the destruction of the sign: "mythoclasm" is succeeded by a "semioclasm" that is much broader and raised to a higher level. The historical field is thereby extended: it is no longer French society, but far beyond it, historically and geographically, the whole of Western (Greco-Judeo-Islamo-Christian) civilization, unified in one and the same theology (essence, monotheism) and identified by the system of meaning it practices, from Plato to *France-Dimanche.*

The science of the signifier contributes a second correction (or a second extension) to contemporary mythology. The world, taken obliquely by language, is written, through and through; signs, constantly deferring their foundations, transforming their signifieds into new signifiers, quoting each other to infinity, nowhere come to a halt: writing is generalized. If society's alienation still compels us to demystify languages (and notably that of the myths), the means of this combat is not—is no longer—a critical decipherment, it is *evaluation.* Faced with the world's writing systems, the tangle of various discourses (didactic, aesthetic, propagandistic, political, etc.), we must determine levels of reification, degrees of phraseological density. Shall we succeed in specifying a notion which seems to me essential: that of a language's *compactness*? Languages are more or less *dense*; some—the most social, the most mythical—present an unshakable homogeneity (there is a power of meaning, there is a war of meanings): woven of habits, of repetitions, of stereotypes, of obligatory fragments and key words, each one constitutes an *idiolect* (a notion which twenty years ago I designated as *writing*); today, more than myths, it is idiolects which we must distinguish, describe; mythologies are succeeded by a more formal, and thereby, I believe, more penetrating, idiolectology, whose operative concepts are no longer sign, signifier, signified, and connotation, but citation, reference, stereotype. Thus, the dense languages (such as mythic discourse) can be apprehended in the cross fire of the trans-writing whose still literary "text," antidote to myth, would occupy the pole, or rather the region—airy, light, open, spaced, decentered, noble, free—where writing deploys itself against the idiolect, i.e., at its limit, and combats it there. Myth in fact must be included in a general theory of the language of writing, of the signifier, and this theory, supported by the formulations of ethnology, psychoanalysis, semiology, and ideological analysis, must extend its object to take in the *sentence*, or better still, to take in *sentences* (the plural of the sentence); by which I mean that the mythic is present wherever *sentences are turned*, where *stories are told* (in every sense of these expressions): from interior monologue to conversation, from the newspaper article to the political speech, from the novel (if there are any left) to the advertising image—all utterances that can be included in the Lacanian concept of the *image-repertoire*.

This is no more than a program, perhaps in fact no more than a "desire." Yet I believe that, even if the new semiology—mainly concerned, recently, with the literary text—is no longer applied to myths of our time since the last text of *Mythologies*, in which I sketched an initial semiotic approach to social speech, it is at least conscious of its task: no longer merely to *reverse* (or to *correct*) the mythic message, putting it right side up, with denotation at the bottom and connotation at the top, nature on the surface and class interest deep down, but to change the object itself, to engender a new object, point of departure for a new science; to shift—making due allowance, of course, for differences in importance, and according to Althusser's scheme—from Feuerbach to Marx, from the young Marx to the great Marx.

Esprit, 1971

Research: The Young

Here is a special issue of *Communications*: it has not been devised to explore a body of knowledge or to illustrate a theme; its unity, at least its original unity, is not in its object but in the group of its authors: these are all students, recently committed to research; deliberately collected here is the first work of young researchers sufficiently free to have determined their research project themselves and yet still subject to an institution, that of the third-cycle doctorate. What I shall discuss here is therefore mainly the research itself, or at least a certain research, research still linked to the traditional realm of arts and letters. It is solely with that research that I shall be concerned.

On the threshold of his work, the student experiences a series of divisions. As a *young* subject he belongs to an economic class defined by its unproductiveness: he is neither an owner nor a producer; he is outside of exchange, and even, one might say, outside of exploitation: socially, he is excluded from any nomination. As an *intellectual* subject, he is brought into the hierarchy of tasks, he is supposed to participate in a speculative luxury he nonetheless cannot enjoy, for he has not yet mastered it, i.e., the availability of communication. As a *researching* subject, he is dedicated to the separation of discourses: on one side the discourse of scientificity (discourse of the Law), and on the other, the discourse of desire, or writing.

The task (of research) must be perceived in desire. If this perception does not occur, the work is morose, functional, alienated, impelled solely by the necessity of passing an examination, of obtaining a diploma, of insuring a career promotion.

For desire to be insinuated into my work, that work must be *demanded* of me not by a collectivity seeking to guarantee my labor and to gain a return on the loans it grants me, but by a living collection of readers expressing the desire of the Other (and not the control of the Law). Now, in our society, in our institutions, what is asked of the student, of the young researcher, of the intellectual worker, is never his desire; he is not asked to write, he is asked to speak, to "report" (with a view to regular verifications).

Here the intention has been that the work of research be *from its inception* the object of a strong demand, formulated outside the institution—a demand which can only be the demand for writing. Of course, only a fragment of utopia can be represented in this issue, for we realize that society is not ready to concede this happiness broadly, institutionally, to the student, and singularly to the student "of letters": that it is not his competence or his future function that is needed, but his present passion.

It is perhaps time to dispose of a certain fiction: the one maintaining that research is reported but not written: here the researcher is essentially a prospector of raw materials, and it is on this level that his problems are raised; once he has communicated his "results," everything is solved; "formulation" is nothing more than a vague final operation, rapidly performed according to a few techniques of "expression" learned in secondary school and whose only constraint is submission to the code of the genre ("clarity," suppression of images, respect for the laws of argument). Yet it is unlikely that, even in the area of simple tasks of "expression," the student of the social sciences is adequately prepared. And when the object of research is the Text (a word to which we shall return), the investigator is faced with a dilemma—a formidable one: either to speak of the Text according to the conventional code of inauthentic writing or *écrivance*, i.e., to remain prisoner of the "image-repertoire" of a scholar who seeks to be or, worse still, believes himself exterior to the object of his study and claims, in all innocence, in all assurance, to put his own language in a position of extraterritoriality; or else to enter the play of the signifier, the infinity of the speech-act, in short "to write" (which does not simply mean "to write well"), to extract the "ego" from its imaginary hull, from that scientific code which protects but also deceives, in a word to cast the subject across the blank page, not to "express" it (nothing to do with "subjectivity") but to disperse it: to overflow the regular discourse of research. It is obviously this overflow, however slight, which we are allowing, in this issue of *Communications*, to come on stage: an overflow variable according to the authors: we have not sought to reward any one kind of writing; the important thing is that at one level or another of his work (knowledge, method, speech-act) the researcher decides not to be imposed upon by the Law of scientific discourse (the discourse of science is not necessarily science: by contesting the scholar's discourse, writing in no way does away with the rules of scientific work).

Research is done in order to be published, though it is rarely published, especially in its early phases, which are not necessarily less important than its conclusion: the success of a piece of research—especially textual research—does not abide in its "result," a fallacious notion, but in the *reflexive* nature of its speech-act; at every moment of its trajectory, a piece of research can turn language back upon itself and thereby overcome the scholar's bad faith: in a word, displace author and reader. However, as we know, the work of students is rarely published: the third-cycle thesis is in fact a repressed discourse. By publishing fragments of initial research, we hope to combat that repression and to release not only the author of the article but his reader, for the reader (and specifically the magazine reader) is also caught up in the division of specialized languages. Research must no longer be that parsimonious task performed either in the researcher's "consciousness" (a painful, autistic form of monologue) or in the impoverished oscillation which makes the "director" of a research project its only reader.

Research must join the anonymous circulation of language, the dispersion of the Text.

These studies are research in that they seek to renew reading (the reading of older texts). To renew reading: not to substitute new scientific rules for the old constraints of interpretation, but rather to imagine that a *free* reading might become, finally, the norm of "literary studies." The freedom in question is of course not just any freedom (freedom is in contradiction with "just any"): the claim of an innocent freedom revives a memorized, stereotyped culture (the spontaneous is the *immediate* field of the already said, the *déja-dit*): this would inevitably be the return of the signified. The freedom "staged" in this issue is the freedom of the signifier: the return of words, of word games and puns, of proper names, of citations, of etymologies, of reflexivities of discourse, of typographies, of combinative operations, of rejections of languages. This freedom *must* be a virtuosity: the kind which ultimately permits us to read within the support text, however ancient, the motto of all writing: *it circulates*.

Interdisciplinary studies, of which we hear so much, do not merely confront already constituted disciplines (none of which, as a matter of fact, consents to *leave off*). In order to do interdisciplinary work, it is not enough to take a "subject" (a theme) and to arrange two or three sciences around it. Interdisciplinary study consists in creating a new object, which belongs to no one. The Text is, I believe, one such object.

The semiotic studies undertaken in France the last fifteen years have in fact stressed a new notion which must gradually be substituted for the notion of the work: this is the Text. The Text—which cannot be allotted to the traditional realm of "Literature"—was theoretically founded by a certain number of initiatory writings: first of all, the Text was theory. The studies (one should like to be able to say, the testimonies) collected here correspond to that moment when theory must be fragmented for the sake of particular investigations. What is put forward here is the passage from theory to research: all these articles deal with a particular, contingent text belonging to historical culture, but all are also the product of that preliminary theory or of the methods of analysis which have prepared it.

With regard to "letters," reflection on research leads to the Text (or, at least, let us admit today, research is free to lead to it): hence the Text, equally with research, is the object of this issue.

The Text: let us make no mistake about either this singular or this capital letter; when we say *the Text,* it is not in order to divinize it, to make it the deity of a new mystique, but to denote a mass, a field requiring a partitive and not a numerative expression: all that can be said of a work is that there is Text in it. In other words, by passing from text to the Text, we must change numeration: on the one side, the Text is not a computable object, it is a methodological field in which are pursued, according to a movement more "Einsteinian" than "Newtonian," the statement and the speech-act, the matter commented on [the *commenté*] and the matter commenting [the *commentant*]; on the other side, there is no necessity that the Text be exclusively modern: there can be Text in ancient works; and it is precisely the presence of this unquantifiable germ that makes it necessary to disturb, to transcend the old divisions of Literary History; one of the immediate, obvious tasks of new research is to proceed to such *accounts of writing,* to explore what Text there can be in Diderot, in Chateaubriand, in Flaubert, in Gide: this is what many of the authors gathered here are doing; as one of them says, speaking implicitly in the name of several of his comrades: "Perhaps our work merely consists in identifying fragments of writing caught up in a discourse still guaranteed by the Father." No better definition of what, in previous work, is Literature, and what is Text. In other words: how can this past work *still* be read? These young researchers must be credited with raising their activity to the level of a critical task: the present evaluation of a past culture.

All these studies form a collective gesture: it is the very territory of the Text which is gradually being drawn, colored in. Let us follow briefly, from article to article, the collective hand which, far from writing the definition of the Text (there is no such thing: the Text is not a concept), *describes* (de-scribes) the practice of writing.

First of all, this, which is necessary in order to understand and to accept the range of articles collected here: the Text frustrates any cultural typology: to show the *limitless* character of a work is to make it a text; even if reflection on the Text begins with literature (i.e., with an object constituted by the institution), the Text does not necessarily stop there; wherever an activity of signifying is staged according to the rules of combination, transformation, and displacement, there is Text: in written productions, of course, but also in the play of images, of signs, of objects: in films, in comic strips, in ritual objects.

Then this: as deployment of the signifier, the Text often dramatically argues with the signified which tends to recrudesce within it: if it succumbs to this recrudescence, if the signified triumphs, the text ceases to be Text, the stereotype within it becomes "truth" instead of being the ludic object of a second combinative operation. Hence, it is logical that the Text engage its operator in what we may call a drama of writing (which we shall see analyzed here apropos of Flaubert), or its reader in preliminary critical evaluation.

However, the main and so to speak massive approach that can be made to the Text consists in exploring all its manifest signifiers: structures which the linguistics of discourse can articulate: phonic configurations (puns, proper names), typographic arrangements, polysemies, enjambments, blanks, collages, associations, everything which calls into question the book's substance, will be recognized here, proposed by various authors, from Flaubert to Claude Simon.

Last, the Text is above all (or after all) that long operation through which an author (a discoursing author) discovers (or makes the reader discover) the *irreparability* of his speech and manages to substitute *it speaks* for *I speak.* To know the image-repertoire of expression is to empty it out, since the image-repertoire is lack of knowledge: several studies, here, attempt to evaluate the image-repertoire of writing (apropos of Chateaubriand, of Gide, of Michel Leiris) or the image-repertoire of the researcher himself (apropos of a research on cinematographic suspense).

It must not be supposed that these various "prospects" help *encircle* the Text; rather, it is to expand the Text that the entire issue functions. Hence, we must resist trying to organize, to program these studies, whose writing remains very diverse (I have been reluctant to acknowledge the necessity of "introducing" this issue of *Communications,* for thereby I risk appearing to give it a unity in which the contributors may not recognize themselves, and lending each of them a voice which is perhaps not entirely his own: any presentation, by its intention of synthesis, is a kind of concession to discourse). Ideally, throughout the issue, independent of what precedes and of what follows, the research of these young scholars should appear both as the revelation of certain structures of speech-acts (even if they are analyzed in the simple language of a report) and the critique (the auto-critique) of any speech-act: moreover it is just when research manages to link its object to its discourse and to dispossess our knowledge by the light it casts on objects not so much unknown as unexpected—it is at just this moment that research becomes a true interlocution, a task in behalf of others, in a word: a social production.

Communications, 1972

The Rustle of Language

Speech is irreversible; that is its fatality. What has been said cannot be unsaid, *except by adding to it*: to correct, here, is, oddly enough, to continue. In speaking, I can never erase, annul; all I can do is say "I am erasing, annulling, correcting," in short, speak some more. This very singular annulation-by-addition I shall call "stammering." Stammering is a message spoiled twice over: it is difficult to understand, but with an effort it can be understood all the same; it is really neither *in* language nor *outside* it: it is a noise of language comparable to the knocks by which a motor lets it be known that it is not working properly; such is precisely the meaning of the *misfire*, the auditory sign of a failure which appears in the functioning of the object. Stammering (of the motor or of the subject) is, in short, a fear: I am afraid the motor is going to stop.

The death of the machine: it can be distressing to man, if he describes it like that of a beast (see Zola's novel). In short, however unsympathetic the machine may be (because it constitutes, in the figure of the robot, the most serious of threats: the *loss of the body*), it still contains the possibility of a euphoric theme: its *good functioning*; we dread the machine when it works by itself, we delight in it when it works well. Now, just as the dysfunctions of language are in a sense summarized in an auditory sign, stammering, similarly the good functioning of the machine is displayed in a musical being: the *rustle*.

The rustle is the noise of what is working well. From which follows this paradox: the rustle denotes a limit-noise, an impossible noise, the noise of what, functioning to perfection, has no noise; to rustle is to make audible the very evaporation of noise: the tenuous, the blurred, the tremulous are received as the signs of an auditory annulation.

Thus, it is happy machines which rustle. When the erotic machine, so often imagined and described by Sade, an "intellectual" agglomerate of bodies whose amorous sites are carefully adjusted to each other—when this machine starts up, by the convulsive movements of the participants, it trembles and rustles: in short, *it works*, and it works well. Elsewhere, when today's Japanese surrender themselves en masse, in huge halls, to the slot-machine game called pachinko, these halls are filled with the enormous rustle of the little balls, and this rustle signifies that something, collectively, is working: the pleasure (enigmatic for other reasons) of playing, of moving the body with exactitude. For the rustle (we see this from the Sadean example and from the Japanese example) implies a community of bodies: in the sounds of the pleasure which is "working," no voice is raised, guides, or swerves, no voice is constituted; the rustle is the very sound of plural delectation—plural but never massive (the mass, quite the contrary, has a single voice, and terribly loud).

And language—can language rustle? Speech remains, it seems, condemned to stammering; writing, to silence and to the distinction of signs: in any case, there always remains *too much meaning* for language to fulfill a delectation appropriate to its substance. But what is impossible is not inconceivable: the rustle of language forms a utopia. Which utopia? That of a music of meaning; in its utopic state, language would be enlarged, I should even say *denatured* to the point of forming a vast auditory fabric in which the semantic apparatus would be made unreal; the phonic, metric, vocal signifier would be deployed in all its sumptuosity, without a sign ever becoming detached from it (ever *naturalizing* this pure layer of delectation), but also—and this is what is difficult—without meaning being brutally dismissed, dogmatically foreclosed, in short castrated. Rustling, entrusted to the signifier by an unprecedented movement unknown to our rational discourses, language would not thereby abandon a horizon of meaning: meaning, undivided, impenetrable, unnamable, would however be posited in the distance like a mirage, making the vocal exercise into a double landscape, furnished with a "background"; but instead of the music of the phonemes being the "background" of our messages (as happens in our poetry), meaning would now be the vanishing point of delectation. And just as, when attributed to the machine, the rustle is only the noise of an absence of noise, in the same way, shifted to language, it would be that meaning which reveals an exemption of meaning or—the same thing—that non-meaning which produces in the distance a meaning henceforth liberated from all the aggressions of which the sign, formed in the "sad and fierce history of men," is the Pandora's box.

This is a utopia, no doubt about it; but utopia is often what guides the investigations of the avant-garde. So there exists here and there, at moments, what we might call certain experiments in rustling: like certain productions of post-serial music (it is quite significant that this music grants an extreme importance to the voice: it is the voice it works with, seeking to denature the meaning in it, but not the auditory volume), certain radiophonic researches; and like the latest texts by Pierre Guyotat or Philippe Sollers.

Moreover, we ourselves can undertake this research around the rustle, and in life, in the adventures of life; in what life affords us in an utterly impromptu manner. The other evening, watching Antonioni's film on China, I suddenly experienced, at the end of a sequence, the rustle of language: in a village street, some children, leaning against a wall, reading aloud, each one a different book to himself but all together; that—that rustled in the right way, like a machine that works well; the meaning was doubly impenetrable to me, by my not knowing Chinese and by the blurring of these simultaneous readings; but I was hearing, in a kind of hallucinated perception (so intensely was it receiving all the subtlety of the scene), I was hearing the music, the breath, the tension, the application, in short something like a *goal.* Is that all it takes—just speak all at the same time in order to make language rustle, in the rare fashion, stamped with delectation, that I have been trying to describe? No, of course not; the auditory scene requires an erotics (in the broadest sense of the term), the élan, or the discovery, or the simple accompaniment of an emotion: precisely what was contributed by the countenances of the Chinese children.

I imagine myself today something like the ancient Greek as Hegel describes him: he interrogated, Hegel says, passionately, uninterruptedly, the rustle of branches, of springs, of winds, in short, the shudder of Nature, in order to perceive in it the design of an intelligence. And I—it is the shudder of meaning I interrogate, listening to the rustle of language, that language which for me, modern man, is my Nature.

Vers une esthétique sans entraves (U.G.E.), 1975

3
LANGUAGES AND STYLE

Rhetorical Analysis

Literature presents itself to us as an *institution* and as a *work*. As an institution, it collects all usages and all practices which govern the circuit of the thing written in a given society: the writer's social status and ideology, modes of circulation, conditions of consumption, sanctions of criticism. As a work, it is essentially constituted by a verbal, written message of a certain type. It is the work-as-object that I wish to deal with, suggesting that we concern ourselves with a still little-explored field (though the word is very old), that of *rhetoric*.

The literary work includes elements which are not special to literature; I shall cite at least one of these, because the development of mass communications permits its incontestable recognition today in films, in comic strips, and perhaps in the news item [the *fait-divers*], i.e., elsewhere than in the novel: this is narrative, story, argument, what Souriau has called, apropos of film, *diegesis*. There exists a diegetic form common to different arts, a form we are beginning to analyze today according to new methods inspired by Propp. However, confronting the element of fabulation it shares with other creations, literature possesses one element which defines it specifically: its language; this specific element the Russian formalist school has already sought to isolate and to treat under the name of *Literaturnost*, "literariness"; Jakobson calls it *poetics*; poetics is the analysis which permits answering this question: What is it that makes a verbal message a work of art? It is this specific element which, for my part, I shall call *rhetoric*, so as to avoid any restriction of poetics to poetry and in order to mark our concern with a general level of language common to all genres, prose and verse alike. My question is whether a confrontation of society and rhetoric is possible, and under what conditions.

For centuries—from antiquity to the nineteenth century—rhetoric has received a definition which is at once functional and technical: it is an art, i.e., a set of constraints which permit either persuasion or, subsequently, expressiveness. This declared goal evidently makes rhetoric into a social institution, and, paradoxically, the link which unites the forms of language to societies is much more immediate than the strictly ideological relation; in ancient Greece, rhetoric is born very specifically in the property trials which followed the exactions of the Tyrants in fifth-century Sicily; in bourgeois society, the art of speaking according to certain rules is both a sign of social power and an instrument of that power; it is not insignificant that the class which concludes secondary studies of the young bourgeois in France is called the *classe de rhétorique*. However, it is not this immediate (and, indeed, quickly exhausted) relation that we shall linger over, for, as we know, if social need engenders certain functons, these functions, once they are set in operation, or, as we say, once they are *determined*, acquire an unforeseen autonomy and acquire new significations. For the functional definition of rhetoric, I shall therefore substitute an immanent, structural definition, or to be still more specific, an *informational* definition.

We know that every message (and the literary work is one of them) includes at least one level of expression, or level of signifiers, and one level of content, or level of signifieds; the junction of these two levels forms the sign (or group of signs). However, a message constituted according to this elementary order can, by an operation of separation or amplification, become the simple expressive level of a second message, which is of the extensive variety; in short, the sign of the first message becomes the signifier of the second. We are then in the presence of two semiotic systems imbricated within each other in a regular fashion. Hjelmslev has called the second system thus constituted *connotative semiotics* (in opposition to the meta-language, in which the sign of the first message becomes the signified and not the signifier of the second message). Now, as language, literature is, from all evidence, a connotative semiotics; in a literary text, a first system of signification, which is language (French, for instance), serves as a simple signifier in a second message, whose signified is different from the signifieds of the language; if I read: *Faites avancer les commodités de la conversation* (Bring forward the comforts of conversation), I perceive a *denotated* message which is the order to move the armchairs closer, but I also perceive a *connotated* message whose signified here is "preciosity." In informational terms, we shall therefore define literature as a double system, denoted-connoted; in this double system, the manifest and specific level, which is that of the signifiers of the second system, will constitute Rhetoric; the rhetorical signifiers will be the connotators.

Defined in informational terms, the literary message can and must be subjected to a systematic exploration, without which we can never confront it with the History which produces it, since the historical being of this message is not only what it says but also the way in which it is fabricated. Of course, the linguistics of connotation—which we cannot confuse with the old stylistics, for the latter, studying means of expression, remained on the level of speech [*parole*], while the former, studying codes, takes its place on the level of the language [*langue*]—is not yet constituted; but certain indications of contemporary linguists permit us to propose at least two directions to rhetorical analysis.

The first has been sketched by Jakobson, who distinguishes six factors in every message: a sender, a receiver, a context or referent, a contact, a code, and finally the message itself; to each of these factors corresponds a function of language; every discourse mixes most of these functions, but it receives its *mark* from the dominance of one function or another over the rest; for instance, if the emphasis is put on the person emitting the message, the expressive or emotive function dominates; if it is put on the receiver, it is the connotative (exhortative or supplicative) function which prevails; if it is the referent which receives the emphasis, the discourse is denotative (as is the case here); if it is the contact (between sender and receiver), the phatic function refers to all the signs intended to maintain communication between the interlocutors; the meta-linguistic function, or function of elucidation, accentuates recourse to the code; last, when it is the message itself, its configuration, the palpable aspect of its signs which are emphasized, the discourse is poetic, in the broad sense of the term: this is obviously the case of literature; we can say that literature (work or text) is specifically a message which puts the emphasis on itself. This definition no doubt permits a better understanding of how it comes about that the communicative function does not exhaust the literary work, but that the latter, resisting purely functional definitions, always presents itself in a certain fashion as a tautology, since the message's intra-mundane functions remain ultimately subject to its structural function. However, the coherence and declaration of the poetic function may vary with History; and further, synchronically, this same function may be "devoured" by other functions, a phenomenon which in a sense diminishes the work's coefficient of literary specificity. Jakobson's definition therefore involves a sociological perspective, since it permits us to evaluate both the process of literary language and its situation in relation to non-literary languages.

Another exploration of the literary message is possible, this time of a distributional type. We know that a whole portion of linguistics is concerned today with defining words less by their meaning than by the syntagmatic associations in which they can take their place; roughly speaking, words associate among themselves according to a certain scale of probability: *dog* is readily associated with *bark* but rarely with *mew*, though syntactically there is nothing that forbids the association of a verb and a subject; this syntagmatic "filling" of the sign is occasionally called *catalysis*. Now, catalysis has a close relation with the special nature of literary language; within certain limits, which are precisely those to be studied, the more aberrant the catalysis, the more patent *literature* becomes. Of course, if we abide by the literal units, literature is not at all incompatible with a normal catalysis; in *the sky is blue as an orange,* no literal association is deviant; but if we refer to a higher level of units, which is precisely that of connotators, we recognize the catalytic disturbance without difficulty, for it is statistically aberrant to associate blueness with an orange. The literary message can therefore be defined as a divergence of association of signs (Guiraud); operationally, for instance, confronting the normative tasks of automatic translation, literature might be defined as the sum of the insoluble cases presented to the machine. We can say in another fashion that literature is essentially a *costly system of information.* However, if literature is uniformly luxurious, there are several luxury economies, which can vary with periods and societies; in our classical literature of the anti-*précieux* generation, syntagmatic associations remain within normal margins on the level of denotation, and it is explicitly the rhetorical level which supports the high cost of the information; on the contrary, in surrealist poetry (to take two extremes), the associations are aberrant and the information costly on the level of the elementary units themselves. We can reasonably hope, here again, that the distributional definition of the literary message will cause certain links to appear between each society and the economy of information it assigns to literature.

Thus, the very form of the literary message is in a certain relation with History and with society, but this relation is special and does not necessarily coincide with the history and sociology of contents. The connotators form the elements of a code, and the validity of this code can be more or less lasting; the classical code (in the broad sense) has lasted for centuries in the West, since it is the same rhetoric which animates an oration by Cicero or a sermon by Bossuet; but it is likely that this code underwent a profound mutation in the second half of the nineteenth century, even if, to this very day, certain traditional writings are subject to it. This mutation is doubtless related to the crisis of bourgeois consciousness; the problem, however, is not to know if the one analogically reflects the other, but if, confronting a certain order of phenomena, history does not somehow intervene to modify the rhythm of their diachrony; as a matter of fact, as soon as we deal with forms (and this is obviously the case with the rhetorical code), the processes of change are more on the order of translation than of evolution: there is successive exhaustion of the possible mutations, and history is called upon to modify the rhythm of these mutations, not these forms themselves; there is perhaps a certain endogenous development of the structure of the literary message, analogous to the one which governs changes of fashion.

There is another way of appreciating the relation between rhetoric and society: by evaluating the degree of "frankness" of the rhetorical code. It is certain that the literary message of the classical period deliberately paraded its connotation, since the figures constituted a code transmissible by apprenticeship (whence the numerous treatises of the period), and since it was not possible to form a recognized message except by drawing on this code. Today, as we know, this rhetoric has exploded; but precisely by studying its debris, its substitutes, or its lacunae, we can doubtless account for the multiplicity of writings and recognize, for each of them, the signification it possesses in our society. We might thus approach quite precisely the problem of the division between *good literature* and the others, whose social importance is considerable, especially in a mass society. But here, too, we must not look for an analogical relation between a group of usages and its rhetoric; our task is rather to reconstitute a general system of sub-codes, each of which is defined in a certain state of society by its differences, its distances, and its identities with regard to its neighbors: elite literature and mass culture, avant-garde and tradition, constitute, formally, different codes simultaneously placed, according to Merleau-Ponty, in a "modulation of coexistence"; it is this set of simultaneous codes, whose plurality has been recognized by Jakobson, which should be studied; and since a code is itself merely a certain way of distributing a closed collection of signs, rhetorical analysis should derive not from sociology strictly speaking, but rather from that socio-logic, or sociology of forms of classification already postulated by Durkheim and Mauss.

Such are, summarily and abstractly presented, the general perspectives of rhetorical analysis. It is an analysis whose project is not new, but to which recent developments of structural linguistics and of information theory afford renewed possibilities of exploration; but, above all, it requires of us a methodological analysis that is perhaps new: for the formal nature of the object it seeks to study (the literary message) obliges us to describe in an immanent and exhaustive fashion the rhetorical code (or codes) before setting this code (or these codes) in relation with the society and the history which produce and consume them.

Goldmann colloquium, 1966

Style and Its Image

I should like to begin with a personal consideration: for some twenty years, my investigations have been concerned with literary language, without my being altogether comfortable in the role either of critic or of linguist. I should like to take advantage of this ambiguous situation in order to deal with an impure notion, one which is at once a metaphoric form and a theoretical concept. This notion is an *image*. I do not believe, as a matter of fact, that scientific work can proceed without a certain *image* of its object (as we know, nothing is more resolutely metaphoric than the language of mathematicians or geographers); nor do I believe that the intellectual image, heir of ancient Pythagorean cosmogonies, at once spatial, musical, and abstract, can be divested of a theoretical value which preserves it from contingency without exaggeratedly deflecting it toward abstraction. Hence, it is an image which I seek to question, or, more specifically, a *vision*: How do we *see* style? What is the image of style which troubles me, what is the one I desire?

Simplifying greatly (the privilege of vision), it seems to me that style (in the current sense of the word) has always been part of a binary system, or, if you prefer, of a mythological paradigm of two terms; these terms have, of course, changed names and even content, according to periods and schools. Let us consider two of these oppositions.

The first, the oldest (it is still with us, at least quite frequently in the teaching of literature), is that of *Content* and *Form*; it derives, we know, from one of the first classifications of classical Rhetoric, the opposition between *Res* and *Verba*: on *Res* (or demonstrative materials of discourse) depends *Inventio*, or research into what one can say about a subject (*quaestio*); on *Verba* depends *Elocutio* (or transformation of these materials into a verbal form); this *Elocutio* is, roughly, our "style." The relation of Form and Content is phenomenological: Form is reputed to be the appearance or garment of Content, which is its truth or body; the metaphors attached to Form (to style) are therefore of a decorative order: *figures, colors, nuances*; or again, this relation of Form and Content is experienced as expressive or alethic: the writer (or the commentator) must establish a *proper* relation between content (truth) and form (appearance), between message (as content) and its *medium* (style); between these two concentric terms (the one being *inside* the other) is assumed a reciprocal guarantee. This guarantee gives rise to a historical problem: can Form *disguise* Content, or must it be subservient to it (so that there can no longer be a "coded" Form)? It is this argument which sets in opposition, down through the centuries, Aristotelian (later Jesuit) rhetoric and Platonic (later Pascalian) rhetoric. This vision subsists, despite terminological change, when we consider the text as the superposition of a *signified* and a *signifier*, the signified then being inevitably experienced (I am speaking here of a more or less assumed vision) as a secret hidden behind the signifier.

The second, much more recent opposition, of a more scientific aspect and largely tributary to the Saussurian paradigm *Langue / Parole* (or *Code / Message*), is that of *Norm* and *Deviance*. Style is then seen as the exception (though coded) to a rule; it is the (individual, yet institutional) aberration of a current usage, sometimes perceived as verbal (if we define the norm by the spoken language), sometimes as prosaic (if we set Poetry in opposition to "something else"). Just as the opposition *Form / Content* implies a phenomenological vision, so the *Norm / Deviance* opposition implies an ultimately moral vision (under cover of a logic of *endoxa*): there is a reduction of the systematic to the sociological (the code is what is statistically guaranteed by the greatest number of users) and of the sociological to the normal, where social nature begins; literature, the space of style, and because it is specifically this space, then assumes a shamanic function, which Lévi-Strauss has well described in his *Introduction to the Work of Marcel Mauss:* it is the site of (verbal) anomaly, as society establishes, recognizes, and assumes it by honoring its writers, in the same way that the ethnic group establishes the supernatural in the person of the witch doctor (the way an abscess marks the limits of a disease), in order to recuperate it in a process of collective communication.

I should like to start from these two visions, less to attack them than to complicate them.

Let us take first the opposition of Content and Form, of Signified and Signifier. No doubt it includes a certain, irreducible portion of truth. Structural analysis of narrative in its achievements and its promises is wholly based on the conviction (and the practical proof) that we can transform a *given* text into a more schematic version, whose meta-language is no longer the integral language of the original text, without changing the narrative identity of this text: in order to enumerate functions, to reconstitute sequences, or to distribute agents—in short, to bring to light a narrative grammar which is no longer the grammar of the vernacular of the text—we must peel off the stylistic (or, more generally, elocutionary, "expressive") film from another layer of secondary (narrative) meaning, to which the stylistic features have no pertinence: they can be varied without affecting the structure. That Balzac should say of a disturbing old man that he "kept upon his bluish lips a fixed and paralyzed smile, as implacable and jeering as the smile of a death's-head," has exactly the same narrative (or, more precisely, semantic) function as if we were to transform the phrase and say that the old man had something funereal and fantastic about him (this *seme* is irreducible, since it is functionally necessary to the sequence of the story).

The error, however—and it is here that we must modify our vision of Content and Form—would be to stop "peeling off" style prematurely; what this (possible, as we have just said) peeling off reveals is not a content, a signified, but another form, another signifer, or if we prefer a more neutral term, another level, *which is never the last* (for the text is always articulated around codes which it does not exhaust); signifieds are forms, as we have known since Hjelmslev and even more clearly from the recent hypotheses of certain psychoanalysts, anthropologists, philosophers. Recently, analyzing a tale by Balzac, I attempted to bring to light—without reference to style, with which I was not concerned, and remaining within the boundaries of the signified—an interplay of five different codes: actional, hermeneutic, semic, cultural, and symbolic; the "citations" which the author (or more exactly the performer of the text) extracts from these codes are juxtaposed, mixed, superimposed within one and the same expressive unit (a single sentence, for example, or, more generally, a "lexia," or unit of reading), so as to form a braid, a fabric, or even (etymologically) a *text*. Here is an example: the sculptor Sarrasine is in love with a prima donna whom he does not know to be a castrato; he abducts her, and the apparent soprano defends herself: "The Italian woman was armed with a dagger. 'If you come closer,' she said, 'I shall be forced to plunge this weapon into your heart.' " Is there, *behind* the statement, a signified? Not at all; the sentence is the "braid" of several codes: a linguistic code (the French language), a rhetorical code (antonomasia, interpolation of an *inquit*, apostrophe), an actional code (the armed defense of the victim is a unit in the sequence *Rape*), a hermeneutic code (the castrato conceals his sex by feigning to defend his virtue as a woman), and a symbolic code (the knife is a symbol of castration).

Hence we can no longer *see* the text as the binary structure of a content and a form; the text is not double, but multiple; in the text, there are only forms, or, more precisely, the text in its totality is only a multiplicity of forms—without (a) content. We can say metaphorically that the literary text is a stereography: neither melodic nor harmonic, it is resolutely contrapuntal; it mingles voices in a volume, not in a line, not even a double one. Doubtless, among these voices (these codes, these systems, these forms), some are more especially attached to verbal substance, verbal *play* (linguistics, rhetoric), but this is a historical distinction, useful only for the literature of the Signified (which is in general the only literature that we have studied); for we need merely think of a few modern texts to see that as the (narrative, logical, symbolic, psychological) signified recedes still further, it is not possible to set in opposition (even with the greatest sensitivity to nuance) systems of Form and systems of Content: style is a historical (and not universal) concept, which has pertinence only for certain historic works. Does it have, within this older literature, a definite function? I believe it does. The stylistic system, which is one system among others, has a function of naturalization, or of familiarization, or of domestication: the units of the codes of content are in effect subjected to a rough pigeonholing (actions are separated, characterial and symbolic notations are disseminated, the march of truth is fragmented, retarded); language, in the elementary aspects of sentence, period, paragraph, superimposes upon this semantic discontinuity established on the level of discourse the appearance of continuity; for however discontinuous language itself may be, its structure is so fixed in the experience of each man that he recognizes it as a veritable *nature*: do we not speak of the "flux of speech"? What is more familiar, more obvious, more natural, than a sentence read? Style "overspreads" the semantic articulations of content; by metonymic means, it naturalizes the story told, declares it innocent.

Now let us turn to the second opposition, that of Norm and Deviance, which is in effect the opposition of Code and Message, since style (or literary effect) is experienced here as an aberrant message which "*surprises*" the code. Here too, we must refine our vision of the opposition rather than destroy it.

The features of style are undeniably drawn from a code, or at least from a systematic space (this distinction seems necessary if we want to respect the possibility of a multi-code, or even the existence of a signifier whose space is governed and yet infinite, i.e., an unsaturatable paradigm): style is a distance, a difference;

but in relation to what? The reference is most often, implicitly or explicitly, to the spoken ("current," "normal") language. This proposition seems to me both excessive and insufficient: excessive because stylistic codes of reference or difference are numerous, and the spoken language is always only one of these codes (which, moreover, there is no reason to privilege as the *princeps* language, the incarnation of the fundamental code, the absolute reference); insufficient because the opposition of spoken and written is never exploited in all its depth. A word on this last point.

We know that the object of linguistics, what determines at once its task and its limits, is the *sentence* (however difficult to define): beyond the sentence, there is no linguistics, for here *discourse* begins, and the combinative rules of sentences are different from those of *monemes*; but, short of this, there is no linguistics either, for then we can expect to find only shapeless, incomplete, "unworthy" syntagms; only the sentence, we feel, guarantees organization, structure, unity. Now, the interior language (the language of thought) is essentially a *sub-sentence* language; of course, it can include complete sentences, but the code of the genre does not require this for the success and advantage of the communication: we constantly talk without finishing our sentences. Listen to a conversation: note how many sentences there are whose structure is incomplete or ambiguous, how many clauses are subordinated with no main clause or with no clear antecedent, how many subjects lack predicates, how many adversatives lack correlatives, etc. To the point where it is abusive to continue speaking of "sentences," even "incomplete" or "defective" ones; better to speak, more neutrally, of syntagms whose "congregation" remains to be described. But if we open a book, there will not be one sentence which is not *ended*, by an overdetermination of operators—structural, rhythmic, and punctuational.

Whence, by rights, two autonomous linguistics: a linguistics of the syntagm and a linguistics of the sentence, a linguistics of the spoken and a linguistics of the written. By carrying this distinction to its conclusions, we shall only be following the recommendations of philosophy, which today assigns speech and writing different ontologies; it is, philosophy says, by a paradoxical abuse that linguistics deals only with the written (language in sentences), while claiming that the canonical form of language is speech, in respect to which writing is only "transcription."

We lack, obviously, a grammar of the spoken language (but is this grammar possible: is it not the very notion of grammar which would be eliminated by this division of communication?), insofar as we have only a grammar of the sentence. This lack determines a new distribution of languages: there are languages of the sentence and all the other kinds. The first are marked by a constraining character, an obligatory rubric: the completion of the sentence. Style is obviously one of these written languages, and its generic feature (which attaches it to the genre of the written but does not yet distinguish it from its neighbors) is its requirement to complete its sentences: by its finitude, by its "*neatness*," the sentence declares itself written, en route to its literary state: the sentence is already, in itself, a stylistic object: the absence of smudging, by which it fulfills itself, is in a sense the first criterion of style; we see this clearly in two properly stylistic values: *simplicity* and *contour*: both are effects of neatness, one litotic, the other rhetorical: if this sentence of Claudel's ("The night is so calm it seems salted") is both simple and "contoured," it is because it completes the sentence in its necessary and sufficient plenitude. This can be related to several historical phenomena: first of all, a certain gnomic inheritance of the written language (divinatory maxims, religious formulas, whose typically sentential closure assures polysemy); then, the humanist myth of the living sentence, effluvium of an organic model, at once closed and generative (a myth discussed in the treatise *On the Sublime*); last, the attempts—though as yet ineffectual, so closely is literature, even subversive literature, linked to the sentence—to explode the limits of the sentence (Mallarmé's *Coup de dés*, hyper-proliferation of the Proustian sentence, destruction of the typographic sentence in modern poetry).

The sentence, in its closure and its "neatness," seems to me, then, the fundamental determination of writing. From which many written codes are possible (though not yet always identified): learned, academic, administrative, journalistic writing, each describable in terms of its clientele, its lexicon, and its syntactical protocols (inversions, figures, clausulae, all features marking the identity of a collective writing by their presence or their absence). Among all these kinds of writing, and even before speaking of style in the individual sense in which we ordinarily understand this word, there is *literary* language, a truly collective writing whose systematic features should be itemized (and not only its historical features, as has been done hitherto): What is it, for instance, which is permitted in a literary text but not in an academic article? Inversions, order of complements, syntactical license, archaisms, figures, lexicon? What we must grasp first is not the idiolect of an author but of an institution (literature).

This is not all. Literary writing must be located not only in relation to its closest neighbors but also in relation to its models. I mean by *models* not sources, in the philological sense of the word (let us note in passing that the problem of sources has been raised almost exclusively on the level of the content), but syntagmatic *patterns*, typical fragments of sentences, formulas, if you like, whose origin is not identifiable but which make up part of the collective memory of literature. *To write* is to let these models come to one and to *transform* them (in the sense this word has acquired in linguistics).

I shall point out, in this regard, three phenomena, taken virtually at random from a recent experiment. The first is personal testimony: having worked for some time on a tale by Balzac, I often catch myself spontaneously carrying over into the circumstances of daily life fragments of sentences, formulations spontaneously taken from the Balzacian text; it is not the memorial (banal) character of the phenomenon which interests me here, but the evidence that I am *writing* daily life (it is true, in my head) through these formulas inherited from an anterior writing; or again, more precisely, life is the very thing which comes *already* constituted as a literary writing: *nascent* writing is a *past* writing. The second phenomenon is an example of external transformation: when Balzac writes: "I was plunged into one of those profound reveries which overcome everyone, even the frivolous, in the midst of the most tumultuous festivities," the sentence, if we except its personal mark (*"I was plunged"*), is merely the transformation of a proverb: *Amidst tumultuous festivities, profound reveries;* in other words, the literary speech-act refers, by transformation, to another syntactic structure: the *first* content of the sentence is another form (here, the gnomic form), and style is established in the effort of transformation applied not to ideas but to forms; it remains, of course, to identify the chief stereotypes (such as the proverb) from which literary language is invented and generated. The third phenomenon is an example of internal transformation (which the author generates from his own formula): at a certain moment of his stay at Balbec, the Proustian narrator tries to engage the young elevator boy of the Grand Hôtel in conversation, but the boy does not answer him, Proust says, "whether from astonishment at my words, attention to his work, concern for etiquette, hardness of hearing, respect for the place, fear of danger, mental torpor, or orders of the director"; the repetition of the same syntactical formula (a noun and its complement) is obviously a game, a "turn," and style then consists in (1) transforming a potential subordinate clause into a nominal syntagm (*because he did not hear well* becomes *his hardness of hearing*); (2) repeating as often as possible this transformational formula through different contents.

From these three random and virtually impromptu remarks, I should merely like to draw a working hypothesis: that we consider stylistic features as *transformations*, derived either from collective formulas (of unrecoverable origin, literary or preliterary) or, by metaphoric interplay, from idiolectal forms; in both cases, what should govern the stylistic task is the search for models, for patterns: sentential structures, syntagmatic clichés, divisions and clausulae of sentences; and what should animate this task is the conviction that style is essentially a citational procedure, a body of formulas, a memory (almost in the cybernetic sense of the word), an inheritance based on culture and not on expressivity. This permits situating the *transformation* to which I allude (and consequently the transformational stylistics I can desire): it certainly has some affinity with transformational grammar, but it differs from it on one fundamental point (where linguistics, inevitably implying a certain *vision* of language, once again becomes ideological): stylistic "models" cannot be identified with "deep structures," with universal forms derived from a psychological logic; these models are only the depositaries of culture (even if they seem very old); they are repetitions, not foundations; citations, not expressions; stereotypes, not archetypes.

To return to that vision of style to which I alluded at the beginning: in my opinion, it must consist today in *seeing* style within the plurality of the text: a plurality of semantic levels (codes), whose "braiding" forms the text, and a plurality of citations deposited in that code we are calling "style" and which I should prefer to call, at least as a first object of study, *literary language*. The problem of style can only be treated in relation to what I shall call the *layered* quality of discourse; and, to continue the alimentary metaphor, I shall sum up these few remarks by saying that, if hitherto we have *seen* the text as a fruit with its pit (an apricot, for instance), the flesh being the form and the pit the content, it would be better to see it as an onion, a superimposed construction of skins (of layers, of levels, of systems) whose volume contains, finally, no heart, no core, no secret, no irreducible principle, nothing but the very infinity of its envelopes—which envelop nothing other than the totality of its surfaces.

Bellagio colloquium, 1969

Pax Culturalis

To say that there is a bourgeois culture is wrong, because it is our entire culture which is bourgeois (and to say that our culture is bourgeois is a tiresome truism, one which is mouthed in all our universities). To say that culture is in opposition to nature is dubious, because we are not sure where the limits of each are: Where is nature in man? If one is to describe himself as man, that man must have a language, i.e., culture itself. In the biological? Today we recognize in the living organism the same structures as in the speaking subject: life itself is constructed as a language. In short, everything is culture, from garment to book, from food to image, and culture is everywhere, from end to end of the social scale. This culture, certainly, is a very paradoxical object: without contours, without oppositional term, *without remainder.*

Let us even add, perhaps: without incident—or at least without schism, subject to a tireless repetition. Here, on television, an American spy serial: cocktails on a yacht, and the characters indulging in a kind of worldly banter (flirtations, double meanings, worldly interests); but *this has already been seen or said*: not only in thousands of popular novels and films, but in earlier works belonging to what might pass for *another* culture, in Balzac, for instance: one might suppose that the Princess de Cadignan has simply *changed places,* that she has left the Faubourg Saint-Germain for the yacht of a Greek shipowner. Thus, culture is not only what returns, it is also and especially what remains in place, like an imperishable corpse: it is a bizarre toy that *History never breaks.*

A unique object, since it never sets itself in opposition to anything, an eternal object, since it never breaks—in short, a peaceable object, in whose bosom everyone is gathered without apparent conflict: then where is culture's reflexive task—where are its contradictions, where is its inadequacy?

To answer, we must, despite the epistemological paradox of the object, risk a definition, the vaguest imaginable of course: culture is a *field of dispersion*. Of what? Of languages.

In our culture, in the *Pax culturalis* to which we are subject, there is an inveterate war of languages: our languages exclude each other; in a society divided (by social class, money, academic origin), language itself divides. What portion of languages can I, as an intellectual, share with a salesman in the Nouvelles Galeries? Doubtless, if we are both French, the language of *communication*; but this is an infinitesimal share: we can exchange pieces of information and truisms; but the rest, i.e., the enormous volume, the entire *play* of language? Since there is no subject *outside* language, since language is what constitutes the subject through and through, the separation of languages is a permanent grief; and this grief, if it does not occur only when we leave our "milieu" (where everyone speaks the same language), is not only the material contact of others, coming from other circles, other professions, which lacerates us—it is precisely that "culture" which, in good democracy, we are all supposed to share: it is precisely when, under the effect of apparently technical determinations, culture seems unified (an illusion rather stupidly reproduced by the expression "mass culture") that the division of cultural languages is excruciated. Spend an evening at your television set (to keep to the commonest forms of culture); you will receive—despite efforts of general banalization undertaken by the producers—several different languages; it is impossible that all of these languages will respond not only to your desire (I use this word in its strongest sense) but even to your intellection: there is always, in culture, a share of language which the Other (hence I myself) does not understand; my neighbor is bored by this Brahms concerto, and I regard this variety sketch as vulgar and that soap opera as idiotic: boredom, vulgarity, stupidity are various names for the secession of languages. The result is that this secession not only separates men from each other, but each man, each individual is in himself lacerated; each day in myself, there accumulate, without communicating, several isolated languages: I am fragmented, severed, scattered (which in other circumstances passes for the very definition of "madness"). And, even if I manage to speak the same language all day long, how many different languages I am compelled to receive! That of my colleagues, of my postman, of my students, of the sports commentator on the radio, of the classical author I read in the evening: it is a linguist's illusion to consider on equal status the language spoken and the language heard, as if they were the same; here we must return to the fundamental distinction proposed by Jakobson between active grammar and passive grammar: the first is monotonous, the second is heteroclite—that is the truth of cultural language; in a divided society, even if it manages to unify its language, each man struggles against the *explosion of listening*: under cover of that total culture institutionally offered to him, the schizophrenic division of the subject is imposed upon him every day; culture is in a sense the pathological field par excellence, in which is inscribed the *alienation* of contemporary man.

Thus, it seems, what is sought by each social class is not the possession of culture—either to obtain or to preserve it—for culture is *there*, everywhere and for everyone; instead, it is the unity of language, the coincidence of speech and listening. How then, today, in our Western society, divided in its languages and unified in its culture, how do the social classes, the ones Marxism and sociology have taught us to recognize—how do they *look toward* the language of the Other? What is the (alas, very disappointing) *interlocutory play* in which, historically, they are involved?

The bourgeoisie in principle possesses all of culture, but it has been a long time (I am speaking for France) since it has possessed any cultural voice of its own. Since when? Since its intellectuals, its writers have dissociated themselves from it; the

Dreyfus Affair seems to have been, in our country, the instituting shock of this dissociation; this was, moreover, the moment when the word *intellectual* appeared: the intellectual is the "clerk" who seeks to break with the good conscience of his class—if not his class of origin (that a writer is "working class" changes nothing about the problem), at least his class of consumption. Here, today, *nothing is invented*: the bourgeois (owner, boss, executive, administrator) no longer accedes to the language of intellectual, literary, artistic research, because this language contests him; he resigns in favor of mass culture; his children no longer read Proust, listen to Chopin, but maybe Boris Vian, pop music. However, the intellectual who threatens him is no longer triumphant for that; try as he will to posit himself as a representative, as a procurator for the proletariat, as an oblate for the socialist cause, his critique of bourgeois culture can use only the old language of the bourgeoisie, which is transmitted to him by university teaching: the idea of *contestation* itself becomes a bourgeois idea; the public of intellectual writers may have shifted (though it is certainly not the proletariat which reads them), but not the language; of course, the intelligentsia seeks to *invent* new languages, but these languages remain *enclosed*: nothing has changed in social interlocution.

The proletariat (the producers) has no culture of its own; in so-called developed countries, its language is that of the petite bourgeoisie, because this is the language offered it by mass communications (popular press, radio, television): mass culture is petit-bourgeois. Of the three typical classes, it is the intermediate class—perhaps because this is the century of its historical promotion, which today is seeking to elaborate an original culture, one that would be *its own*: it is incontestable that important work is being done on the level of so-called mass culture (i.e., petit-bourgeois culture)—which is why it would be ridiculous to hold aloof from it. But by what means is such work being done? By the *already known* means of bourgeois culture: it is by taking and degrading the models (the patterns) of bourgeois language (its narratives, its types of reasoning, its psychological values) that petit-bourgeois culture creates and implants itself. The idea of *degradation* may seem "moral," the product of a bourgeois which regrets the excellence of past culture; I am giving it, quite the contrary, an objective, structural content: there is degradation because there is no invention; models are *repeated* on the spot, *banalized,* because petit-bourgeois culture (censored by the state) excludes even the contestation the intellectual can contribute to bourgeois culture: it is immobility, submission to stereotypes (conversion of messages into stereotypes) which defines such degradation. One can say that in petit-bourgeois culture, in mass culture, it is bourgeois culture which returns to the stage of History, *but as a farce* (Marx's image will be recalled).

A game of hunt-the-slipper thereby seems to govern the cultural war: the languages are indeed separated, like partners in the game, sitting beside each other; but what is passed from hand to hand is always the same object, the same culture: tragic immobility of culture, dramatic separation of languages—such is the double alienation of our society. Can we trust socialism to undo this contradiction, at once to "fluidify," to pluralize culture, and to put an end to the war of meanings, to the exclusion of languages? Certainly; what hope elsewhere? Yet we must not blind ourselves to the threat of a new enemy which lies in wait for *all* modern societies. Indeed, it seems that a new historical entity has appeared, has established itself, and is developing pathologically, complicating (without outdating) Marxist analysis: this new figure is the state (here, moreover, was the enigmatic point of Marxist science): the state apparatus is tougher than revolutions—and so-called mass culture is the direct expression of this state presence: in France, for example, the state now seeks to dissociate itself from the university, to turn its interest elsewhere, to concede the institution to the communists and the protesters, for it realizes that it is not here that a conquering culture will be created; but for nothing in the world will it release its hold of television or radio; by possessing these means of culture, it governs real culture, and, by governing it, makes it into *its own*: a culture within which must gather together the intellectually "resigning" class (the bourgeoisie), the promotional class (the petite-bourgeoisie), and the silent class (the proletariat). Thus, we understand why *on the other side,* even if the problem of the state is far from being settled, the People's Republic of China has named the radical transformation of society it has undertaken a "cultural revolution."

The Times Literary Supplement, 1971

The War of Languages

While out walking one day in my region, which is southwestern France, a peaceable terrain of retired minor officials, I had occasion to read, within a few hundred yards, on the doors of three villas, three different signs: *Vicious Dog, Dangerous Dog, Watchdog.* This region, evidently, has a very lively sense of property. But that is not of such interest as this: these three expressions constitute one and the same message: *Do Not Enter* (or you will be bitten). In other words, linguistics, which is concerned only with messages, could say nothing about them but what is very simple, very banal; it would by no means exhaust the meaning of these expressions, for *this meaning is in their difference*: *Vicious Dog* is aggressive; *Dangerous Dog* is philanthropic; *Watchdog* is apparently objective. In still other words, through one and the same message, we read three choices, three commitments, three mentalities, or again, three image-repertoires, three alibis of ownership; by the language of his sign—by what I should call his *discourse,* since the language is the same in the three cases—the villa's owner is sheltered and reassured behind a certain representation, even a certain system of ownership: here fierce (the dog, i.e., the owner, of course, is vicious), here protective (the dog is dangerous, the villa is armed), here finally legitimate (a dog is guarding the property, a statutory right). Thus, on the level of the simplest message (*Do Not Enter*), language (discourse) explodes, fragments, diverges: there is a *division* of languages, for which no simple science of communication can account; society, with its socio-economic and neurotic structures, intervenes, constructing language like a battleground.

Of course, it is the possibility of saying one and the same

thing in several ways, it is synonymy, which permits language to divide itself up; and synonymy is a statutory, structural, "natural" datum of language; but the war of languages is not "natural": it occurs where society transforms difference into conflict; one might say that there was a convergence of origin between the division of social classes, symbolic dissociation, the division of languages, and neurotic schism.

I have deliberately chosen my example *a minimo,* out of the language of a single class, that of small landowners, whose discourse sets in opposition certain *nuances* of appropriation. *A fortiori,* on the level of *social* society, if I may put it that way, language appears divided into great masses. However, one must be convinced of three things which are not simple: the first is that the division of languages does not match the division of classes term for term: from one class to the next, there are skids, borrowings, grids, relays; the second is that the war of languages is not the war of subjects: it is linguistic systems which are in opposition, not individualities—*sociolects,* not *idiolects*; the third is that the division of languages is marked against an apparent background of communication: the national idiom; more specifically, I should say that, on the scale of the nation, we understand each other but we do not communicate: putting things at their best, we have a *liberal* practice of language.

In contemporary societies, the simplest division of languages bears on their relation to Power. There are languages which are articulated, which develop, and which are marked in the light (or the shadow) of Power, of its many state, institutional, ideological machineries; I shall call these *encratic* languages or discourses. And facing them, there are languages which are elaborated, which feel their way, and which are themselves outside of Power and/or against Power; I shall call these *acratic* languages or discourses.

These two major forms of discourse do not have the same character. *Encratic* language is vague, diffuse, apparently "natural," and therefore not easily discerned: it is the language of mass culture (popular press, radio, television) and it is also, in a sense, the language of conversation, of public opinion (of the *doxa*); encratic language is both (a contradiction which constitutes its strength) *clandestine* (it is not easily recognizable) and *triumphant* (it is inescapable): I shall say that it is *sticky*.

Acratic language, on the other hand, is separate, severed from the *doxa* (hence, it is *paradoxical*); its schismatic strength derives from the fact that it is *systematic*, it is constructed around thought, not around ideology. The most immediate examples of this acratic language would be, today, Marxist discourse, psychoanalytic discourse, and, to a lesser degree but statutorily perceptible, structuralist discourse. But what is perhaps most interesting is that, even in the acratic sphere, there occur, once again, certain divisions, regionalities, and antagonisms of language: critical discourse is fragmented into dialects, enclaves, systems. I am tempted to call these discursive systems *Fictions*, adopting Nietzsche's word, and to regard intellectuals as those who form, again according to Nietzsche, the *sacerdotal class*, the caste responsible for elaborating, as artists, these Fictions of language (has not the priestly class, for a very long time, been the owner and the technician of formulas, i.e., of language?).

Whence certain relations of force between the discursive systems. What is a strong system? It is a system of language which can function in all situations, and whose energy subsists, whatever the mediocrity of the subjects using it: the stupidity of certain Marxists, of certain psychoanalysts, or of certain Christians in no way jeopardizes the force of the corresponding systems, of the corresponding discourses.

How do we account for the aggressive force, the power of domination of a discursive system, of a Fiction? Since the old Rhetoric, now permanently alien to our world of language, no *applied* language has yet revealed the weapons of linguistic combat: we do not know for certain the physics or the dialectic or the strategy of what I shall call our *logosphere*—though not a day passes when each of us is not subject to the intimidations of language. It seems to me that these discursive weapons are at least of three kinds.

1. Every strong system of discourse is a *representation* (in the theatrical sense: a show), a staging of arguments, aggressions, retorts, formulas, a mimodrama, in which the subject can engage his hysteric gratification.

2. There certainly exist *figures of system* (as we used to say *figures of rhetoric*), partial forms of discourse, set up with a view to giving the sociolect an absolute consistency, to closing the system, to protecting it and to excluding the adversary from it irremediably: for example, when a psychoanalyst says: "The rejection of psychoanalysis is a resistance which itself relates to psychoanalysis," that is a figure of system. In a general way, figures of system aim at including the Other in discourse as a simple object, the better to exclude him from the community of subjects speaking the strong language.

3. Last, going still further, we can speculate whether the sentence, as a practically closed syntactic structure, is not itself, already, a weapon, an operator of intimidation: every complete sentence, by its assertive structure, has something imperative, something comminatory about it. The disorganization of the subject, his timorous subjection to the masters of language, is always translated by incomplete sentences, with vague contours, undecided being. As a matter of fact, in ordinary, apparently free life, we do not speak in sentences. And conversely, there is a mastery of the sentence which is very close to power: to be strong is *first of all* to finish one's sentences. Does not grammar itself describe the sentence in terms of power, of hierarchy: *subject, subordinate, complement,* etc.?

Since the war of languages is general, what are we to do? By "we" I mean we intellectuals, writers, practitioners of discourse. Everything suggests that we cannot escape: by culture, by political choice, we must be committed, engage in one of the particular languages to which our world, our history compels us. And yet we cannot renounce the gratification—however utopian—of a de-situated, dis-alienated language. Thus, we must hold in the same hand the two reins of commitment and gratification, must assume a plural philosophy of languages.

Now, this *elsewhere* which remains, so to speak, *within*, has a name: it is the *Text*. The Text, which is no longer *the work,* is a production of writing, whose social consumption is certainly not neutral (the Text is little read), but whose production is supremely free, insofar as (Nietzsche again) it does not respect the Whole (the Law) of language.

Only writing, as a matter of fact, can assume the *fictional* character of the most serious, even the most violent dialects, can replace them in their theatrical distance; for example, I can borrow psychoanalytic speech in its wealth and its extent, but make use of it *in petto* as of a language of fiction.

Moreover, only writing can *mix* languages (psychoanalytic, Marxist, structuralist, for example), can constitute what is called a *heterology* of knowledge, can give language a festive dimension.

Last, only writing can be deployed *without a site of origin*; only writing can baffle every rhetorical rule, every law of genre, every arrogance of system: writing is *atopic*; in relation to the war of languages, which it does not suppress but *displaces*, writing anticipates a state of reading and writing practices where it is desire which circulates, not domination.

Le Conferenze dell'Associazione
Culturale Italiana, 1973

The Division of Languages

Is our culture divided? Indeed not; everyone, in our France today, can *understand* a television broadcast, an article in *France-Soir,* the arrangement of a banquet; moreover, one can say that, aside from a little group of intellectuals, everyone consumes these cultural products: objective participation is total; and if we define the culture of a society by the circulation of symbols which occurs there, our culture appears as homogeneous and united as that of some little ethnic society. The difference is that it is only *consumption* which is general in our culture, not *production*: we all understand what we hear in common, but we do not all speak the same thing that we hear; "tastes" are divided, sometimes even opposed, quite inveterately: I like this broadcast of classical music which my neighbor cannot endure, while I cannot bear the boulevard comedies he adores; each of us turns on his television precisely when the other turns it off. In other words, this culture of our time, which seems so general, so peaceable, so communal, rests on the division of two activities of language: on one side a—national—listening, or, if one prefers, acts of intellection; on the other, if not speech, at least creative participation, and, to be still more specific, *the language of desire,* which remains divided: I listen on one side, I love (or do not love) on the other: *I understand and I'm bored*: the unity of mass culture corresponds, in our society, to a division not only of languages but of language itself. Certain linguists—concerned, however, only with language and not with discourse—have had a presentiment of this situation: they have suggested—without being followed, so far—that we distinguish two grammars: an *active* grammar, or a grammar of the language as it is spoken, emitted, produced, and a *passive* grammar, or a grammar of simple listening. Raised, by a trans-linguistic mutation, to the level of discourse, this division would nicely account for the paradox of our culture, unitary in its code of listening (of consumption), fragmented in its codes of production, of desire: "cultural peace" (no apparent conflict on the level of culture) refers to the (social) division of languages.

Scientifically, till now this division has been relatively uncensored. Of course, linguists know that a national idiom (French, for example) includes a certain number of species; but the specification which has been studied is geographic (dialects, patois), not social; doubtless such a thing is postulated, though minimized, reduced to "fashions" of expression (argots, jargons, pidgins); and in any case, it is assumed, idiomatic unity is reconstituted on the level of the speaker, provided with his own language, an individual constant of speech known as an *idiolect*: *species* of language are only intermediary, floating, "amusing" states (derived from a kind of social folklore). This construction, which originated in the nineteenth century, nicely corresponds to a certain ideology—from which Saussure himself was not exempt—which sets, on one side, society (idiom, language) and, on the other, individual (idiolect, style); the tensions between these two poles can only be "psychological": the individual is supposed to struggle for recognition of his language—or to avoid being completely smothered by the language of others. Yet the sociology of this period could not grasp the conflict on the level of language: Saussure was more of a sociologist than Durkheim was a linguist. It is literature which anticipated the division of languages (even if it remained psychological), more than sociology (we shall hardly be astonished: literature contains all knowledges, though in a non-scientific state: it is a *Mathesis*).

The novel, once it became realistic, inevitably encountered the copy of collective languages; but in general the imitation of group languages (socio-professional languages) has been delegated by our novelists to secondary characters, to supernumeraries responsible for "fixing" social realism, while the hero continues speaking a timeless language whose "transparency" and neutrality are supposed to match a psychological universality of the human soul. Balzac, for instance, has an acute awareness of social languages; but, when he reproduces them, he *frames* them, a little like set pieces, rhetorically produced; he marks them with a folkloric, picturesque index; these are caricatures of languages, such as the jargon of Monsieur de Nucingen, whose phonetism is scrupulously reproduced, or the concierge language of Madame Cibot, Cousin Pons's housekeeper; yet there is another *mimesis* of language in Balzac, a more interesting one, first of all because it is more naïve, then because it is more cultural than social: this is the mimesis of the *codes of public opinion* which Balzac often adopts as his own, when he is commenting incidentally on the story he is telling: if, for example, Balzac slips the figure of Brantôme into the anecdote (in *Sur Catherine de Médicis*), Brantôme will speak of women exactly as public opinion (the *doxa*) expects Brantôme to honor his cultural "role" of "specialist" in stories about women—without our being able to swear, alas, that Balzac himself is quite conscious of his own procedure: for he believes he is reproducing Brantôme's language, whereas in fact he is copying only the (cultural) copy of that language. This suspicion of naïveté (some will say, of vulgarity) we cannot attach to Flaubert, who does not include himself in reproducing simple tics (phonetic, lexical, syntactical); he uses imitation to capture the most subtle and diffuse linguistic values and to grasp what we might call *figures of discourse*; and above all, if we consider Flaubert's most "profound" book, *Bouvard and Pécuchet,* the *mimesis* is without basis or prop: the cultural languages—languages of sciences, of technologies, of classes too: the bourgeoisie—are *cited* (Flaubert does not take them for ready money), but, by an extremely subtle mechanism, one which only today is beginning to be discovered, the author who copies (contrary to Balzac) remains unrecoverable, insofar as Flaubert never gives us a sure means of knowing whether he puts himself definitively *outside* the discourse he is "borrowing": an ambiguous situation which makes somewhat illusory the Sartrian or Marxist analysis of

Flaubert's *bourgeoisie*; for if Flaubert, a bourgeois, speaks the language of the bourgeoisie, we never know from what site this speech-act functions: A critical site? A distant one? Or an associated one? In truth, Flaubert's language is *utopic*, and this is what constitutes its modernity: are we not in the process of learning (from linguistics, from psychoanalysis) precisely that *language is a site with no exterior*? After Balzac and Flaubert—to mention only the greatest—in order to confront this problem of the division of languages, we can cite Proust, because we find in his work a true encyclopedia of language; without returning to the general problems of signs in Proust—which Deleuze has treated so remarkably—and remaining on the level of articulated language, we find in this author every state of verbal *mimesis*, i.e., characterized pastiches (the letter from Gisèle, which mimics academic jargon, the Goncourts' Journal), idiolects of character, each participant in the *Search for Lost Time* having his simultaneously characterial and social language (Charlus the medieval seigneur, Legrandin the snob), a clan language (the jargon of the Guermantes), a class language (Françoise and the "folk," though one reproduced here mainly by reason of its allegiance to the past), a catalogue of linguistic *anomalies* (the distorting, "outlandish" language of the manager of the Grand Hôtel de Balbec), the scrupulous collection of phenomena of acculturation (Françoise contaminated by her daughter's "modern" language) and linguistic diaspora (the Guermantes language's "swarms"), a theory of etymologies and of the founding power of the name as signifier; there is even, in this subtle and complete panorama of the types of discourse, a (deliberate) *absence* of certain languages: the narrator, his parents, Albertine do not have a language of their own. Whatever advance literature has made in the description of divided languages, one sees the limits of literary *mimesis*: on one hand, the language reported does not manage to emerge from a folklorist (one might say, colonial) view of exceptional languages; the language of the *Other* is framed, the author (except perhaps in Flaubert's case) speaks it in a situation of extraterritoriality; the division of languages is often recognized by these "objective" authors with a perspicacity socio-linguistics might well envy, but it remains external to the describer: in other words, contrary to the acquisitions of modern, relativist science, the observer does not utter his place in the observation; the division of language *stops* at the one who describes (if he does not denounce) it; and on the other hand, the social language reproduced by literature remains *univocal* (still the division of grammars denounced earlier): Françoise speaks by herself, we understand her, but no one, in the book, answers her; the language observed is monologic, it never participates in a dialectic (in the proper sense of the term); the result is that the fragments of language are in fact treated as so many *idiolects*—and not as a total and complex system of *production* of languages.

Hence, let us turn to the "scientific" treatment of the question: How does (socio-linguistic) science see the division of languages?

The postulation of a link between the division of classes and the division of languages is obviously not a recent insight: the division of labor engenders a division of lexicons; it can even be said (Greimas) that a lexicon is precisely the outline imposed upon the semantic mass by the practice of a certain labor: no lexicon without a corresponding labor (there are no grounds for making an exception for that general, "universal" lexicon, which is merely a lexicon "outside labor"); socio-linguistic investigation would therefore be easier to conduct within ethnic societies than in our historical and "developed" societies, where the problem is extremely complex; for us, in effect, the social division of languages seems blurred both by the weight, the unifying force of the national idiom, and by the homogeneity of so-called mass culture, as has been suggested; a simple phenomenological observation suffices, however, to attest to the validity of linguistic separations: one need merely emerge for a minute from one's own milieu and to have the task, if only for an hour or two, not only to listen to other languages besides one's own but also to participate in the conversation as actively as possible, in order to perceive, always with embarrassment, sometimes with laceration, the extremely hermetic nature of languages within the French idiom; the failure of these languages to communicate (except about "the weather") occurs not on the level of language, understood by all, but on the level of discourse (an object which is beginning to join linguistics); in other words, lack of communication is not strictly speaking of an informational order but of an interlocutory order: from one language to another, there is indifference, lack of curiosity: in our society, the language of the *same* suffices us, we have no need of the *Other*'s language in order to live: *to each his own language suffices.* We lock ourselves into the language of our own social, professional cell, and this sequestration has a neurotic value: it permits us to adapt ourselves as best we can to the fragmentation of our society.

Obviously, in the historic conditions of sociality, the division of labor is not refracted directly, as a simple mirror-image within the division of lexicons and the separation of languages: there is *complexization,* overdetermination or contrariety of factors. And, even in countries of relatively equal development, differences, generated by history, can persist; I am convinced that, compared to other countries no more "democratic" than ours, France is particularly divided: there is in France, perhaps by classical tradition, an intense awareness of the *identities* and *properties* of language; the other's language is perceived according to the most extreme qualities of its otherness: whence the frequent accusations of "jargon" and an old tradition of irony with regard to closed languages which are quite simply *other* languages (Rabelais, Molière, Proust).

Confronting the division of languages, do we possess a scheme of scientific description? Yes, and it is obviously socio-linguistics. Without wanting to lodge a contestation of this discipline, we must nonetheless acknowledge a certain disappointment: socio-linguistics has never dealt with the problem of the *social* language (as a divided language); on the one hand, there have been certain rapprochements (though episodic and indirect) between macro-sociology and macro-linguistics, the phenomenon "society" being put in relation with the phenomenon "language"; on the other hand, and one might say at the other end of the scale, there have been few attempts at a sociological description of speech communities: language of prisons, parishes, formulas of politeness, baby talk; socio-linguistics (and it is on this point that we can register our disappointment) refers to the separation of social groups *insofar as they are struggling for power*; the division of languages is not conceived as a total fact, involving the very roots of the economic system, of culture, of civilization, even of history, but only as the empirical (and not at all symbolic) attribute of a half-sociological, half-psychological arrangement: the desire for *promotion*—a narrow view, to say the least, and one which does not correspond to our expectations.

Has linguistics (and, no longer, sociology) done any better? It has rarely brought languages and social groups into relation, but it has ventured to make historical investigations into vocabularies, into lexicons endowed with a certain social or institutional autonomy: we may instance, here, the work of Meillet on the Indo-European religious vocabulary; of Benveniste on Indo-European institutions; of Matoré, who attempted, some twenty years ago, to establish a veritable historical sociology of the vocabulary (or lexicology); more recently, of Jean Dubois, who has described the vocabulary of the Commune. The attempt which best shows the interest and the limits of socio-historical linguistics is perhaps that of Ferdinand Brunot; in Volumes X and XI of his monumental *Histoire de la langue française dès origines à 1900,* Brunot studied in great detail the language of the French Revolution. The interest of his work is this: what is studied is a *political* language, in the full sense of the word; not a group of verbal tics intended to "politicize" language from outside (as often occurs today), but a language elaborated in the very movement of a political *praxis*; whence the more *productive* than *representative* character of this language: words, whether discarded or promoted, are linked almost magically to a real effectiveness: by abolishing the word, one believes one is abolishing the referent; with the banning of the word *noblesse,* it is apparently the nobility which is being banned; the study of this political language might furnish a fine context for an analysis of our own political (or *politicized*?) discourse: affectivized words, marked with a taboo or a countertaboo, cherished words (Nation, Law, *Patrie*, Constitution), execrated words (Tyranny, Aristocracy, Conspiracy), exorbitant power of certain words, however "pedantic" (Constitution, Federalism), terminological "translations," substitutive creations (*clergy→"prêtraille," religion→fanaticism, religious object→religious baubles, enemy soldiers→vile satellites of the despots, taxes→contribution, servant→"homme de confiance," informers→police agents, "comédiens"→artists*, etc.), unrestrained connotations (*revolutionary* ends by signifying *prompt, accelerated*). As for the limit, it is the following: the analysis bears only on the *lexicon*; it is true that French *syntax* was little affected by the Revolutionary shock (which in fact made every effort to govern it and to maintain classic "good usage"); but perhaps it would be better to say that linguistics does not yet have the means to analyze that fine structure of discourse which is located between grammatical "construction" (too loose) and the vocabulary (too limited), and which doubtless corresponds to the region of frozen syntagms (for instance: "the pressure of the Revolutionary masses"); the linguist is then obliged to reduce the separation of the social languages to phenomena of the lexicon—even of fashion.

Hence, the most interesting situation, i.e., the very opacity of the social relation, seems to escape traditional scientific analysis. The basic reason, it seems to me, is of an epistemological order: confronting discourse, linguistics has remained, one might say, at a Newtonian stage: it has not yet experienced its Einsteinian revolution; it has not theorized the linguist's place in the field of observation. It is this relativization that must first be postulated.

It is time to give a name to these social languages outlined within the idiomatic mass, and whose hermeticism, however existentially we have experienced it, follows, through every conceivable nuance and complication, the division and the opposition of classes; let us call these group languages *sociolects* (in evident opposition to the *idiolect* or jargon of a single individual). The main character of the sociolectal field is that no language can be exterior to it: all speech is inevitably included in a certain sociolect. This constraint has an important consequence for the analyst: he himself participates in the interplay of sociolects. It will be said that in other cases this situation in no way prevents scientific observation: this is the case of the very linguist who must describe a national idiom, i.e., a field which no language (including his own) escapes; but precisely: the idiom is a unified field (there is only one French language), the one who speaks it is not obliged to situate himself within it. Whereas the sociolectal field is defined by its division, its inveterate secession, and it is *within* this division that the analysis must take place. It follows that sociolectal research (which does not yet exist) cannot begin without an initial, founding action of *evaluation* (I should like this word to be understood in the critical sense Nietzsche gave it). This means we cannot pour all sociolects (all social jargons), whatever they are, whatever their political context, into a vague undifferentiated corpus, whose very lack of differentiation, whose *equality*, would be a guarantee of objectivity, of scientificity; here we must refuse the *adiaphoria* of traditional science, we must accept—a paradoxical order, in the eyes of many—that the *types* of sociolects govern the analysis, and not the converse: *typology is anterior to definition.* Let us specify further that *evaluation* cannot be reduced to *appreciation*: quite objective scholars have accorded themselves the (legitimate) right to *appreciate* the phenomena they were describing (this is precisely what Brunot did with the French Revolution); to *evaluate* is not a subsequent but a founding act; it is not a "liberal" order of behavior, but on the contrary a violent one; sociolectal evaluation, from the start, experiences the conflict of groups and of languages; by *positing* the sociolectal concept, the analyst must *immediately* account both for social contradiction and for the fragmentation of the scholarly subject (I refer here to the Lacanian analysis of the "subject supposed to know"—*sujet supposé savoir*).

Hence, no scientific description of the social languages (of the sociolects) without a founding *political* evaluation. Just as Aristotle, in his *Rhetoric,* distinguished two groups of proofs: proofs *within the technè (entechnoï)* and proofs *outside the technè (atechnoï),* I am suggesting we distinguish from the start two groups of sociolects: discourses *within power* (in the shadow of power) and discourses *outside power* (or without power, or even in the light of non-power); resorting to pedantic neologisms (but how else to proceed?), let us call the former, *encratic* discourses, and the latter, *acratic* discourses.

Of course, the relation of a discourse to power (or to exclusion from power) is very rarely direct, immediate; cetainly the law *forbids,* but its discourse is already mediatized by a whole juridical culture, by a *ratio* almost universally admitted; and only the fabulous figure of the Tyrant could produce a speech which would instantaneously adhere to his power ("*the King ordered that* . . ."). As a matter of fact, the language of power is always furnished with structures of mediation, conduction, transformation, inversion (as is ideological discourse, whose *inverted* character, in relation to bourgeois power, Marx has indicated). Similarly, *acratic* discourse does not always stand declaratively *against* power; to take a specific and current example, psychoanalytic discourse is not directly linked (at least in France) to a critique of power, and yet it can be classified among the acratic sociolects. Why? Because the mediation which intervenes between power and language is not of a political order but of a cultural order: adopting an old Aristotelian notion, that of the *doxa* (public opinion, the general, the "probable," but not the "true," the "scientific"), we shall say that the *doxa* is the cultural (or discursive) mediation through which power (or non-power) speaks: encratic discourse is a discourse that conforms to the *doxa,* subject to codes which are themselves the structuring lines of its ideology; and acratic discourse always speaks out, to various degrees, against the *doxa* (whatever it is, acratic discourse is *paradoxical*). This opposition does not exclude nuances within each type; but, structurally, its simplicity remains valid as long as power and non-power are in their place; it can be (provisionally) blurred only in the rare cases where there is a mutation of power (of the sites of power); thus, in the case of the political language in a revolutionary period: revolutionary language issues from the preceding acratic language; in shifting over to power, it retains its acratic character, as long as there is an active struggle within the Revolution; but once this struggle dies down, once the state is in place, the former Revolutionary language itself becomes *doxa*, encratic discourse.

Encratic discourse—since we have subjected its definition to the mediation of the *doxa*—is not only the discourse of the class in power; classes out of power or attempting to take power by reformist or promotional means can borrow it—or at least receive it consentingly. Encratic language, supported by the state, is everywhere: it is a diffused, widespread, one might say osmotic discourse which *impregnates* exchanges, social rites, leisure, the socio-symbolic field (above all, of course, in societies of mass communication). Not only does encratic discourse never describe itself as systematic, but it always constitutes itself as *an opposition to system*: alibis of nature, of universality, of good sense, of clarity—the anti-intellectualist resistances—become the tacit figures of the encratic system. Further, it is a *full* discourse: *there is no room* in it for the Other (whence the sensation of smothering, of stifling which it can provoke in someone who does not participate in it). Finally, if we refer to the Marxian schema ("Ideology is an *inverted* image of the real"), encratic discourse—as fully ideological—presents the real as the reversal of ideology. In short, it is a *non-marked* language, producer of a masked intimidation, so that it is difficult to assign it morphological *features*—unless we manage to reconstitute with rigor and precision what is something of a contradiction in terms: *the figures of the masked.* It is the very nature of the *doxa* (diffuse, full, complete, "natural") that makes an internal typology of encratic sociolects difficult; there is an *atypia* of the discourses of power: this genus knows no species.

The acratic sociolects are doubtless easier and more interesting to study: they are all the languages which are elaborated outside the *doxa* and are consequently rejected by it (ordinarily under the name of *jargons*). By analyzing encratic discourse, we know more or less in advance what we shall find (which is why, *today*, the analysis of mass culture is visibly marking time); but acratic discourse is by and large our own (that of the researcher, the intellectual, the writer); to analyze it is to analyze ourselves insofar as we speak: always a risky operation and yet one that must be undertaken: what do Marxism, Freudianism, structuralism, or the science of the so-called human sciences—insofar as each of these group languages constitutes an acratic (*paradoxical*) sociolect—what do they think of their own discourse? This question, which is never assumed by the discourse of power, is obviously the founding act of any analyst who claims not to exteriorize himself from his object.

The principal advantage of a sociolect (outside the advantages which the possession of a language gives to any power one seeks to preserve or to gain) is obviously the security it affords: like any closure, that of a language exalts, reassures all the subjects *inside*, rejects and offends those *outside*. But how does a sociolect act outside itself? As we know, there is no longer, today, an art of persuasion, there is no longer a rhetoric (at least no longer one not ashamed to assume itself openly); it will be noted in this regard that Aristotelian rhetoric, being founded on the opinion of the greatest number, was by rights, and one may say voluntarily, declaratively, an endoxal, hence encratic rhetoric (which is why, by an only apparent paradox, Aristotelianism can still furnish very good concepts to the sociology of mass communications); what has changed is that, in modern democracy, "persuasion" and its *technè* are no longer theorized, because the systematic is censored and because, under the effect of a strictly modern myth, language is reputed to be "natural," "instrumental." We can say that by a single impulse our society rejects rhetoric and "forgets" to theorize mass culture (a flagrant oversight in Marxist theory posterior to Marx).

As a matter of fact, the sociolects do not derive from a *technè* of persuasion, but they *all* include figures of intimidation (even if acratic discourse seems more brutally terrorist): fruit of social division, witness to the war of meaning, every sociolect (encratic or acratic) aims at keeping the Other from speaking (this is also the fate of the liberal sociolect). Hence, the division of the two great types of sociolects merely sets types of intimidation, or, if you prefer, modes of pressure, in opposition: the encratic sociolect acts by *repression* (of endoxal superfluity, of what Flaubert would have called *Bêtise*); the acratic sociolect (being outside power, it must resort to violence) acts by *subjection*, it mounts offensive figures of discourse, intended to *constrain* rather than to invade the Other; and what sets these two intimidations in opposition is once again the acknowledged role of system: declared recourse to an elaborated system defines acratic violence; the blurring of the system, the inversion of thought into "experience" (and non-thought) defines encratic repression: there is an inverted relation between the two systems of discursivity: *patent / hidden, overt / covert.*

A sociolect has an intimidating character not only for those excluded from it (by reason of their social, cultural situation): it also constrains those who participate in it (or, rather, who receive it as their lot). This results, structurally, from the fact that the sociolect, on the level of discourse, is a true language; following Boas, Jakobson has nicely remarked that a language is defined not because it *permits* saying . . . but because it *compels* saying . . . ; so every sociolect involves "obligatory rubrics," great stereotyped forms outside which the clientele of this sociolect cannot speak (cannot think). In other words, like every language, the sociolect implies what Chomsky calls a *competence*, within which variations of performance become structurally insignificant: the encratic sociolect is not broached by differences of *vulgarity* established between its locutors; and on the other side, everyone knows that the Marxist sociolect can be spoken by imbeciles: the sociolectal *language* is not called upon to change according to individual accidents, but only if there occurs in history a *mutation of discursivity* (Marx and Freud were themselves such mutants, but since them, the discursivity they founded is merely repeating itself).

To conclude these remarks, situated ambiguously between the essay and the research program, may I observe that, as I see it, the division of social languages, sociolectology, if you like, is linked to an apparently unsociological theme which has hitherto been the special realm of theoreticians of literature; this theme is what is today called *writing*. In our society of divided languages, writing is becoming a value worthy to institute a continuing debate and a constant theoretic exploration, because it constitutes a *production of undivided language*. Having lost every illusion, we know today that the writer cannot speak the "language of the people," as Michelet nostalgically claimed; nor can we align writing with the language of the greatest number, for in an alienated society the greatest number is not the universal, and to speak such a language (as in mass culture, where one is on the statistical hunt for the greatest number of listeners or telespectators) is still to speak a special language—even if a majority language. We know that language cannot be reduced to simple communication, it is the whole human subject that is committed to speech and is constituted through it. In modernity's "progressive" attempts, writing holds an eminent place, not as a consequence of its (extremely reduced) clientele, but as a consequence of its practice: it is because writing attacks the relations of the subject (always social: is there any other?) and language, the outdated distribution of the symbolic field and the process of the sign, that writing appears as a practice of *counterdivision* of languages: probably a utopian, in any case a mythic image, since it rejoins the old dream of an innocent language, the *lingua adamica* of the first romantics. But does not history, in Vico's splendid metaphor, move in a *spiral*? Must we not renew (which does not mean repeat) the old images in order to give them new contents?

From *Hommage à Georges Friedmann* (Gallimard), 1973

4
FROM HISTORY TO REALITY

The Discourse of History

The formal description of groups of words superior to the sentence (which will for convenience's sake be called *discourse*) is not of recent date: from Gorgias to the nineteenth century, it was the specific object of the old rhetoric. Recent developments of linguistic science nonetheless give it a new actuality and new means: a linguistics of discourse may henceforth be possible; by reason of its effects on literary analysis (whose importance in teaching is familiar to us), it even constitutes one of the first tasks of semiology.

This second linguistics, at the same time that it must seek out the universals of discourse (if they exist), in the form of units and general rules of combination, must obviously decide if structural analysis permits retaining the old typology of discourse, if it is indeed legitimate still to oppose poetic discourse to fictional discourse, fictive narrative to historical. It is on this last point that I should like to offer some reflections: the narration of past events, commonly subject in our culture, since the Greeks, to the sanction of historical "science," placed under the imperious warrant of the "real," justified by principles of "rational" exposition—does this narration differ, in fact, by some specific feature, by an indubitable pertinence, from imaginary narration as we find it in the epic, the novel, the drama? And if this feature—or this pertinence—exists, in what site of the discursive system, at what level of the speech-act, must we locate it? In order to answer this question, we shall observe here, in a free and by no means exhaustive fashion, the discourse of several great classical historians, mainly Herodotus, Machiavelli, Bossuet, and Michelet.

1. Speech-act

And first of all, under what conditions is the classical historian led—or authorized—to designate, in his discourse, the very act by which he utters it? In other words, what are, on the level of discourse—and no longer of language—the *shifters* (in the sense Jakobson has given this word) which assure transition from statement to speech-act (or conversely)?

It seems that historical discourse involves two regular types of shifters. The first type we might call *shifters of listening*. This category has been observed, on the level of language, by Jakobson, under the name *testimonial* and under the formula $C^eC^{a1}C^{a2}$: besides the event reported (C^e), the discourse mentions both the act of the informant (C^{a1}) and the speech of the "writer" who refers to it (C^{a2}). This shifter therefore designates all mention of sources, of testimony, all reference to a *listening* of the historian, collecting an *elsewhere* of his discourse and speaking it. Explicit listening is a choice, for it is possible not to refer to it; it relates the historian to the ethnologist who mentions his informant; we therefore find this shifter of listening abundant in such historian-ethnologists as Herodotus. The forms they employ vary from interpolations of the type *as I have heard, to our knowledge*, to the historian's present (a tense which attests to the speaker's intervention) and to any mention of the historian's personal experience; this is Michelet's case, who "listens" to the History of France starting from a subjective illumination (the July Revolution of 1830), and accounts for it in his discourse. The *shifter of listening* is obviously not pertinent to historical discourse: we find it frequently in conversation and in certain artifices of the novel (anecdotes recounted as "heard from" certain fictive informants who are mentioned).

The second type of shifter covers all the declared signs by which the "writer," in this case the historian, organizes his own discourse, revises it, modifies it in the process of expression; in short, arranges explicit references within it. This is an important shifter, and the "organizers" of discourse can receive many different expressions; they can all be reduced, however, to the indication of a movement of the discourse in relation to its substance, or more precisely throughout this substance, something like such temporal or locative deictics as *voici / voilà*; hence we have, in relation to the flow of the speech-act: immobility (*as we have said earlier*), harking back (*altius repetere, replicare da più alto luogo*), the return (*ma ritornando all' ordine nostro, dico come* . . .), the halt (*on this point, we shall say no more*), the declaration (*here are the other memorable actions he performed during his reign*). The *shifter of organization* raises a notable problem, which we can only mention here: it is generated by coexistence or, to put it better, by the conflict of two time spans: the time of the speech-act and the time of the material stated. This conflict gives rise to important phenomena of discourse; we shall cite three. The first refers to all the acceleration phenomena of history: an equal number of "pages" (if such is the crude measure of time in the speech-act) cover varying lapses of time (time of the material stated): in Machiavelli's *History of Florence*, the same measure (a chapter) covers several centuries here and some twenty years there; the closer we come to the historian's own time, the more powerful the pressure of the speech-act becomes, and the more history slows down; there is no isochrony—the result of which is implicitly to attack the linearity of discourse and to reveal a possible "paragrammatism" of historical speech.* The second phenomenon also suggests, in its way, that the discourse, though materially linear, when confronted with historical time apparently determines to explore this time, producing what we might call zigzag history: thus, with each character who appears in his *History*, Herodotus goes back to the newcomer's ancestors, then returns to his point of departure, in order to continue a little further—and to begin all over again. Finally, a third phenomenon of discourse, and a considerable

* Following J. Kristeva ("Bakhtine, le mot, le dialogue et le roman," *Critique*, no. 239, April 1967), we shall designate as *paragrammatism* (derived from Saussure's Anagrams) the double writings which contain a dialogue of the text with other texts and postulate a new logic.

one, attests to the destructive role of the *shifters of organization* in relation to history's *chronicle time*: this involves inaugurations of historical discourse, places where the beginning of the material stated and the exordium of the speech-act are united.* The discourse of history knows, in general, two forms of inauguration: first of all, what we might call the *performative opening*, for in it speech is actually a solemn act of foundation; the model of this is poetic, the *I sing* of the poets; thus, Joinville begins his history by a religious appeal ("In the name of God Almighty, I, Jehan, Sire de Joinville, cause to be written the life of our Holy King Louis"), and even the socialist Louis Blanc does not disdain the purifying *introit*,† so difficult does the inception of speech remain—or so sacred, let us say; subsequently, a much more common unit, the Preface, a characteristic speech-act, prospective when it announces discourse to come, or retrospective when it judges that discourse (as in the great Preface with which Michelet crowned his *Histoire de France* once it was completely written and in fact published). Our review of these units tends to suggest that the entrance of the speech-act into historical statement, through *shifters of organization*, has as its goal not so much to give the historian a chance to express his "subjectivity" as to "complicate" history's chronicle time by confronting it with another time, that of discourse itself, a time we may identify as *paper time*; in short, the presence, in historical narration, of explicit speech-act signs tends to "de-chronologize" the historical "thread" and to restore, if only as a reminiscence or a nostalgia, a complex, parametric, non-linear time whose deep space recalls the mythic time of the ancient cosmogonies, it too linked by essence to the speech of the poet or the

* The exordium (of any discourse) raises one of the most interesting problems of rhetoric, insofar as it is a codification of the breaks in silence and a struggle against aphasis.

† "Before taking up my pen, I have questioned myself closely, and since I discerned neither partisan affections nor implacable hatreds, I have decided that I could judge of men and things without neglecting justice and without betraying the truth."—Louis Blanc, *Histoire de dix ans* (Paris, 1842)

soothsayer; in effect, the shifters of organization attest—if only by certain apparently rational detours—to the historian's predictive function: it is insofar as he *knows* what has not yet been recounted that the historian, like the agent of myth, needs to double the chronic splitting of events by references to the actual time of his speech.

The signs (or shifters) we have just mentioned bear uniquely on the speech-act's actual process. There are others which no longer concern the speech-act but, in Jakobson's terminology, its protagonists (T^a), addressee, or "writer." It is a notable and rather enigmatic fact that literary discourse very rarely includes signs of the "reader"; we might even say that what specifies it as literary discourse is that it is—apparently—a discourse without *you*, though in reality the whole structure of this discourse implies a "subject" of the reading. In historical discourse, the signs of reception or destination are commonly absent: we find them only when History gives itself out as a lesson; this is the case with Bossuet's *Histoire universelle*, a discourse nominally addressed by the tutor to the prince, his student; yet this schema is possible, in a sense, only insofar as Bossuet's own discourse is supposed to reproduce homologically the discourse God Himself offers men precisely in the form of History He gives them: it is because the History of men is Scripture that Bossuet, mediator of this Scripture, can establish a relation of destination between the young prince and himself.

Signs of the "writer" (or sender) are obviously much more frequent; here we must list all the fragments of discourse in which the historian, an empty subject of the speech-act, gradually fills himself with various predicates intended to establish him as a *person*, provided with a psychological plenitude, with a *countenance*. We shall indicate here one particular form of this "filling," which relates more directly to literary criticism. This occurs when the historian intends to "absent himself" from his discourse and where there is, consequently, a systematic absence of any sign referring to the sender of the historical message: history seems to *tell itself*. This accident has had a considerable career, since it corresponds in fact to so-called objective historical discourse (in which the historian never intervenes). As a matter of fact, in this case, the speaker annuls his emotive person, but substitutes for it another person, the "objective" person: the subject subsists in his plenitude, but as an objective subject; this is what Fustel de Coulanges called, significantly (and rather naïvely), the "chastity of History." On the level of discourse, objectivity—or lack of signs of the "speaker"—thus appears as a special form of image-repertoire, the product of what we might call the *referential illusion*, since here the historian claims to let the referent speak for itself. This illusion is not proper to historical discourse: how many novelists—in the realistic period—imagine they are being "objective" because they suppress signs of the *I* in the discourse! The combination of linguistics and psychoanalysis has increased our lucidity with regard to a privative speech-act: we know that the absence of signs has a meaning, too.

To conclude with the speech-act, we must mention the special case—anticipated by Jakobson, on the level of language, in the grid of his shifters—in which the speaker (or writer) of the discourse is at the same time a participant in the process spoken (or written), in which the protagonist of the text is the same as the protagonist of the speech-act (T^e / T^a), in which the historian, an actor at the time of the event, becomes its narrator; thus, Xenophon participates in the retreat of the Ten Thousand and becomes their historian after the fact. The most illustrious example of this conjunction of the spoken *I* and the speaking *I* is doubtless the *he* of Julius Caesar. This famous *he* belongs to the statement; when Caesar becomes explicitly the "writer," he shifts to *we* (*ut supra demonstravimus*). The Caesarian *he* seems at first glance swamped among the other participants of the spoken process and, on this account, we have seen it as the supreme sign of objectivity; it seems, however, that we can formally differentiate it; how? by observing that its predicates are consistently selected: the Caesarian *he* supports only certain syntagms which we might call *syntagms of the leader* (*to give orders, to hold meetings, to visit, to have done, to congratulate, to explain, to think*), quite close, as a matter of fact, to certain performatives, in which speech is identified with action. There are other examples of this *he*, past-tense actor and present-tense narrator (notably in Clausewitz): they show that the choice of the a-personal pronoun is merely a rhetorical alibi and that the true situation of the "writer" is manifested in the choice of syntagms with which he surrounds his past actions.

2. Statement

The historical statement must lend itself to a figuration destined to produce units of content, which we can subsequently classify. These units of content represent what history *speaks about*; as signifieds, they are neither pure referent nor complete discourse: their totality is constituted by the referent discerned, named, already intelligible, but not yet subjected to a syntax. We shall not undertake to explore these classes of units here, such an effort would be premature; we shall limit ourselves to a few preliminary remarks.

Historical statement, like sentential statement, includes "existents" and "occurrents," beings, entities, and their predicates. Now, a first inspection suggests that the former and the latter (separately) can constitute relatively closed, consequently controllable lists, in a word, *collections* whose units ultimately repeat themselves in obviously variable combinations; thus, in Herodotus, existents are reduced to *dynasties, princes, generals, soldiers, peoples*, and *places*, and occurrents to actions such as *to devastate, to subjugate, to make alliances, to make an expedition, to reign, to employ a stratagem, to consult the oracle*, etc. These collections, being (relatively) closed, must be accessible to certain rules of substitution and transformation, and it must be possible to structure them—a more or less easy task, obviously, depending largely on a single lexicon, that of warfare; we must determine whether, in modern historians, we must expect more complex associations of different lexicons, and if, even in that case, historical discourse is not always based, finally, on "strong" collections (better to speak of *collections*, not *lexicons*, for we are here uniquely on the level of content). Machiavelli seems to have had an intuition of this structure: at the beginning of his *History of Florence*, he presents his "collection," i.e., the list of juridical, political, ethnic objects which will subsequently be mobilized and combined in his narration.

In the case of more fluid collections (in historians less archaic than Herodotus), the units of content can still receive a strong structuration, not from the lexicon, but from the author's personal thematics; such thematic (recurrent) objects are numerous in a romantic historian like Michelet; but we can quite easily find them in so-called intellectual authors: in Tacitus, *fama* is a personal unit, and Machiavelli bases his history on a thematic opposition, that of *mantenere* (a verb which refers to the fundamental energy of the man of government) and *ruinare* (which, on the contrary, implies a logic of the decadence of things). It follows that, by these thematic units, generally confined in a single word, we discover units of discourse (and no longer of content alone); here we touch on the problem of the *nomination* of historical objects: the word can economize a situation or a series of actions; it favors structuration insofar as, projected into content, it is itself a little structure; thus, Machiavelli employs *conspiracy* to economize explicitation of a complex datum designating the only remaining possibility of struggle when a government triumphs over all openly declared enmities. Nomination, by permitting a strong articulation of the discourse, reinforces its structure; strongly structured histories are substantive histories: Bossuet, for whom the history of human beings is structured by God, makes abundant use of successions of substantive shortcuts.*

* Example: "Here we see the innocence and the wisdom of young Joseph . . . his mysterious dreams . . . his jealous brothers . . . the selling of this great man . . . the loyalty he maintained to his master . . . his admirable chastity; the persecutions it drew upon him; his prison and his constancy . . ."—Bossuet, *Discours sur l'histoire universelle*

These remarks concern the occurrents as much as the existents. The historical processes themselves (whatever their terminological development) raise—among others—this interesting problem: that of their status. The status of a process can be assertive, negative, interrogative. Now, the status of historical discourse is uniformly assertive, constative; historical fact is linguistically linked to a privilege of being: one recounts what has been, not what has not been or what has been questionable. In a word, historical discourse does not know negation (or very rarely, in an eccentric fashion). This fact may be curiously—but significantly—related to the arrangement we find in a "writer" quite different from the historian, the psychotic, who is incapable of subjecting a statement to a negative transformation; we might say that, in a sense, "objective" discourse (this is the case of positivist history) joins the situation of schizophrenic discourse; in either case, there is a radical censorship of the speech-act (in which feeling alone permits a negative transformation), a massive reflux of discourse toward statement and even (in the historian's case) toward the referent: no one is there to assume the statement.

In order to approach another, essential aspect of historical statement, we must say a word about the classes of units of content and about their succession. These classes are, as is apparent from a first exploration, the very ones we supposed we could discover in the narrative of fiction. The first class covers all the segments of discourse which refer to an implicit signified, according to a metaphoric process; thus, Michelet describes the motley of garments, the fading of blazons, and the mixture of architectural styles at the beginning of the fifteenth century as so many signifiers of a single signified, which is the moral division of the waning Middle Ages; this class is that of indices, or more precisely of signs (a very abundant class in the classical novel). The second class of units is constituted by the fragments of discourse of a reasoning, syllogistic, or more precisely enthymematic nature, since it is almost always imperfect, approximative syllogisms which are involved.* Enthymemes are not proper to historical discourse; they are frequent in the novel, where bifurcations of the anecdote are generally justified in the reader's eyes by pseudo-reasonings of syllogistic type. The enthymeme arranges, in historical discourse, a non-symbolic intelligibility, and this is what is interesting: does it subsist in recent histories, whose discourse attempts to break with the classical, Aristotelian model? Last, a third class of units—and not the least—receives what since Propp we have called the "functions" of the narrative, or cardinal points from which the anecdote can take a different course; these functions are grouped syntagmatically into closed, logically saturated series or sequences; thus, in Herodotus, we frequently find a sequence *Oracle*, composed of three terms, each of which is an alternative (to consult or not, to answer or not, to follow or not), and which can be separated from each other by units foreign to the sequence: these units are either the terms of another sequence—and then the schema is one of imbrication—or else minor expansions (times of information, indices)—and then the schema is one of a catalysis which fills the interstices of the nuclei.

By generalizing—perhaps abusively—these few remarks on the structure of statements, we can suggest that historical discourse oscillates between two poles, according to the respective density of its indices and its functions. When, in a historian's work, indicial units predominate (constantly referring to an implicit signified), the History is inflected toward a metaphorical form, and borders on the lyric and the symbolic: this is the case, for instance, with Michelet. When on the contrary it is functional units which prevail, the History takes a metonymic form, it is related to the epic: we might cite as a pure example of this tendency the narrative history of Augustin Thierry. A third History, it is true, exists: one which, by the structure of its discourse, attempts to reproduce the structure of the choices

* Here is the syllogistic schema of a passage in Michelet (*Histoire de Moyen Age*, Vol. III, Book VI, chapter II): 1. In order to distract the people from rebellion, they must be kept occupied. 2. Now, the best means is to throw them a man. 3. Hence, the princes chose old Aubriot, etc.

experienced by the protagonists of the process related; in it the reasonings dominate; this is a reflexive history, which we can also call a strategic history, and Machiavelli is the best example of it we know.

3. Signification

For history not to signify, discourse must be limited to a pure unstructured series of notations: these will be chronicles and annals (in the pure sense of the word). In constituted historical discourse, the facts related irresistibly function either as indices or as nuclei whose very succession has an indicial value; and even though facts are presented in an anarchic manner, they at least *signify* anarchy and refer to a certain negative idea of human history.

The signifieds of historical discourse can occupy at least two different levels. There is, first of all, a level immanent to the material stated; this level retains all the meanings the historian deliberately gives to the facts he reports (the motley of fifteenth-century garments for Michelet, the importance of certain conflicts for Thucydides, etc.); such can be the moral or political "lessons" the narrator draws from certain episodes (in Machiavelli, in Bossuet). If the "lesson" is continuous, we reach a second level, that of a signified transcending the entire historical discourse, transmitted by the historian's thematics, which we are thereby entitled to identify with the form of the signified; thus, the very imperfection of Herodotus's narrative structure (generated by certain *series* of facts without closure) ultimately refers to a certain philosophy of History, which is the accessibility of the world of men under the law of the gods; thus again, in Michelet, the very "strong" structuration of particular signifieds, articulated in oppositions (antitheses on the level of the signifier), has as its ultimate meaning a Manichaeistic philosophy of life and death. In the historical discourse of our civilization, the process of signification always aims at "filling" the meaning of History: the historian is the one who collects not so much facts as signifiers and relates them, i.e., organizes them in order to establish a positive meaning and to fill the void of pure series.

As we see, by its very structure and without there being any need to appeal to the substance of the content, historical discourse is essentially an ideological elaboration or, to be more specific, an *imaginary* elaboration, if it is true that the image-repertoire is the language by which the speaker (or "writer") of a discourse (a purely linguistic entity) "fills" the subject of the speech-act (a psychological or ideological entity). Hence, we understand why the notion of historical "fact" has so often given rise to a certain mistrust. Nietzsche has written: "There are no facts *as such*. We must always begin by introducing a meaning in order for there to be a fact." Once language intervenes (and when does it not intervene?), a fact can be defined only tautologically: the *noted* issues from the *notable*, but the *notable* is—since Herodotus, where the word loses its mythic acceptation—only what is worthy of memory, i.e., worthy to be *noted*. Hence, we arrive at that paradox which governs the entire pertinence of historical discourse (in relation to other types of discourse): fact never has any but a linguistic existence (as the term of discourse), yet everything happens as if this linguistic existence were merely a pure and simple "copy" of *another* existence, situated in an extra-structural field, the "real." This discourse is doubtless the only one in which the referent is addressed as external to the discourse, though without its ever being possible to reach it outside this discourse. Hence, we must inquire more closely into the place of the "real" in discursive structure.

Historical discourse supposes, one might say, a double operation, one that is extremely complex. In a first phase (this decomposition is, of course, only metaphorical), the referent is detached from the discourse, it becomes exterior to it, grounds it, is supposed to govern it: this is the phase of *res gestae*, and the discourse simply claims to be *historia rerum gestarum*: but in a second phase, it is the signified itself which is repulsed, merged in the referent; the referent enters into direct relation with the signifier, and the discourse, meant only to *express* the real, believes it elides the fundamental term of imaginary structures, which is the signified. Like any discourse with "realistic" claims, the discourse of history thus believes it knows only a two-term semantic schema, referent and signifier; the (illusory) merging of referent and signified defines, as we know, *sui-referential* discourses (such as performative discourse); we can say that historical discourse is a fake performative discourse in which the apparent constative (descriptive) is in fact only the signifier of the speech-act as an act of authority.*

In other words, in "objective" history, the "real" is never anything but an unformulated signified, sheltered behind the apparent omnipotence of the referent. This situation defines what we might call the *reality effect*. The extrusion of the signified outside the "objective" discourse, letting the "real" and its expression apparently confront each other, does not fail to produce a new meaning, so true is it, once more, that within a system any absence of an element is itself a signification. This new meaning—extensive to all historical discourse and ultimately defining its pertinence—is reality itself, surreptitiously transformed into a "shamefaced" signifier: historical discourse does not follow the real, it merely signifies it, constantly repeating *this happened*, without this assertion ever being anything but the signified *wrong side* of all historical narration.

The prestige of *this happened* has a truly historical importance and scope. Our entire civilization has a taste for the reality effect, attested to by the development of specific genres such as the realistic novel, the private diary, documentary literature, the news item [*fait divers*], the historical museum, the exhibition of ancient objects, and, above all, the massive development of photography, whose sole pertinent feature (in relation to drawing) is precisely to signify that the event represented has *really* taken place. Secularized, the relic no longer has anything sacred about it, except that sacred quality attached to the enigma of

* Thiers has expressed, with great purity and naïveté, this referential illusion, or this merging of referent and signified, by thus defining the historian's ideal: "To be simply true, to be what things are and nothing more than that, and nothing except that."

what has been, is no more, and yet offers itself as present sign of a dead thing. Conversely, the profanation of relics is in fact a destruction of reality itself, starting from the intuition that the real is never anything but a meaning, revocable when history requires it and demands a veritable destruction of the very foundations of civilization.*

Since it refuses to assume the real as a signified (or even to detach the referent from its simple assertion), it is understandable that history, at the privileged moment when it attempted to constitute itself as a genre, i.e., in the nineteenth century, should have come to see in the "pure and simple" relation of facts the best proof of these facts, and to institute narration as a privileged signifier of the real. Augustin Thierry made himself the theoretician of this narrative history, drawing its "truth" from the very solicitude of its narration, the architecture of its articulations, and the abundance of its expansions (called, in this case, "concrete details").†

Thus, we close the paradoxical circle: narrative structure, elaborated in the crucible of fictions (through myths and early epics), becomes both sign and proof of reality. Hence, it will be understood that the effacement (if not the disappearance) of narration in contemporary historical science, which prefers to speak of structures rather than of chronologies, implies much more than a simple change of school: a veritable ideological transformation; historical narration is dying because the sign of History is henceforth not so much *the real* as *the intelligible*.

Information sur les sciences sociales, 1967

* This is doubtless the meaning, beyond any strictly religious subversion, which we must give to the act of the Red Guards profaning the temple at Confucius's birthplace (January 1967); let us recall that the expression *cultural revolution* is a very inadequate translation of "destruction of the foundations of civilization."

† "It has been said that the historian's goal was to recount, not to prove; I do not know, but I am certain that in history the best proof, the kind most capable of arousing and convincing all minds, the kind which permits the least resistance and leaves the fewest doubts, is complete narration . . ."—Augustin Thierry, *Récits des temps mérovingiens*, Vol. II (Paris, 1851)

The Reality Effect

When Flaubert, describing the room occupied by Mme Aubain, Félicité's employer, tells us that "an old piano supported, under a barometer, a pyramidal heap of boxes and cartons" ("A Simple Heart," from *Three Tales*); when Michelet, recounting the death of Charlotte Corday and reporting that, before the executioner's arrival, she was visited in prison by an artist who painted her portrait, includes the detail that "after an hour and a half, there was a gentle knock at a little door behind her" (*Histoire de France: La Révolution*)—these authors (among many others) are producing notations which structural analysis, concerned with identifying and systematizing the major articulations of narrative, usually and heretofore has left out, either because its inventory omits all details that are "superfluous" (in relation to structure) or because these same details are treated as "filling" (catalyses), assigned an indirect functional value insofar as, cumulatively, they constitute some index of character or atmosphere and so can ultimately be recuperated by structure.

It would seem, however, that if analysis seeks to be exhaustive (and what would any method be worth which did not account for the totality of its object, i.e., in this case, of the entire surface of the narrative fabric?), if it seeks to encompass the absolute detail, the indivisible unit, the fugitive transition, in order to assign them a place in the structure, it inevitably encounters notations which no function (not even the most indirect) can justify: such notations are scandalous (from the point of view of structure), or, what is even more disturbing, they seem to correspond to a kind of narrative *luxury*, lavish to the point of offering many "futile" details and thereby increasing the cost of narrative information. For if, in Flaubert's description, it is just possible to see in the notation of the piano an indication of its owner's bourgeois standing and in that of the cartons a sign of disorder and a kind of lapse in status likely to connote the atmosphere of the Aubain household, no purpose seems to justify reference to the barometer, an object neither incongruous nor significant, and therefore not participating, at first glance, in the order of the *notable*; and in Michelet's sentence, we have the same difficulty in accounting structurally for all the details: that the executioner came after the painter is all that is necessary to the account; how long the sitting lasted, the dimension and location of the door are useless (but the theme of the door, the softness of death's knock have an indisputable symbolic value). Even if they are not numerous, the "useless details" therefore seem inevitable: every narrative, at least every Western narrative of the ordinary sort nowadays, possesses a certain number.

Insignificant notation* (taking this word in its stong sense: apparently detached from the narrative's semiotic structure) is related to description, even if the object seems to be denoted only by a single word (in reality, the "pure" word does not exist: Flaubert's barometer is not cited in isolation; it is located, placed in a syntagm at once referential and syntactic); thus is underlined the enigmatic character of all description, about which a word is necessary: the general structure of narrative, at least as it has been occasionally analyzed till now, appears as essentially *predictive*; schematizing to the extreme, and without taking into account numerous detours, delays, reversals, and disappointments which narrative institutionally imposes upon this schema, we can say that, at each articulation of the narrative syntagm, someone says to the hero (or to the reader, it does not matter which): if you act in this way, if you choose this alternative, this is what will happen (the *reported* character of these predictions does not call into question their practical nature). Description

* In this brief account, we shall not give examples of "insignificant" notations, for the insignificant can be revealed only on the level of an immense structure: once cited, a notion is neither significant nor insignificant; it requires an already analyzed context.

is entirely different: it has no predictive mark; "analogical," its structure is purely summatory and does not contain that trajectory of choices and alternatives which gives narration the appearance of a huge traffic-control center, furnished with a referential (and not merely discursive) temporality. This is an opposition which, anthropologically, has its importance: when, under the influence of von Frisch's experiments, it was assumed that bees had a language, it had to be realized that, while these insects possessed a predictive system of dances (in order to collect their food), nothing in it approached a *description*. Thus, description appears as a kind of characteristic of the so-called higher languages, to the apparently paradoxical degree that it is justified by no finality of action or of communication. The singularity of description (or of the "useless detail") in narrative fabric, its isolated situation, designates a question which has the greatest importance for the structural analysis of narrative. This question is the following: Is everything in narrative significant, and if not, if insignificant stretches subsist in the narrative syntagm, what is ultimately, so to speak, the significance of this insignificance?

First of all, we must recall that Western culture, in one of its major currents, has certainly not left description outside meaning, and has furnished it with a finality quite "recognized" by the literary institution. This current is Rhetoric, and this finality is that of the "beautiful": description has long had an aesthetic function. Very early in antiquity, to the two expressly functional genres of discourse, legal and political, was added a third, the epideictic, a ceremonial discourse intended to excite the admiration of the audience (and no longer to persuade it); this discourse contained in germ—whatever the ritual rules of its use: eulogy or obituary—the very idea of an aesthetic finality of language; in the Alexandrian neo-rhetoric of the second century A.D., there was a craze for ecphrasis, the detachable set piece (thus having its end in itself, independent of any general function), whose object was to describe places, times, people, or works of art, a tradition which was maintained throughout the

Middle Ages. As Curtius has emphasized, description in this period is constrained by no realism; its truth is unimportant (or even its verisimilitude); there is no hesitation to put lions or olive trees in a northern country; only the constraint of the descriptive genre counts; plausibility is not referential here but openly discursive: it is the generic rules of discourse which lay down the law.

Moving ahead to Flaubert, we see that the aesthetic purpose of description is still very strong. In *Madame Bovary*, the description of Rouen (a real referent if ever there was one) is subject to the tyrannical constraints of what we must call aesthetic verisimilitude, as is attested by the corrections made in this passage in the course of six successive rewritings. Here we see, first of all, that the corrections do not in any way issue from a closer consideration of the model: Rouen, perceived by Flaubert, remains just the same, or more precisely, if it changes somewhat from one version to the next, it is solely because he finds it necessary to focus an image or avoid a phonic redundance condemned by the rules of *le beau style*, or again to "arrange" a quite contingent felicity of expression;* next we see that the descriptive fabric, which at first glance seems to grant a major importance (by its dimension, by the concern for its detail) to the object *Rouen*, is in fact only a sort of setting meant to receive the jewels of a number of rare metaphors, the neutral, prosaic excipient which swathes the precious symbolic substance, as if, in Rouen, all that mattered were the figures of rhetoric to which the sight of the city lends itself—as if Rouen were notable only by its substitutions (*the masts like a forest of needles, the islands like huge motionless black fish, the clouds like aerial waves silently breaking against a cliff*); last, we see that the whole description is *constructed* so as to connect Rouen to a painting: it is a painted scene which the language takes up ("Thus, seen from above, the whole

* A mechanism distinguished by Valéry, in *Littérature*, commenting on Baudelaire's line "*La servante au grand coeur* . . .": "This line *came* to Baudelaire . . . And Baudelaire continued. He buried the cook out on the lawn, which goes against the custom, but goes with the rhyme," etc.

landscape had the motionless look of a painting"); the writer here fulfills Plato's definition of the artist as a maker in the third degree, since he imitates what is already the simulation of an essence. Thus, although the description of Rouen is quite irrelevant to the narrative structure of *Madame Bovary* (we can attach it to no functional sequence nor to any characterial, atmospheric, or sapiential signified), it is not in the least scandalous, it is justified, if not by the work's logic, at least by the laws of literature: its "meaning" exists, it depends on conformity not to the model but to the cultural rules of representation.

All the same, the aesthetic goal of Flaubertian description is thoroughly mixed with "realistic" imperatives, as if the referent's exactitude, superior or indifferent to any other function, governed and alone justified its description, or—in the case of descriptions reduced to a single word—its denotation: here aesthetic constraints are steeped—at least as an alibi—in referential constraints: it is likely that, if one came to Rouen in a diligence, the view one would have coming down the slope leading to the town would not be "objectively" different from the panorama Flaubert describes. This mixture—this interweaving—of constraints has a double advantage: on the one hand, aesthetic function, giving a meaning to "the fragment," halts what we might call the vertigo of notation; for once, discourse is no longer guided and limited by structural imperatives of the anecdote (functions and indices), nothing could indicate why we should halt the details of the description here and not there; if it were not subject to an aesthetic or rhetorical choice, any "view" would be inexhaustible by discourse: there would always be a corner, a detail, an inflection of space or color to report; on the other hand, by positing the referential as real, by pretending to follow it in a submissive fashion, realistic description avoids being reduced to fantasmatic activity (a precaution which was supposed necessary to the "objectivity" of the account); classical rhetoric had in a sense institutionalized the fantasmatic as a specific figure, *hypotyposis*, whose function was to "put things before the hearer's eyes," not in a neutral, constative manner, but by imparting to representation all the luster of desire (this was the vividly illuminated sector of discourse, with prismatic outlines: *illustris oratio*); declaratively renouncing the constraints of the rhetorical code, realism must seek a new reason to describe.

The irreducible residues of functional analysis have this in common: they denote what is ordinarily called "concrete reality" (insignificant gestures, transitory attitudes, insignificant objects, redundant words). The pure and simple "representation" of the "real," the naked relation of "what is" (or has been) thus appears as a resistance to meaning; this resistance confirms the great mythic opposition of the *true-to-life* (the lifelike) and the *intelligible*; it suffices to recall that, in the ideology of our time, obsessive reference to the "concrete" (in what is rhetorically demanded of the human sciences, of literature, of behavior) is always brandished like a weapon against meaning, as if, by some statutory exclusion, what is alive cannot not signify—and vice versa. Resistance of the "real" (in its written form, of course) to structure is very limited in the fictive account, constructed by definition on a model which, for its main outlines, has no other constraints than those of intelligibility; but this same "reality" becomes the essential reference in historical narrative, which is supposed to report "what really happened": what does the non-functionality of a detail matter then, once it denotes "what took place"; "concrete reality" becomes the sufficient justification for speaking. History (historical discourse: *historia rerum gestarum*) is in fact the model of those narratives which consent to fill in the interstices of their functions by structurally superfluous notations, and it is logical that literary realism should have been—give or take a few decades—contemporary with the regnum of "objective" history, to which must be added the contemporary development of techniques, of works, and institutions based on the incessant need to authenticate the "real": the photograph (immediate witness of "what was here"), reportage, exhibitions of ancient objects (the success of the Tutankhamen show makes this quite clear), the tourism of monuments and historical sites.

All this shows that the "real" is supposed to be self-sufficient, that it is strong enough to belie any notion of "function," that its "speech-act" has no need to be integrated into a structure and that the *having-been-there* of things is a sufficient principle of speech.

Since antiquity, the "real" has been on History's side; but this was to help it oppose the "lifelike," the "plausible," to oppose the very order of narrative (of imitation or "poetry"). All classical culture lived for centuries on the notion that reality could in no way contaminate verisimilitude; first of all, because verisimilitude is never anything but *opinable*: it is entirely subject to (public) opinion; as Nicole said: "One must not consider things as they are in themselves, nor as they are known to be by one who speaks or writes, but only in relation to what is known of them by those who read or hear"; then, because History was thought to be general, not particular (whence the propensity, in classical texts, to functionalize all details, to produce strong structures and to justify no notation by the mere guarantee of "reality"); finally, because, in verisimilitude, the contrary is never impossible, since notation rests on a majority, but not an absolute, opinion. The motto implicit on the threshold of all classical discourse (subject to the ancient idea of verisimilitude) is: *Esto* (*Let there be, suppose* . . .) "Real," fragmented, interstitial notation, the kind we are dealing with here, renounces this implicit introduction, and it is free of any such postulation that occurs in the structural fabric. Hence, there is a break between the ancient mode of versimilitude and modern realism; but hence, too, a new verisimilitude is born, which is precisely *realism* (by which we mean any discourse which accepts "speech-acts" justified by their referent alone).

Semiotically, the "concrete detail" is constituted by the *direct* collusion of a referent and a signifier; the signified is expelled from the sign, and with it, of course, the possibility of developing a *form of the signified*, i.e., narrative structure itself. (Realistic literature is narrative, of course, but that is because its realism is only fragmentary, erratic, confined to "details," and because the most realistic narrative imaginable develops along unrealistic lines.) This is what we might call the *referential illusion.** The truth of this illusion is this: eliminated from the realist speech-act as a signified of denotation, the "real" returns to it as a signified of connotation; for just when these details are reputed to *denote* the real directly, all that they do—without saying so—is *signify* it; Flaubert's barometer, Michelet's little door finally say nothing but this: *we are the real*; it is the category of "the real" (and not its contingent contents) which is then signified; in other words, the very absence of the signified, to the advantage of the referent alone, becomes the very signifier of realism: the *reality effect* is produced, the basis of that unavowed verisimilitude which forms the aesthetic of all the standard works of modernity.

This new verisimilitude is very different from the old one, for it is neither a respect for the "laws of the genre" nor even their mask, but proceeds from the intention to degrade the sign's tripartite nature in order to make notation the pure encounter of an object and its expression. The disintegration of the sign—which seems indeed to be modernity's grand affair—is of course present in the realistic enterprise, but in a somewhat regressive manner, since it occurs in the name of a referential plenitude, whereas the goal today is to empty the sign and infinitely to postpone its object so as to challenge, in a radical fashion, the age-old aesthetic of "representation."

Communications, 1968

* An illusion clearly illustrated by the program Thiers assigned to the historian: "To be simply true, to be what things are and nothing more than that, and nothing except that."

Writing the Event

To describe the event implies that the event has been written. How can an event be written? What can it mean to say "Writing the event"? The event of May '68 seems to have been written in three fashions, three writings, whose polygraphic conjunction forms, perhaps, its historical originality.

1. Speech

Every national shock produces a sudden flowering of written commentary (press, books). This is not what I want to speak of here. The spoken words of May '68 had original aspects, which must be emphasized.

1. Radiophonic speech (that of the "peripheral" stations) clung to the event, as it was occurring, in a breathless, dramatic fashion, imposing the notion that knowledge of present reality is no longer the business of print but of the spoken word. "Hot" history, history in the course of being made, is an auditive history,* and hearing becomes again what it was in the Middle Ages: not only the first of the senses (ahead of touch and sight), but the sense which establishes knowledge (as, for Luther, it established the Christian faith). Nor is this all. The (reporter's) informative word was so closely involved with the event, with the very opacity of its present, as to become its immediate and consubstantial meaning, its way of acceding to an instantaneous intelligibility; this means that in terms of Western culture, where nothing can be perceived without meaning, it was the event

* One recalls streets filled with motionless people seeing nothing, looking at nothing, their eyes down, but their ears glued to transistor radios, thus representing a new human anatomy.

itself. The age-old distance between act and discourse, event and testimony, was reduced; a new dimension of history appeared, immediately linked to its discourse, whereas all historical "science" had the task to acknowledge this distance, in order to govern it. Not only did radiophonic speech inform the participants as to the very extension of their action (a few yards away from them), so that the transistor became the bodily appendage, the auditory prosthesis, the new science-fiction organ of certain demonstrators, but even, by the compression of time, by the immediate resonance of the act, it inflected, modified the event; in short, wrote it: fusion of the sign and its hearing, reversibility of writing and reading which is sought elsewhere, by that revolution in writing which modernity is attempting to achieve.

2. The relations of force between the different groups and parties engaged in the crisis were essentially *spoken,* in the sense that the tactical or dialectical displacement of these relations during the days of May occurred *through* and *by* (confusion of the means and of the cause which marks language) the communiqué, the press conference, the declaration, the speech. Not only did the crisis have its language, but in fact the crisis *was* language: it is speech which in a sense molded history, made it exist like a network of traces, an operative writing, displacing (it is only stale prejudice that considers speech an illusory activity, noisy and futile, and set in opposition to actions); the "spoken" nature of the crisis is all the more visible in that it has had, strictly speaking, no murderous, irremediable effect (speech is what can be "corrected"; its rigorous antonym, to the point of defining it, can only be death).*

3. The students' speech so completely overflowed, pouring out everywhere, written everywhere, that one might define superficially—but also, perhaps, essentially—the university revolt as a *Taking of Speech* (as we say *Taking of the Bastille*). It seems

* The insistence with which it was repeated, on either side, that, whatever happens, *afterwards* can no longer be like *before* doubtless translates, negatively, the fear (or the hope) that in fact *afterwards* would become *before*: the event being speech, it can, mythically, cross itself out.

in retrospect that the student was a being frustrated of speech; frustrated but not deprived: by class origin, by vague cultural practice, the student has the use of language; language is not unknown to him, he is not (or is no longer) afraid of it; the problem was to assume its power, its active use. Hence, by a paradox which is only apparent, just when the students' speech made its claims in the sole name of content, it actually involved a profoundly ludic aspect; the student had begun to wield speech as an activity, a free labor, and not, despite appearances, as a simple instrument. This activity took different forms, which correspond perhaps to phases of the student movement throughout the crisis.

a) "Wild" speech, based on "invention," consequently encountering quite naturally the "finds" of form, rhetorical shortcuts, the delights of formula, in short *felicity of expression*; very close to writing, this discourse (which affected public opinion intensely) logically assumed the form of *inscription*; its natural dimension was the wall, fundamental site of collective writing.

b) "Missionary" speech, conceived in a purely instrumental fashion, intended to transport "elsewhere" (to factory gates, to beaches, into the street, etc.) the stereotypes of political culture.

c) "Functionalist" speech, conveying the reform projects, assigning to the university a social function, here political, there economic, and thereby rediscovering some of the watchwords of a previous technocracy ("adaptation of teaching to society's needs," "collectivization of research," primacy of the "result," prestige of the "interdisciplinary," "autonomy," "participation," etc.).

"Wild" speech was quite rapidly eliminated, embalmed in the harmless folds of (surrealist) "literature" and the illusions of "spontaneity"; as writing, it could only be useless (until it became intolerable) to any form of power, whether possessed or claimed; the other two kinds remain mixed: a mixture which rather nicely reproduces the political ambiguity of the student movement itself, threatened, in its historical and social situation, by the dream of a "social-technocracy."

2. Symbol

There was no lack of symbols in this crisis, as was often remarked; they were produced and consumed with great energy; and above all, a striking phenomenon, they were *sustained* by a general, shared willingness. The paradigm of the three flags (red / black / tricolor), with its pertinent associations of terms (red and black against tricolor, red and tricolor against black), was "spoken" (flags raised, brandished, taken down, invoked, etc.) by everyone, or just about: a fine agreement, if not as to the symbols, at least as to the symbolic system itself (which, *as such*, should be the final target of a Western revolution). The same symbolic avatar for the barricade: itself the symbol of revolutionary Paris, and itself a significant site of an entire network of other symbols. Complete emblem, the barricade made it possible to irritate and unmask other symbols; that of property, for example, henceforth lodged, for the French, in the fact that it appeared much more in the car than in the house. Other symbols were mobilized: monument (Bourse, Odéon), demonstration, occupation, garment, and of course language, in its most coded (i.e., symbolic, ritual*) aspects. This inventory of symbols should be made; not so much because it is likely to produce a very eloquent list (this is improbable, despite or because of the "spontaneity" which presided over their liberation), but because the symbolic system under which an event functions is closely linked to the degree of this event's integration within the society of which it is both the expression and the violation: a symbolic field is not only a junction (or an antagonism) of symbols; it is also formed by a homogeneous set of rules, a commonly acknowledged recourse to these rules. A kind of almost unanimous adherence† to one and the same symbolic discourse

* For instance: lexicon of revolutionary work ("committees," "commissions," "motions," "points of order," etc.), ritual of communication (second-person-singular forms, first names, etc.).

† The most important aspect of this inventory would ultimately be to discover how each group played or did not play the symbolic game: rejection of the (red or black) flag, refusal of the barricade, etc.

seems to have finally marked partisans and adversaries of the contestation: almost all played the same symbolic game.

3. Violence

Violence, which in modern mythology is linked, as if it followed quite naturally, with spontaneity and effectiveness—violence, symbolized here concretely, then verbally, by "the street," site of released speech, of free contact, counter-intellectual space, opposition of the immediate to the possible ruses of all mediation—violence is a writing: it is (a Derridian theme) the trace in its profoundest gesture. Writing (if we no longer identify it with style or with literature) is itself violent. It is, in fact, the violence of writing that separates it from speech, reveals the force of inscription in it, the weight of an irreversible trace. Indeed, this writing of violence (an eminently collective writing) possesses a code; however one decides to account for it, tactical or psychoanalytic, violence implies a language of violence, i.e., of signs (operations or pulsions) repeated, combined into figures (actions or complexes), in short, a system. Let us take advantage of this to repeat that the presence (or the postulation) of a code does not intellectualize the event (contrary to what anti-intellectualist mythology constantly states): the intelligible is not the intellectual.

Such at first glance are the orientations that a description of the traces which constitute the event might take. Yet such a description risks being inert if we do not attach it, from the start, to two postulates whose bearing is still polemical.

The first consists in rigorously separating, according to Derrida's proposition, the concepts of speech and of writing. Speech is not only what is actually spoken but also what is transcribed (or rather transliterated) from oral expression, and which can very well be printed (or mimeographed); linked to the body, to the person, to the will-to-seize, it is the very voice of any "revendication," but not necessarily of the revolution. Writing is integrally "what is to be invented," the dizzying break with the old symbolic system, the mutation of a whole range of language. Which is to say, on the one hand, that writing (as we understand it here, which has nothing to do with "style" or even literature) is not at all a bourgeois phenomenon (what this class elaborated was, in fact, a printed speech), and, on the other, that the present event can only furnish marginal fragments of writing, which as we saw were not necessarily printed; we will regard as suspect any eviction of writing, any systematic primacy of speech, because, whatever the revolutionary alibi, both tend to *preserve* the old symbolic system and refuse to link its revolution to that of society.

The second postulate consists in not expecting written description to afford a "decoding." Considering the event from the viewpoint of whatever symbolic mutation it can imply means, first of all, breaking as much as possible (this is not easy, it requires the sort of continuous labor begun in various quarters, it must be recalled, some years ago) with the system of meaning which the event, if it seeks to be revolutionary, must call into question. The critical aspect of the old system is *interpretation*, i.e., the operation by which one assigns to a set of confused or even contradictory appearances a unitary structure, a deep meaning, a "veritable" explanation. Hence, interpretation must gradually give way to a new discourse, whose goal is not the revelation of a unique and "true" structure but the establishment of an interplay of multiple structures: an establishment itself *written*, i.e., uncoupled from the truth of speech; more precisely, it is the relations which organize these concomitant structures, subject to still unknown rules, which must constitute the object of a new theory.

Communications, 1968

5
THE LOVER OF SIGNS

Revelation

The Berliner Ensemble came to France the first time in 1954. Some of us who saw the company then had the revelation of a new system, one which cruelly dated our whole theater. Such novelty had nothing provocative about it, and did not borrow the habitual manners of the avant-garde. It was what could be called a *subtle revolution.*

That revolution proceeded from the fact that the playwright (in this case, Brecht himself) regarded as quite compatible certain values which our theater had always been reluctant to combine. Brechtian theater, as we know, is *intellectual* theater, a practice elaborated from an explicit theory, at once materialist and semantic. Longing for a political theater enlightened by Marxism and an art which rigorously governs its signs, how could we help being dazzled by the work of the Berliner Ensemble? Another paradox: this political work did not reject beauty; the merest blue spot, the most discreet substance, a belt buckle, a gray rag—formed, each time, a scene which never copied painting and yet would not have been possible without the most refined taste: this theater which insisted on its "commitment" was not afraid to be *distinguished* (a word we should release from its usual triviality, so as to give it a meaning close to Brechtian *distancing*). The product of these two values generated what we can regard as a phenomenon unknown in the West (perhaps precisely because Brecht had learned it from the East): *a theater without hysteria.*

Finally, an ultimate flavor, this intelligent, political theater of an ascetic sumptuousness was also—according, moreover, to one of Brecht's precepts—an amusing theater: no tirades, no preaching, never, even, that edifying Manichaeanism which commonly opposes, in all political art, the good proletarians to the wicked bourgeois; but always an unexpected argument, a social criticism conducted outside the tedium of stereotypes and mobilizing pleasure's most recent resource: subtlety. A theater at once revolutionary, signifying, and voluptuous—who could ask for anything better?

This surprising conjunction, however, had nothing magical about it; it would not have been possible without a material datum, one which was lacking—and which is lacking still—in our theater. For a long time there has prevailed among us, inherited from a spiritualist tradition which Copeau perfectly symbolized, the convenient conviction that one can have excellent theater without money: poverty of means thus became a "sublime" value, converted actors into officiants. Now, Brechtian theater is an expensive theater, it pays for the unprecedented attention given to staging, for the elaboration of costumes—whose careful treatment costs infinitely more than the wildest luxury of our spectacles—for the number of rehearsals, for the actors' professional security, so necessary to their art. This theater, at once popular and refined, is impossible in a private economy, where it could be supported by neither the bourgeois public which makes money nor the petit-bourgeois public which makes spectators. Behind the success of the Berliner Ensemble, behind the perfection of its work—a thing everyone could observe—we had to see a whole economy, a whole political determination.

I do not know what the Berliner Ensemble has become since Brecht's death, but I know that the Berliner Ensemble of 1954 taught me a great many things—and much more than theater.

Le Monde, 1971

A Magnificent Gift

Jakobson made literature a magnificent gift: he gave it linguistics. Of course, Literature did not wait to know it was Language; all of classical Rhetoric until Valéry attests to the fact; but once a *science* of language was sought (initially in the form of a historical and comparative linguistics of languages), it was oddly negligent of the *effects* of meaning, it too succumbing in that century of positivism (the nineteenth) to the taboo of specialized realms: on one side, Science, Reason, Fact; on the other, Art, Sensibility, Impression. Jakobson was involved since his youth in the amendment of this situation: because this linguist has persisted in his great love of poetry, of painting, of cinema, because, at the heart of his scientific research, he never censored his pleasure as a cultivated man, he realized that the authentic scientific phenomenon of modernity was not *fact* but *relationship*. At the origin of the generalized linguistics he outlined was a decisive *opening* gesture of classifications, castes, disciplines: these words lost, with him, their separatist, penal, racist taint; there are no more owners (of Literature, of Linguistics), the watchdogs are sent back to their pens.

Jakobson endowed Literature in three ways. First of all, he created within linguistics itself a special department, *Poetics*; this sector (and this is what is new in his work, his historical contribution), he did not define from Literature (as if Poetics still depended on the "poetic" or on "poetry") but from the analysis of the functions of language: every speech-act which accentuates the form of the message is poetic; therefore, he was able, *starting from a linguistic position*, to join the vital (and often the most emancipated) forms of Literature: the right to ambiguity of meanings, the system of substitutions, the code of figures (metaphor and metonymy).

Subsequently, even more strongly than Saussure, he promoted a pansemiotics, a generalized (and not only general) science of signs; but here again his position was doubly avant-garde: on the one hand he maintained a preeminent place in that science for articulated language (being well aware that language is *everywhere*, and not simply *close by*), and on the other he immediately united the realms of Art and Literature to semiotics, thereby postulating from the start that semiology is a science of signification—and not of mere communication (thus freeing linguistics of any risk of technocratic intent).

Finally, his linguistics itself admirably grounds our present concept of the Text: i.e., that a sign's meaning is only its translation into another sign, which defines meaning not as a final signified but as *another* signifying level; and also that the commonest language involves an important number of metalinguistic utterances, which attests man's necessity to conceive his language at the very moment he speaks: a crucial activity which Literature merely carries to its highest degree of incandescence.

The very style of his thought, a brilliant, generous, ironic, expansive, cosmopolitan, flexible style which we might call *devilishly intelligent*, predisposed Jakobson to this historical function of opening—of abolishing disciplinary ownership. Another style is doubtless possible, based at once on a more historical culture and on a more philosophical notion of the speaking subject: I am thinking here of the unforgettable (and yet somewhat forgotten, it seems to me) work of Benveniste, whom we must never dissociate (and Jakobson would agree with me here) from any *homage* we pay to the decisive role of Linguistics in the birth of that *other thing* operative in our age. But Jakobson, through all the new and irreversible propositions that constitute his work of fifty years, is for us that historic figure who, by a stroke of intelligence, definitively shoved *into the past* some highly respectable things to which we were attached: he converted prejudice into anachronism. All his work reminds us that "each of us must realize, once and for all, that the linguist deaf to poetic function, like the specialist in literature indifferent to the problems and ignorant of methods of linguistics, is henceforth, in either case, a flagrant anachronism."

Le Monde, 1971

Why I Love Benveniste

1

The present emphasis on problems of language irritates some, who regard it as an excessive fashion. Yet they will have to resign themselves to the inevitable: we are probably only beginning to speak of language: along with other sciences which tend, today, to be attached to it, linguistics is entering the dawn of its history: we have yet to discover language, as we are in the process of discovering space: our century will perhaps be marked by these two explorations.

Every work of general linguistics therefore answers an imperious need of today's culture as well as a demand for knowledge formulated by every science whose object is to any degree involved with language. Now, linguistics is difficult to expound, divided as it is between a necessary specialization and an explosive anthropological project. Therefore, works of general linguistics are few in number, at least in French: Martinet's *Elements* and Jakobson's *Essays*; Hjelmslev's *Prolegomena* are soon to be translated. And today there is the work of Benveniste.

This is a collection of articles (normal units of linguistic research), some of which are already famous (on the arbitrariness of the sign, on the function of language in Freudian discovery, on the levels of linguistic analysis). The first group constitute a description of contemporary linguistics: especially to be recommended here is the splendid article on Saussure, who in fact wrote nothing after his memorandum on Indo-European vowels, being unable, he believed, to effect that total subversion of past linguistics he required to construct his own linguistics, and whose "silence" has the greatness and the bearing of a writer's silence. The articles that follow occupy the cardinal points of linguistic space: *communication,* or again the articulated sign, situated in relation to thought, to animal language, and to oneiric language; *structure* (I have mentioned the crucial text on the levels of linguistic analysis: I must also point out the text—fascinating in its clarity—in which Benveniste establishes the sub-logical system of Latin prepositions; if only we had had such an explanation in the days when we were making our Latin translations: everything is illuminated by structure); *signification* (for it is always from the point of view of meaning that Benveniste interrogates language); *person,* to my mind the decisive part of the work, in which Benveniste, essentially, analyzes the organization of pronouns and tenses. The work concludes with several lexical studies.

All of which forms the program of an impeccable scholarship, answers with clarity and power the questions of fact likely to be raised by anyone with some interest in language. But this is not all. This book not only satisfies a present demand of culture: it anticipates it, forms it, directs it. In short, this is not merely an indispensable book; it is also an important book, an unlooked-for book: it is a very beautiful book.

When the science in which one has specialized is solicited by the curiosity of amateurs of every kind, it is quite tempting to defend the specialty of that science rather jealously. Quite the contrary, Benveniste has the courage deliberately to place linguistics at the point of origin of a very wide movement and to divine in it the future development of a veritable science of culture, insofar as culture is essentially language; he does not hesitate to note the birth of a new objectivity, imposed upon the scholar by the symbolic nature of cultural phenomena; far from abandoning language on society's doorstep as if it were merely a tool, he hopefully asserts that "it is society which is beginning to acknowledge itself as language." Now, it is crucial for a whole set of investigations and revolutions that a linguist as rigorous as Benveniste should himself be conscious of his discipline's powers, and that, refusing to constitute himself as its owner, he should recognize in it the germ of a new configuration of the human sciences.

This courage is paired with a profound vision. Benveniste—this is his success—always grasps language at that crucial level where, without ceasing to be language to the full, it gathers up everything we were accustomed to consider as external or anterior to language. Take three contributions, among the most important: one on the middle voice of Indo-European verbs, the second on the structure of the personal pronouns, the third on the system of tenses in French; all three deal in various ways with a crucial notion in psychology: that of person. Now, Benveniste magisterially manages to *root* this notion in a purely linguistic description. In a general manner, placing the subject (in the philosophic sense of the word) in the center of the great categories of language, showing, on the occasion of extremely diverse phenomena, that this subject can never be distinguished from an "instance of discourse," unlike the instance of reality, Benveniste establishes linguistically, i.e., scientifically, the identity of subject and language, a position at the heart of many contemporary investigations and of as much interest to philosophy as to literature; such analyses may show the way out of an old antinomy, one that has not yet been liquidated: that of subjective and objective, of individual and society, of science and discourse.

Books of scholarship, of research, have their "style" too. This one is of a very high order. There is a beauty, an experience of the intellect, which gives the work of certain scholars that *inexhaustible clarity* which also goes into the making of great literary works. Everything is clear in Benveniste's book, everything can be immediately recognized as true; and yet everything in it is only beginning.

La Quinzaine littéraire, 1966

2

Benveniste's place in the concert of great linguists whose influence marks all intellectual work of our times is quite original—to the point of being, it seems to me, occasionally underestimated. Even today, his work is paradoxical twice over: with regard to the tradition, and with regard to what I shall call the *easy avant-garde*, the one which repeats instead of exploring.

What is it, then, that Benveniste tells us? First of all, this: that language can never be separated from a sociality. This pure linguist, whose objects of study apparently belong to the apparatus of general, transcendent linguistics, actually never ceases apprehending language in which we might call its *concomitances*: work, history, culture, institutions; in short, everything that constitutes human reality. The *Vocabulary of Indo-European Institutions*, the studies of agent names, of the verbal prefixes *prae-* and *vor-*, are texts which denature the linguistic discipline, achieve that subversive moment by which the disciplinary outline is erased and a new, as yet unnamed, science appears; this is the moment when linguistics ceases to take a theatrical leadership and becomes in fact a universal "sociology": the science of a society which speaks, which is a society *precisely because it speaks*. On this level, Benveniste's work is always critical; a demystifier, he is tirelessly concerned to *reverse* scholarly prejudices and implacably to illuminate (for this man of science is rigorous) language's social basis. This power Benveniste possesses because of the precise—but today rare, and underrated—situation of his work: he is a linguist of *languages*, not just of language.

At the other end of the chain (but the hiatus will astonish only those frivolous minds who imperturbably continue to set history in opposition to structure), Benveniste has given scientific body to a notion which has assumed the greatest importance in the work of the avant-garde: the speech-act. The speech-act [*énonciation*] is not, of course, the statement [*énoncé*], nor is it (a much subtler and more revolutionary proposition) the simple presence of subjectivity in discourse; it is the renewed act by which the locutor takes possession of the language (appropriates it, Benveniste says quite accurately): the subject is not anterior to language; he becomes subject only insofar as he speaks; in short, there is no "subject" (and consequently no "subjectivity"), there are only locutors; moreover—and this is Benveniste's incessant reminder—there are only *interlocutors*.

From this point of view, Benveniste considerably widens the notion of *shifter*, which Jakobson advanced with such brio; he establishes a new linguistics, which exists nowhere else but in his work (and, above all, not in Chomsky's): the linguistics of interlocution, language, and consequently the whole world, is articulated around this form: *I / you*. Hence, we understand Benveniste's insistence on dealing, throughout his work, with the so-called personal pronouns, with temporality, with diathesis, with composition (the privileged appropriation of the lexicon). We also understand why Benveniste could so early establish a bridge between linguistics and psychoanalysis; why, again, this specialist in Old Persian was able, without forcing himself, to understand—or at least specifically to keep himself from censoring—the new investigations of semiology (Metz, Schefer) and the work of the avant-garde on language. The direct interest of Benveniste's new book is here: it is the book of the speech-act.

A scholar's intellectual gifts (not what is given to him, but what he gives us) derive, I am convinced, from a power which is not only that of knowledge and rigor but also that of writing, or, to adopt a word whose radical acceptation we now know, from the speech-act. The language Benveniste appropriates (since that is his definition of the speech-act) is not *altogether* that of ordinary scholars, and this slight displacement is sufficient to constitute a writing. Benveniste's writing is very difficult to describe because it is *almost* neutral; only occasionally does a word—by dint of being accurate, one might say, so much does accuracy seem to accumulate in him—gleam out, delight like a charm, swept away by a syntax whose measure, proportion, and exactitude (all virtues of a cabinetmaker) attest to the pleasure which this scholar has taken in forming his sentences. Benveniste's writing thus presents that subtle mixture of expenditure and reserve which founds the text or, better still, music. Benveniste writes *silently* (is not music an art of intelligent silence?), the way the greatest musicians play: there is something of Richter in Benveniste.

Working with him, with his texts (which are never mere articles), we always recognize the generosity of a man who seems to listen to the reader and to lend him his intelligence, even in the most special subjects, the most improbable ones. We read other linguists (and indeed we must), but we love Benveniste.

La Quinzaine littéraire, 1974

Kristeva's *Semeiotike*

Although recent, semiology already has a history. Derived from a quite Olympian formulation of Saussure's ("A science is conceivable which would study the life of signs at the very heart of social life"), it continues to experiment with itself, to split itself up, to de-situate itself, to enter into that great carnival of languages Julia Kristeva describes. Its historical role is at present to be the intruder, the third party, the one who upsets those exemplary households we hear so much about and which are formed, it appears, by History and Revolution, Structuralism and Reaction, determinism and science, *progressisme* and the critique of content. Of this upset, Julia Kristeva's work is today the ultimate orchestration: it activates its tendencies and supplies its theory.

Already greatly in Kristeva's debt (and from the beginning), I have just experienced once more, and this time in its entirety, the force of her work. Here *force* means *displacement*. Julia Kristeva changes the place of things: she always destroys the *last prejudice*, the one you thought you could be reassured by, could take pride in; what she displaces is the *already-said*, the *déjà-dit*, i.e., the instance of the signified, i.e., stupidity; what she subverts is authority—the authority of monologic science, of filiation. Her work is entirely new, exact, not by scientific puritanism, but because it takes up the whole of the site it occupies, fills it *exactly*, obliging anyone who excludes himself from it to find himself in a position of resistance or censorship (this is what we call, with a very shocked expression, terrorism).

Since I have reached the point of speaking of a *site* of research, let me say that for me Kristeva's work constitutes this admonition: that we are still going too slowly, that we are wasting time in "believing," i.e. in repeating and humoring ourselves, that often a supplement of freedom in a new thought would suffice to gain years of work. In Julia Kristeva, this supplement is theoretical. What is theory? It is neither an abstraction nor a generalization nor a speculation: it is a reflexivity; it is in some sense the reversed gaze of a language upon itself (which is why, in a society deprived of socialist practice, thereby condemned to *discourse,* theoretical discourse is transitorily necessary). It is in this sense that, for the first time, Julia Kristeva is giving us a theory of semiology: *Any semiotics must be a criticism of semiotics.* Such a proposition is not to be taken as a pious and hypocritical wish ("Let us criticize the semioticians who precede us") but as the affirmation that, in its very discourse, and not on the level of a few phrases, the work of semiotic science is shot through with destructive returns, with countered coexistences, with productive disfigurations.

The science of languages cannot be Olympian, positive (still less positivist), indifferent, adiaphoric, as Nietzsche says; it is itself (because it is the language of language) dialogic—a notion borrowed by Kristeva from Bakhtine, whom she has introduced to us. The first act of this dialogism is, for semiotics, to conceive itself at once and contradictorily as science and as writing—which, I believe, has never been done by any science, except perhaps by the materialist science of the pre-Socratics, and which may permit us, let it be said in passing, to escape from the impasse *bourgeois science* (spoken) / *proletarian science* (written, at least postulatively).

The value of Kristevian discourse is that it is homogeneous to the theory it enunciates (and this homogeneity is the theory itself): in it, science is writing, the sign is dialogic, the basis is destructive; if it seems "difficult" to some, this is precisely because it is *written.* Which means what? First of all, that it asserts and practices both formalization and its displacement, mathematics becoming, in short, analogous to the work of dreams (whence many complaints). Next, that it assumes *as theory* the terminological slippage of so-called scientific definitions. Finally, that it institutes a new type of transmission of knowledge (it is not knowledge which constitutes the problem, but its transmission): Kristeva's writing possesses at once a discursivity, a "development" (we should like to give this word a *bicyclist* meaning rather than a rhetorical one), and a formulation, a *frappe* (trace of shock and of inscription), a germination; it is a discourse which functions not so much because it "represents" a thought as because, immediately, without the mediation of dim *écrivance* (inauthentic writing), it produces thought and aims it. This means that only Julia Kristeva is able to produce semio-analysis: her discourse is not propaedeutic, it does not offer the possibility of a "teaching"; but this also means, conversely, that this discourse transforms us, displaces us, gives us words, meanings, sentences which permit us to work and to release in ourselves the creative movement itself: permutation.

In short, what Julia Kristeva produces is a critique of *communication* (the first, I believe, since that of psychoanalysis). Communication, she shows, the darling of the positive sciences (such as linguistics), of the philosophies and the politics of "dialogue," of "participation," and of "exchange"—communication is *merchandise*. Are we not constantly told that a "clear" book sells better, that a communicative temperament more easily finds a job? Hence, it is a political task, the very one Kristeva is performing, to undertake to reduce communication theoretically to the mercantile level of human relations and to integrate it, as a simple fluctuating level, to significance, to the Text, an apparatus outside of meaning, victorious affirmation of Expenditure over Exchange, of Numbers over Reckoning.

Will all of this "get anywhere"? That depends on French *inculture*, which today seems to be gently lapping, rising around us. Why? For political reasons, no doubt; but these reasons seem to affect precisely those who should resist them best: there is a petty nationalism of the French intelligentsia; one that does not bear on nationalities, of course (is not Ionesco, after all, the Pure and Perfect French Petit-Bourgeois?), but on the stubborn rejection of *the other language*. The other language is the one spoken from a politically and ideologically uninhabitable place: an interstitial site, oblique, on the edge—the verge—of irregular action: a *cavalier* site, since it traverses, straddles, panoramizes, and offends. The woman to whom we owe a new knowledge, from the East and from the Far East, and new instruments of analysis and commitment (paragram, dialogism, text, productivity, intertextuality, number, formula), teaches us to work *in difference,* i.e., above the differences in whose name we are forbidden to conjugate writing and science, History and form, the science of signs and the destruction of the sign: it is all these fine antitheses, comfortable, conformist, stubborn, and self-assured, which the work of Julia Kristeva cuts across, scarring our young semiotic science with a *foreign* mark, in accord with the first sentence of *Semeiotike*: "*To make language into work,* to work in the *materiality* of what, for society, is a means of contact and of comprehension—is this not to make oneself, from the start, foreign to language?"

La Quinzaine littéraire, 1970

The Return of the Poetician

When he sits down in front of the literary work, the poetician does not ask himself: What does this mean? Where does this come from? What does it connect to? But, more simply and more arduously: *How is this made?* This question has already been asked three times in our history: Poetics has three patrons: Aristotle (whose *Poetics* provides the first structural analysis of the levels and the parts of the tragic oeuvre), Valéry (who insisted that literature be established as an object of language), Jakobson (who calls *poetic* any message which emphasizes its own verbal signifier). Poetics is therefore at once very old (linked to the whole rhetorical culture of our civilization) and very new, insofar as it can today benefit from the important renewal of the sciences of language.

Gérard Genette—and this defines the personality of his work—masters both the past and the present of Poetics: he is by one and the same impulse a rhetorician and a semiotician; *figures* are for him logical forms, manners of discourse, whose field is not only a little group of words but the structure of the text in its entirety; it is therefore appropriate that his written work be called *Figures* (I, II, III); for what belongs to the Figure is not only the poetic image but also, for instance, the form of the narrative, present object of narratology. Genette's work thereby takes its place within a huge and contemporary space: it is a work at once critical (related to literary criticism), theoretical (militating for a theory of literature, that object so neglected in France), practical (applied to specific works), epistemological (proposing, thanks to the text, a new dialectic of the particular and the general), and pedagogic (seeking to renew the teaching of literature and providing the means to do so).

The poetician: until quite recently, this character might have passed for the poet's poor relation. But precisely, the poetics practiced by Genette has as its object all the *praxis* of language—or the *praxis* of all language. Not only does poetics include in its field the narrative forms (whose analysis is well developed) and doubtless tomorrow the essay, intellectual discourse—insofar as it chooses to be *written*—but also, turning back to its own language, it consents, it is compelled to consider itself, in a certain fashion, as an object of poetics. This return, which is much more important than a simple expansion, tends to make the poetician into a writer, to abolish the hierarchical distance between "creator" and "commentator." In other words, the poetician accepts the return of the signifier in his own discourse. At least, this is what happens in Genette's case. I am not here passing judgment on writing in the name of "style" (though Genette's is perfect), but on the kind of fantasmatic power which makes a *scriptor* give himself over to the demon of classifying and naming, consent to put his discourse on stage. Genette possesses this power in the guise of an extreme discretion—a discretion, moreover, sufficiently wily to enjoy such power (crucial attribute of the pleasure of writing and of reading).

Genette classifies, vigorously and rigorously (notably the narrative figures in Proust, since that is the chief object of his *Figures III*): he divides and subdivides forms, and this is the first point where the poetician becomes a poet, for he creates, in the profile of the work (here Proust's novel), a second *tableau*, deriving less from a meta-language than, more simply, from a second language (which is not the last, since I myself, among others, am writing on Genette). Genette's description of the modes of Proustian narrative reminds me of that text in which Poe simultaneously describes, discredits, and *creates* "Maelzel's Chess-Player": a man is hidden in the automaton, but *he is not seen*; the problem (for Poe, and by proxy for Genette) is not to describe the man (hidden object), or even, strictly speaking, how he is hidden (since the machine's interior is apparently always visible), but the subtle shifting of screens, doors, and shutters which arranges matters so that the man *is never where one is looking*; in the same way, Genette sees Proust where we are not looking for him; and from that moment on, it is of little importance whether or not he is there: it is not the occupant of meaning which determines the work, it is *his place*; and, also from that moment on, Proust, the Proustian aroma, returns in force and circulates in Genette's machine; the quotations pass in a new light, they engender a different *vibrato* from the one to which we had been accustomed by a *compact reading* of the work.

Then, too, Genette *names* what his classification finds: he argues against received acceptations, he creates neologisms, he vivifies old names, he constructs a terminology, i.e., a network of subtle and distinct verbal objects; now, neological concern (or courage) is what most directly establishes what I shall call the great critical fictivity [*romanesque*]. To make the work of analysis into an elaborated fiction is perhaps today's crucial enterprise: not against truth and in the name of subjective impressionism, but, on the contrary, because the truth of critical discourse is not of a referential but of a linguistic order: language has no truth except to acknowledge itself as language; good critics, useful scholars will be those who announce the color of their discourse, those who clearly affix to it the signature of the signifier. That is what Genette does (his "*après-propos*" leaves no doubt as to his intention).

Here is how Genette's project concerns us: what he discerns in Proust, with predilection (as he himself underlines), are narrative deviances (by which the Proustian narrative counters our possible notion of a simple, linear, "logical" narrative). Now, deviances (from a code, a grammar, a norm) are always manifestations of writing: where the rule is transgressed, there writing appears as excess, since it takes on a language *which was not foreseen*. In short, what interests Genette in Proust is writing, or, to be more precise, the difference which separates style from writing. The term *deviance* would doubtless be troublesome if we believed that there exists an anthropological model of narrative (whose creator "would withdraw"), or even a narrative ontology (whose "work" would be some monstrous abortion); in reality, the narrative "model" is itself only an "idea" (a fiction), a memory of reading. I should prefer to say that Genette dips into the Proustian reservoir and shows us the places where the story "*skids*" (this metaphor aims at respecting the text's movement, its productivity). Now, a theory of "skidding" is necessary *precisely today*. Why? Because we are in that historical moment of our culture when narrative cannot yet abandon a certain readability, a certain conformity to narrative pseudo-logic which culture has instilled in us and in which, consequently, the only possible novations consist not in destroying the story, the anecdote, but in *deviating* it: making the code skid while seeming to respect it. It is this very fragile state of the narrative, at once conforming and deviant, that Genette has been able to see and to make us see in Proust's work. His work is at once structural and historical because he specifies the conditions on which narrative novation is possible without being suicidal.

La Quinzaine littéraire, 1972

To Learn and to Teach

Even before the curtain goes up on his book, Christian Metz gives us what is inimitable in his voice. Listen to the overture of his latest work: "Volume I of this collection, elaborated in 1967 and published in 1968 (2nd edition, 1971), grouped certain articles written between 1964 and 1967, published between 1964 and 1968. This second volume consists of subsequent texts (written between 1967 and 1971, published between 1968 and 1972), as well as two unpublished texts written in 1971 (texts no. 8 and 9)."*

These numerical specifications are of course required by the scientific—or at least by the scholarly—code of exactitude; but who could fail to notice that, in the mixture of insistence and elegance which marks the statement, there is something *more*? What is it? Precisely, the subject's very voice. Dealing with any message, Metz *adds on*; but what he adds on is neither idle nor vague nor digressive nor verbose: it is a matte supplement, the idea's insistence that it be expressed completely. Anyone who knows Metz in the triple aspect of writer, teacher, and friend is always struck by this paradox, which is merely apparent: a radical demand for precision and clarity generates a free, somehow dreamy tone, a tone I should say sounds almost drugged (did not Baudelaire make hashish the source of an unexampled *precision*?): here an *enraged* exactitude prevails. Henceforth, we are in Expenditure—and not in mere knowledge: when Metz gives figures, references, when he summarizes, when he classifies, when he clarifies, when he invents, when he proposes (and in all these operations his labor is active, tireless, efficacious), he does not merely communicate, he *gives*, in the full sense of the term: there is a veritable *gift* of

* *Essais sur la signification au cinéma,* Vol. II (Paris, 1972).

knowledge, of language, of the subject insofar as he is concerned to speak (though his work issues so explicitly from linguistics, does he not tell us, in his way, that the error of this science is to make us believe that messages are "exchanged"—always the ideology of Exchange—whereas the *reality* of speech is precisely to give or to take itself back, in short to *demand*?). There are two ways of subverting the legality of knowledge (inscribed in the Institution): either to disperse it or to *give* it. Metz chooses to give; the way in which he treats a problem of language and/or of cinema is always generous: not by the invocation of "human" ideas, but by his incessant solicitude for the reader, patiently anticipating his demand for enlightenment, which Metz knows is always a demand for love.

There are perhaps two ways of avoiding mastery (is this not the stake today of all teaching, of any intellectual "role"?): either to produce a perforated, elliptical, drifting, skidding discourse; or, conversely, to load knowledge with an excess of clarity. This is the way chosen (savored?) by Metz. Christian Metz is a marvelous didactician; when we read him, we know everything, as if we had learned it ourselves. The secret of this effectiveness is not difficult to find: when Metz teaches a piece of knowledge, a classification, a synthesis, when he explicates certain new concepts, he always demonstrates, by the didactic perfection of his utterance, that *he is teaching himself* what he is supposed to be communicating to others. His discourse—this is his characteristic, his idiolectal virtue—manages to unite two tenses: that of assimilation and that of exposition. Hence, we understand why the *transparency* of this discourse is not reductive: the (heteroclite) substance of knowledge is clarified before our eyes; what remains is neither a scheme nor a type, but rather a "solution" of the problem, briefly suspended before us solely so that we can traverse and inhabit it ourselves. Metz knows and invents many things, and these things he says very well: not by mastery (Metz never sets anyone else right), but by *talent*: by this old word, I mean not some innate disposition but the artist's or scholar's happy submission to the effect he wants to produce, to the encounter he wants to provoke: even to the *transference* he thus accepts, lucidly, outside any scientific image-repertoire, as the very principle of writing.

A theoretical work—which is only just beginning—is thus constructed from a movement (as we say: a movement of the heart); Metz has sought to break down the fatigue of a stereotype: "*Cinema is a language.*" What if we were to look and see? What if, suddenly, we were to grasp the metaphor—nonsensical by dint of being repeated—in the implacable light of the Letter? From this wager, new and somehow innocent (is not any return to the letter innocent?), Metz has drawn a work whose rings uncoil according to an implacable and flexible project: for, in our time, when sensibility to language changes so rapidly, Metz follows its twists and turns, its explosions; he is not the man of a semiology (of a grid), but of an object: the filmic text, a shimmer in which different intentions may be read, according to the moment of our intellectual discourse. Such, I think, is Metz's historic place (there is no minor history): he has been able to give what was (or risked being) merely a metaphor the plenitude of a scientific pertinence: in this he is a founder, as is attested by his singular and acknowledged place in general semiotics and in the analysis of the cinematographic phenomenon; yet, having founded, he shifts ground: now he is at grips with psychoanalysis. It is perhaps in this that semiology owes and will owe him so much: for having conquered for it, in his chosen realm, a right of mutation. By his work, Metz makes us realize that semiology is not a science like the others (which does not keep it from being rigorous), and that it has no intention of substituting itself for the great *epistemes* which are our century's historical truth, but rather that it is their servant: a vigilant servant who, by representing the snares of the Sign, keeps them from falling victim to what these great new knowledges claim to denounce: dogmatism, arrogance, theology; in short, that monster: the Last Signified.

Ça, 1975

6
READINGS

ONE

Cayrol and Erasure

"I'll never have time, if I must keep erasing what I have to say."

In all of Jean Cayrol's work, *someone is speaking to you,* but you never know who it is. Is the speaker an individual narrator, whose individuality is renewed in novel after novel, and does Gaspard differ from Armand the way Fabrizio does from Julien Sorel? Is he a single narrator whose voice extends from book to book? Is it Cayrol himself, half concealed behind this speaking Other? The narrator's person, in this entire oeuvre, remains technically indeterminate; we find neither the narrative duplicity of the classical novel nor the complexity of the Proustian "I" nor the poet's ego; in literature, ordinarily, the person is a completed idea (even if it manages to make itself ambiguous): no novelist can begin writing if he has not chosen the profound person of his narrative: to write is, in short, to decide (to be able to decide) *who* is going to speak. Now, Cayrolian man is scarcely a character; he possesses no pronominal certainty; either he falls far short of identity (in the early novels) or, apparently constituted, he nonetheless keeps undoing his person by continual deception of memory and narrative; he is never anything but a voice (which we cannot even call anonymous, for that would be to qualify it), and yet this voice does not entrust its indecision about origins to any novelistic technique: neither collective nor named, it is the voice of *someone.*

Constantly posited and withdrawn, the narrative's person is in fact merely the support parsimoniously granted to a very mobile, *ill-attached* language, which shifts from place to place, from object to object, from memory to memory, while everywhere remaining a pure articulated substance. This is anything but a metaphor; there is, in Cayrol, a veritable imagination of the voice substituted for the visual sensibility of writers and poets. First of all, the voice can rise, emanate from no one knows where; unsituated, it is nonetheless there, somewhere, around you, behind you, beside you, but actually never *in front of* you; the real dimension of the voice is indirect, lateral; it takes others obliquely, brushes against them and goes off; it can touch without telling its origins; hence, it is the very sign of the *unnamed*, what is born or what remains of man if we take from him the materiality of his body, the identity of his face, or the humanity of his gaze; it is the substance at once most human and most inhuman; without it, no communication among men, but with it, too, the discomfort of a *double*, insidiously appearing from a (chthonic or celestial) super-nature, in short from an alienation; a well-known test tells us that everyone is uncomfortable hearing his own voice (on tape, for example) and often fails even to recognize it; this is because the voice, if we detach it from its source, always establishes a kind of strange familiarity which is, ultimately, the very familiarity of the Cayrolian world, a world which offers itself to recognition by its exactitude and yet denies itself to recognition by its uprootedness. The voice is still another sign: that of time; no voice is motionless, no voice ceases *to pass*; furthermore, the time the voice manifests is not a serene time; however smooth and discrete it may be, however continuous its flux, every voice is *threatened*; symbolic substance of human life, there is always at its origin a cry and at its end a silence; between these two moments develops the fragile time of speech; fluid and threatened, the voice is therefore life itself, and it is perhaps because a novel by Cayrol is always a novel of the voice that it is also always a novel of life—of fragile—jeopardized—life.

It is said of certain voices that they are *caressing*. The Cayrolian voice gives an abusive caress to the world, a lost caress. Like the caress, language here remains on the surface of things; the surface is its realm. This superficial description of objects has been made into a feature common to a certain number of contemporary novelists; yet, unlike Robbe-Grillet, for example, Cayrol's surface is not the object of a perception which exhausts its existence; his way of describing is often *profound*, it gives things a metaphorical radiance which does not break with a certain romantic writing; this is because the surface, for Cayrol, is not a quality (optic, for instance) but a *situation* of things. This superficial situation of objects, of landscapes, of memories, even, is *low*, as we might say of a world seen from floor level; we shall not find here, on the writer's part, any sentiment of power or *elevation* with regard to the things described; the gaze and the voice which follow them *on the level* remain captives (and we with them) of their surface; all the objects (and there are many of them in Cayrol's novels) are minutely scrutinized, but his minuteness is a captive, in it something cannot *rise*, and the very complete world which the writing caresses remains stricken by a kind of sub-familiarity; man does not enter completely into the use of the things he encounters in the course of his life, not because he sublimates them (as would be the case in a traditional novel, lapsed into psychology), but on the contrary because he cannot raise himself to this use—because he remains doomed to a certain *unattainability* of objects whose exact altitude he cannot reach.

This *literature at floor level* (Cayrol himself has already used the expression) might have the mouse for its totem animal. For the mouse, like Cayrolian man, deals with things; it omits little on its way, concerned with everything its oblique gaze, proceeding from the ground up, can encounter; a tiny stubbornness, never triumphant and never discouraged, animates it; remaining on the level of things, it sees them all; the same is true of Cayrolian description, which in its fragile and insistent way scrutinizes the countless objects modern life stuffs into the narrator's existence; this busy, mouselike progress, at once incidental and continuous, gives its ambiguity to Cayrolian description (such description is important, for Cayrol's novels are essentially *exterior*); this description spares nothing, it slides across the surface of everything, but its sliding lacks the euphoria of flight or swimming, it acquires no resonance from the noble substances of the poetic image-repertoire, the aerial or the liquid; it is a terrestrial sliding, a sliding across of the floor, whose apparent movement consists of tiny jerks, of a rapid and modest discontinuity: the "holes" in such description are not even loaded silences, but merely a human impotence to link the accidents of things: there is a Cayrolian misfortune in not being able to institute a familiar logic, a rational order among the phenomena with which time and the journey confront the narrator. It is here that we rediscover, in a mocking form, the theme of the caress: in opposition to it, though proceeding from it, we discover a kind of scratchy perception of things, a grating touch bestowed upon the world of objects (but silk, too, can grate, and often nothing could be more sumptuous, in its modesty, than a Cayrolian description); whence so many images of the rough, the nibbled, and the acid, mocking forms of a sensation which never manages to regain the euphoric continuity of the caress; the *smooth*, elsewhere a miraculous theme of the "seamless," is here an element which "turns," covering itself with a kind of superficial harshness: the surface of things begins to vibrate, to grate slightly.

This theme of the rough, of the failed caress, disguises a still more disturbing image, that of a *certain coldness*. The touchy is, after all, merely the active world of the chilly, the susceptibility to cold. In Cayrol, where seascapes abound, from Dieppe to Biarritz, the wind is always sharp; it is faintly cutting, but, more certainly than deep cold, causes constant shivering, without, however, altering the progress of events, without astonishing . . . The world continues, familiar and close at hand, and yet one feels the cold. This Cayrolian cold is not that of the great immobilities, it leaves life intact, even agile, yet fades it, ages it; Cayrolian man, vulnerable as he may be, is never frozen stiff, paralyzed; he still walks, but his physical milieu keeps him continually on edge: the world is to be *warmed up*. This sustained cold is, as Cayrol says somewhere, a forgotten wind. This is because at bottom all the chilly edginess of the Cayrolian habitat is that of *forgetting*; in Cayrol, there are no noble ruins, *standing* remains, solid and well-planted fragments of ancient sumptuous edifices; not even—or very few—dilapidated, crumbling residences; on the contrary, everything is in place, but stricken with a kind of open oblivion which makes us shiver (is this not one of the themes of his film *Muriel*?); nothing in this Cayrolian world is broken, objects function, but everything is *disinherited*, like that room in *Foreign Bodies** which the narrator one day discovers in his own house, papered over, where objects of the past (perhaps even a corpse?) are in place, motionless, forgotten, enchanted without magic, shivering in the "shrill" wind of the fireplace.

Perhaps we must go further and abandon this last image, still too poetic, of the *chilly*, to give these themes of insistent and disappointed life another name, at once more vulgar and more terrible—the name of *fatigue*. Fatigue is a mode of existence we have neglected; it is rarely spoken of; it is a color of life which does not even have the prestige of the dreadful or the accursed: what language are we to use for fatigue? Yet fatigue is the very dimension of time: infinite, it is infinity itself. The superficial perception of Cayrolian man, that suspended, jerky caress so quickly turned into edginess, by which he attempts to follow the world—perhaps this is nothing but a certain contact with fatigue. ("Why does everything become complicated as soon as you touch it?" asks one of Cayrol's characters.) What exhausts is inexhaustible—such is perhaps the truth of this intense, persistent consciousness which never releases the world and yet can never rest in it. Fatigue, but not lassitude: Cayrolian man is neither depressed nor indifferent, he does not efface himself, he does not leave the scene; he surveys, he combats, he participates, he has the very energy of fatigue. "You seem in pain," someone

* English translation of *Les Corps étrangers* by Richard Howard published in 1960 by Putnam's, New York.

says in *La Gaffe*, "and yet I know no one more impervious to pain than you . . . You are impregnable when someone attacks your secret reserves." This fragile, sensitive world is a resistant world; beneath the harshness and the piercing wind, behind the oblivion which fades things, behind that tense footstep, something (or someone) *burns* whose reserves nonetheless remain secret, like a strength which never knows its own name.

This strength is secret because it is not in the hero described by the book but in the book itself. As a shortcut, we can say that it is Cayrol's own strength, the strength which makes him write. Our culture has long wondered what it was that passed from the author into a work; here we see that, even more than his life or his times, it is the writer's *strength* which passes into his work. In other words, literature is itself a moral dimension of the book: to be able to write a story is the final meaning of that story. This explains how, with an extremely disarmed world, Cayrol can present a power, even a violence (I am thinking of *Muriel*), but this power is not interior to this world, it is the power of the writer Cayrol, the power of literature: we can never sever the meaning of a fictive world from the very meaning of the novel. Hence, it is futile to ask by what philosophy—interior to Cayrolian man but modestly silenced—the default of this world can be recuperated, for once literature takes over "what doesn't work in the world" (as it does here), the absurd ceases. Led to the brink of the cold and the futile, every reader of Cayrol also finds himself endowed with warmth and a sense of being alive which are given by the very spectacle of someone who writes. Thus, what can be asked of this reader is to entrust himself to the work, not for what philosophy it may afford, but for what literature . . .

Just as substances in Cayrol never present themselves except to a kind of failed caress, to a discontinuous and somehow slighted perception, similarly Cayrolian time is a *devoured* time, insidiously nibbled in places. And when the object of this time is a man's life (as in *Foreign Bodies*), something appears which constitutes the entire Cayrolian novel (this theme will be apparent to viewers of *Muriel*): the bad faith of memory.

Every novel by Cayrol might be called *Memoirs of an Amnesiac.* Not that the narrator makes an enormous effort to recall his life: it seems to come to his memory quite naturally, as happens with ordinary recollections; yet the more the narrative develops, the more *perforated* it appears; episodes do not connect properly, something grates in the distribution of actions (one ought to say, more specifically, with regard to a novel: in their *dispatching*); but above all, without our ever being able to catch the narrator out in his preterition (or lie), the whole of an apparently regular narrative gradually refers to the sensation of a major forgetting, settled somewhere in existence and unluckily resonant within it, devouring it, branding it with a *false* movement. In other words, Cayrolian narrative is subject to a montage whose speed and dispersion designate a very special disorganization of time, which Cayrol himself anticipated in *Lazare* and which we find illustrated in the montage of *Muriel.* This forgetting, in which the characters struggle without quite knowing it, is not a censoring; the Cayrolian universe is not burdened with a concealed fault, forever unnamed; confronted with this world, there is nothing to decipher; what is lacking here are not fragments of culpable time but only fragments of pure time, what it is necessary for the novelist *not* to say in order to separate a little man from his own life and the life of others, in order to render him at once familiar and unattached.

Another form of this nibbled time: memories are interchangeable within one and the same life, they constitute the object of a swap, analogous to that of the dealer and fence Gaspard (a camembert for an air-chamber rifle): memory is at once a substance for concealment and for deals; the hero of *Foreign Bodies* has two childhoods, which he cites as necessary, depending on whether he wants to endow himself with a rural origin or with that of an abandoned child; Cayrolian time consists of transferred—one might even say *stolen*—fragments, and between these fragments there is an *interplay* which constitutes the entire novel. *Foreign Bodies* begins with a review of all the objects which can enter the body, by negligence or misfortune; but for Cayrolian man, the real foreign body is ultimately time: this man is not hewn within the same duration as other men; time is transferred to him, sometimes too short when he forgets, sometimes too long when he invents. For this unjust (unadjusted) time must be struggled against, and the entire novel consists in telling one man's efforts to regain the exact time of other men. Thus is generated, throughout the Cayrolian monologue (especially in *Foreign Bodies*), a disclaiming utterance whose function is not to deny faults but in a more elementary, less psychological fashion, *to erase time*. Cayrolian erasure is nonetheless secondary: the narrator does not try to rub out what exists, to invoke oblivion of what has been, but, quite the contrary, to repaint the void of time with bright colors, to paper the holes in his memory with an invented memory, destined much less to justify his time (though the collaborator Gaspard desperately needs an organized time) than to make it rejoin *the time of others*, i.e., *to humanize* time.

For this is basically the great task of the Cayrolian novel: to say—with all of literature's power of recuperation, of which we have spoken—how a man is separated from other men, not by the romantic singularity of his destiny, but by a kind of vice of his temporality. The singularity of this Cayrolian world is in fact that the beings in it are by the same impulse *mediocre and unwonted, natural and incomprehensible*. Hence, we never know if the hero of this world is "sympathetic"—if we can care for him to the end. All our traditional literature has played on the positivity of the fictive hero, but here we do not feel alienated in the presence of a being whose world we know well but of whose secret time we are ignorant: his time is not ours, yet he speaks to us quite familiarly of the places, objects, and stories we share with him: he is at home with us, yet he comes from "somewhere" (but from where?). Confronting this ordinary and singular hero, we experience a sentiment of solitude, but such solitude is not simple; for when literature offers us a solitary hero, it is his very solitude which we understand, which we love, and which thereby we put an end to: neither the hero nor his reader is alone any longer, since they are alone together. Cayrol's art goes further: he makes us see a solitude and yet keeps us from participating in it; not only does literature not recuperate Cayrolian solitude but it goes about purifying it of any positive complicity: it is not a solitary man whom we see living (in which case he would not be altogether alone), it is a man who imposes upon us, in relation to himself, that *tenacious insensibility* Cayrol has spoken of in *Lazare.* Thus, by a final achievement of the work, the reader experiences the Cayrolian hero exactly as the latter experiences the world: sensitive and insensitive, installed in that "parasitical" sympathy characterizing a world in which we can never love except by proxy.

We know just where this work comes from: from the concentration camps. The proof of which is that *Lazare parmi nous,* a work which creates the first junction between experience of the camps and literary reflection, contains in germ, with great exactitude, all of Cayrol's subsequent work. *Pour un romanesque lazaréen* is a program which is still being carried out today in a virtually literal fashion: the best commentary on *Muriel* is *Lazare.* What must be suggested, if not explicated, is how such a work—whose germ is in a specific, dated history—is nonetheless entirely a literature of today.

The first reason for this may be that the mind of the concentration camps is not dead; there occur in the world odd "concentrative" impulses—insidious, deformed, familiar—cut off from their historical model but spread in the fashion of a style; Cayrol's novels are the very passage from the concentrative event to the concentrative "life style": in them we rediscover today, twenty years after the Camps, a certain form of human *malaise,* a certain quality of the dreadful, of the grotesque, or of the absurd, whose shock we receive in the presence of certain events or, worse still, in the presence of certain images of our time.

The second reason is that Cayrol's oeuvre, from its beginning, has been immediately modern; all the literary techniques with which we credit today's avant-garde, and singularly the New Novel, are to be found not only in Cayrol's entire oeuvre but even, as a conscious program, in *Pour un romanesque lazaréen* (1950): the absence of anecdote, the disappearance of the hero, giving way to an anonymous character reduced to his voice or to his gaze, the promotion of objects, the affective silence which we cannot call either modesty or insensitivity, the Ulyssean character of the work, which is always a man's long march through labyrinthine space and time. If, however, Cayrol's oeuvre has remained outside recent theoretical discussions concerning the novel, it is because its author has always refused to systematize his work, and also because the technical community just mentioned is far from being complete; the New Novel (granting that we can unify it) posits matte descriptions, the character's insensibility communicating itself to things he speaks of, so that the New Novel's world (which I should be glad to reduce, as I see it, to the world of Robbe-Grillet) is a neutral one. Cayrol's world, on the contrary, even if love is here merely parasitical (the author's expression), is a world vibrant with adjectives, radiant with metaphors; granted, objects are promoted to a new fictive rank, but man continues to touch them with a subjective language, he gives them not only a name but also a reason, an effect, a relation, an image. It is this *commentary* on the world, which is no longer merely uttered but *embellished*, that makes Cayrol's oeuvre such an individual communication: deprived of any experimental intention yet audacious, at once emancipated and integrated, violent without the theater of violence, "concentrative" and of the moment, it is an oeuvre which unceasingly escapes forward, impelled by its own fidelity to itself, toward the *new* our times call for.

Postscript to Jean Cayrol's *Les Corps étrangers* (U.G.E.), 1964

Bloy

Leaving the Grande-Chartreuse, where he has just made a retreat, Marchenoir (alias Léon Bloy) receives a thousand-franc note from the Father-General. This is odd: usually alms are bestowed *in nature, not in cash*; Marchenoir is not deceived; he perceives in the Carthusian's gesture a true scandal: one which consists in regarding money directly, as a metal, not as a symbol.

Bloy always considers money not in its causes, its consequences, its transformations, and its substitutions, but in its opacity, as a stubborn object, subject to the most painful of movements: repetition. Bloy's *Journals* have, in truth, only one interlocutor: money. Unceasing complaints, invectives, schemes, failures, pursuits of the few louis necessary for food, warmth, rent; the poverty of the man of letters is here anything but symbolic; it is a calculable poverty whose tireless description matches up with one of the harshest moments of bourgeois society. This desirable character of money (and not of wealth) is expressed by Léon Bloy through a conduct whose avowal remains singular: with assurance, even pride, the writer never stops "touching" everyone, friends, relations, strangers. It follows that to the "borrower" Léon Bloy corresponds an army of "rebuffers" ("I am the man who must be rebuffed"): motionless, engorged, money rejects the most elementary of transformations: circulation.

By ceaseless requests and refusals, Bloy thereby constructs a profound (because archaic) experience of money: object of an immediate and repeated demand (psychoanalysis would doubtless have no great difficulty in discovering a maternal relation here), money for Bloy resists all reason. When Paul Bourget ventures to write that "it is not lack of money which makes the poor poor, but their character, which makes it impossible to change anything about them," Bloy does not fail to reply sharply to this disgraceful remark—for Bloy, poverty cannot be reduced by any discourse—psychological, political, or moralizing; it persists in being nothing but itself and pitilessly rejects any kind of sublimation. "True poverty is involuntary, and its essence is to be eternally incapable of being desired." Bloy could make this profound remark only because money is, at bottom, the great and only idea of his work: he constantly returns to the secret of the metal ("The sensation of mystery which this astonishing word produces has never been expressed"), ceaselessly reveals its opacity, exploring by his words, like every poet, in the manner of a man running his hands over a wall, what he does not understand—and what fascinates him.

Money, in Bloy's work, has two faces: one which, if not positive (that would be to sublimate it), is at least interrogative, manifested in Prostitution: ". . . that figurative prostitution of Woman of which only hypocrites have an ostensible horror and which I persist in believing mysterious and unexplained"; and an imbecilic face: "Have you noticed the astounding imbecility of money, the infallible stupidity, the eternal delusion of all those who possess it?" Beneath this double face, money forms the explicit argument of *Le Désespéré* (1886), Bloy's key work, structured at one and the same time around the disfiguration of the prostitute (symbolically achieved at the moment when she ceases to prostitute herself) and around the cruel poverty of the artist (when he refuses to prostitute himself).

Here we reach the core of all of Bloy's works: the separation of the writer and his society, which is the bourgeoisie. All of Bloy's chronicles portray a kind of pandemonium of the writer who has arrived, i.e., prostituted himself to the bourgeoisie (". . . that fierce, adipose, and cowardly bourgeoisie which we find to be the vomit of the ages"). As we know, at the nineteenth century's end, the word designated an aesthetic disease, a disgusting vulgarity, intolerable to the artist; this has subsequently been shown to be a partial one, and the entire literature of the period (since Flaubert) has been compromised by the blindness which failed to discern, within the bourgeois, the capitalist. Yet can literature be anything other than *indirectly* lucid? In order to constitute his discourse, in order to invent and develop it within his own truth, the writer can speak only of what alienates *himself*, for one cannot write by proxy; and what alienates the writer, in the bourgeois, is stupidity; bourgeois vulgarity is doubtless only the sign of a deeper malady, but the writer is doomed to work with signs, to vary and elaborate them, not to deflower them: his form is metaphor, not definition.

Hence, Bloy's labor has been to metaphorize the bourgeois. His disgusts invariably and specifically designate the parvenu writer, as the bourgeoisie acknowledges and delegates him. It suffices to be *recognized* by bourgeois institutions (the press, the salons, the Church) in order to be condemned by art. Bloy's virulent demystifications therefore aim at all ideologies without distinction, once they appear *privileged*, from Veuillot to Richepin, from Père Didon to Renan. Bloy sees no difference whatever between the populism of Vallès and the charities of the Duchess of Galliera, crudely praised by the press for the fabulous benefaction of millions which she had only, Bloy says, to *restore*. Conversely, none of the (few) writers he supported were on the side of Property; or more specifically, Bloy's glance at Barbey d'Aurevilly, at Baudelaire, at Verlaine is a way of galvanizing these writers, of making them inapt for any bourgeois purpose. Bloy's discourse does not consist of ideas; nonetheless, his work is critical insofar as it could discern in the literature of his time its resistances to order, its power of inadaptation, the permanent scandal it constituted with regard to collectivities and to institutions, in short the infinite recession of the questions it raised, or in still another word: its *irony*. Because he always saw art as anti-money, he almost never made a mistake: the writers he vilified (Dumas *fils*, Daudet, Bourget, Sarcey) certainly look to us today like absurd puppets; on the other hand, Bloy was one of the very first to recognize Lautréamont, and, in Lautréamont, a singularly penetrating prophecy, the irreversible transgression of literature itself: "As for literary form, there is none here. It is a liquid lava. It is senseless, black, and corrosive." Did he not see in Sade "a maddened craving for the absolute," thus prefiguring by a word, doubtless unique in his times, the entire inverted theology of which Sade has been the subsequent object?

Who knows? Perhaps this negative state of literary discourse was what Bloy himself was seeking through that outrageous and concocted style which ultimately never says anything but the passion of words. In his bourgeois fin-de-siècle, destruction of style could perhaps be achieved only through excesses of style. Systematic invective, wielded without respect to its objects (the surrealist insult to Anatole France's corpse is quite timid alongside Bloy's profanations), constitutes a radical experience of language: felicity of invective is merely a variety of that *felicity of expression* which Maurice Blanchot correctly reversed into an *expression of felicity*. Confronting a calculating society in which money is surrendered only under the regime of compensation (of prostitution), the impoverished writer's discourse is essentially *an expenditure*, an extravagance; in Bloy, such discourse, infinitely obliging, gives itself *unsalaried*; it thus appears not as a sacerdotal ministry, an art, or even as an instrument, but as an activity, linked to the profound zones of desire and of pleasure. It is doubtless this invincible delight of language, attested to by an extraordinary "wealth" of expression, which gives Bloy's ideological choices a kind of inconsistent antirealism: that Bloy was furiously Catholic, that he promiscuously insulted the conformist and modernist Church, the Protestants, the Freemasons, the British, the democrats; that this demon of incongruity declared his infatuation for Louis XVIII or for Mélanie (the shepherdess of la Salette)—this is nothing more than a variable, impugnable substance, which deceives no reader of Bloy; illusion is the contents, the ideas, the choices, the beliefs, the professions, the causes; reality is the words, the erotics of language which this impoverished, *unsalaried* writer practiced with frenzy and whose passion he makes us share even today.

Tableau de la littérature française (Gallimard), 1974

Michelet, Today

Twenty years ago, reading Michelet, I was struck by the thematic insistence of his work: each figure recurs, decked out with the same epithets, products of a reading at once somatic and ethical; ultimately, these are "epithets of nature," which relate Michelet to the Homeric epic: Bonaparte is waxen and phantasmagorical, exactly as Athena is the gray-eyed goddess. Today, doubtless because my reading is impregnated with notions that have modified the conception of the text over twenty years (let us roughly characterize the sum of these notions as "structuralism" or "semiology"), I am struck by something else (alongside the thematic attestation, still as lively): a certain discursive disorder. If we abide by our impression as readers, Michelet, when he tells a story (history), is often *not clear* (I am thinking of his last work, *Histoire du xixe siècle*, which is actually only the history of the Consulate and the Empire); one has difficulty understanding, at least at first glance, the interconnection of events; I defy anyone with only a vestigal, schoolboy knowledge of French history to understand the scenario of the 18th Brumaire as Michelet outlines it: Which were the participants? Where were they? In what order did the operations succeed each other? The whole scene is full of holes: intelligible on the level of each sentence (nothing clearer than Michelet's style), it becomes enigmatic on the level of discourse.

There are three reasons for this disorder. First of all, Michelet's discursivity is continuously elliptical; Michelet excessively indulges in asyndeton, omission of conjunctions, he skips the links, is unconcerned with the distance established between his sentences (this has been called his *vertical style*); what we have here—a stylistic phenomenon of great interest and one that has been little studied, I believe—is an *erratic* structure which privileges certain blocks of utterance, without the author's bothering about the visibility of the interstices, the gaps: each idea is present without that anodyne excipient by which we ordinarily consolidate our discourse; this structure is obviously "poetic" (we are familiar with it in poetry and in aphorism) and is entirely in accord with the thematic structure I mentioned earlier; what thematic analysis found, semiological analysis would no doubt confirm and extend.

Next, as we know, the statement is steeped in judgments; Michelet does not posit first in order to judge thereafter; he creates an immediate confusion, a veritable contraction, between the *notable* and the *reprehensible* (or the *praiseworthy*): "Two very sincere men, Daunou and Dupont de l'Eure . . ." "And now to complete an absurd comedy . . ." "Sieyès courageously replied . . ." Etc. Michelet's account is openly *to the second degree*; it is a narration (it would be better to say a discourse) grafted on a subjacent account which is supposed to be already known; here again, we have a constant: what interests Michelet is the *predicate*, what is added to the event (to the "subject"); one might say that for Michelet statutory discourse begins only with the attribute; language's being is not constative (thetic) but appreciative (epithetic); all of Michelet's grammar is optative; as we know, the indicative, which our teaching procedures have made into a simple, fundamental mode—all verbs are first conjugated in the indicative—is in fact a complicated mode (the zero degree of the subjunctive and of the optative, so to speak), one probably acquired very late; Michelet's "lyricism" derives less from his subjectivity than from the logical structure of his discourse: he thinks by attributes—predicates—not by beings, constatations, and this accounts in his work for these disorders in discursive rationality; reasoning, or rational, "clear" exposition, consists in progressing from thesis to thesis (from verb to verb), and not in deploying the whirlwind of adjectives *on the spot*; for Michelet, the predicates, no longer held by the subject's being, can be contradictory: if a certain "bad" hero (Bonaparte) performs a "good" action, Michelet simply says it is "inexplicable"; this is because the tyranny of the predicate produces a kind of deficiency of the subject (in logic; but in relation to discourse, the logical meaning is not far from the psychological meaning: is not a purely predicative discourse the very discourse of paranoiac delirium?).

Finally, and perhaps this is the most disturbing, it is not only the concatenation of events which vacillates in Michelet, but the event itself. *What is an event?* This is a problem of philosophical dimensions, the *pons asinorum* of historical epistemology. Michelet accepts the disorder of the notion. It is not that his history lacks facts, events, frequently the most precise sort; but these events are never where one expects them to be; or again, it is their moral resonance which is evaluated, *not their extent*; the Micheletist fact oscillates between excess of specificity and excess of evanescence; it never has its *exact* dimension: Michelet tells us that on the 18th Brumaire (November 10) stoves were lit in the great hall of the Orangerie and that in front of the door was a tapestried drum: but Barras's resignation? the two phases of the operation? the role of Sieyès, of Talleyrand? No mention of these facts, or at least no mention which "extracts" from a strange discourse (strange for our ways of reading history) some frankly narrative element. In short, what Michelet disorders is the *proportion* of facts (need we recall that the critique of *relations* is much more subversive than that of *notions*?). Philosophically, at least from the viewpoint of a certain philosophy, it is Michelet who is right. Here he stands, quite paradoxically, beside Nietzsche: "There is no fact *in itself*. What happens is a group of phenomena, selected and grouped by a being who interprets them . . . There is no state-of-fact in itself; on the contrary, a meaning *must be introduced even before there can be a state of fact*." Michelet is, in short, the writer (the historian) of the *even before*: his history is impassioned not because his discourse is rapid, impatient, not because its author is hotheaded, but because it does not arrest language at the fact; because, in that enormous staging of an age-old reality, *language precedes fact to infinity*: a proposition outrageous to a classical historian (but, once History is structuralized, does it not come closer to our present philosophy of language?), a proposition promising to the modern theoretician who thinks that, like any science (and this is the problem of the "human sciences"), the science of history, not being algorithmic, inevitably encounters a discourse, and it is *here that everything begins.* We must be grateful to Michelet (among other gifts he has given us—gifts ignored or suppressed) for having represented to us, through the pathos of his period, the *real conditions* of historical discourse, and for inviting us to transcend the mythic opposition between "subjectivity" and "objectivity" (such a distinction is merely propaedeutic: necessary on the level of research), in order to replace it with the opposition between *statement* [*énoncé*] and *speech-act* [*énonciation*], between the product of investigation and production of the text.

Criticism of Michelet by many historians and by popular opinion itself—whose arguments have been ironically summarized by Lucien Febvre in his little book *Traits* (1946)—is not only, of course, a scientific criticism (bearing on the historian's facts and interpretations) but also a criticism of *writing*: for many, Michelet is a bad historian *because he writes*, instead of simply "reporting," "chronicling," etc. Today we no longer understand writing as the simple product of stylistic mastery. What makes Michelet a writer (practitioner of writing, operator of the text) is not his style (which is not invariably first-rate, being on occasion merely the *parading* of style) but what we today call the *excess of the signifier.* This excess is to be read *in the margins of representation.* Of course, Michelet is a classic (readerly) writer: he recounts what he knows, he describes what he sees, his language imitates reality, he adjusts the signifier to the referent and produces *clear* signs thereby (no "clarity" without a classical conception of the sign, the signifier on one side, the referent on the other, the former in the latter's service). Michelet's readerliness, however, is not certain; it is often jeopardized, compromised by excesses, blurs, breaks, leaks;

between what Michelet claims to see (the referent) and his description (the tissue of signifiers), there is often a remainder—or a hole. We have seen that Michelet's *narrativity* is readily disturbed by ellipses, asyndetons, the very indeterminacy of the concept of "fact." The signifier (in the semio-analytic sense of the word: half semiologic, half psychoanalytic) produces a pressure at many other points. As an emblem of this royalty of the signifier, we can cite the realm of what we might call etymological temptation. A name's etymology is, from the signifier's viewpoint, a privileged object because it represents both *letter* and *origin* (a whole history of etymological science, of etymological philosophy, from Cratylus to Proust's Brichot is yet to be written); and just as a whole part of Proust's novel emerges from the name *Guermantes*, the whole Micheletist History of the nineteenth century emerges from an etymological play on words: Buonaparte, *la bonne part*, the first prize; Napoleon is reduced to his name, that name to its etymology, and that etymology, like a magical sign, commits the name's bearer to a fatal thematics: that of lottery, of the sinister operations of chance, of the gambler, a phantasmagorical figure whom Michelet substitutes without nuance for the national hero; twenty years of our History depend on this *origin* of Bonaparte: an origin (and this is the wild excess of the text) not historical, sociological, or political (which would have been a referential origin), but *literal*: it is the Name's letters which establish the Micheletist account; hence, this account is actually a *dream* as contemporary psychoanalysis might analyze it.

If we read Michelet, we must not use this weight, this zest of the signifier against him. We may know—at least we know better today than yesterday—what the science of history is, but its discourse? History, today, is no longer *told*, its relation to discourse is different. Michelet is condemned in the name of a new discursivity, which could not be his own, that of his own time; there is in short a complete heterogeneity between these two histories (and not only the former's defects or inadequacies in relation to the latter). Michelet is right against all the historians of his time, and this "rightness" represents, in his work, the share which today seems to us correct. Michelet has not "distorted" "reality" (or he has done much more than that), he has located the surfacing point of that "reality" and of his discourse in an unexpected place; he has shifted history's level of perception; in his historical work, examples abound (phenomena of collective mentality, mores, ecological realities, material history, everything which has flourished in subsequent history), but the example I want to cite, of this "perceptual decision," comes from his natural history (*La Mer*). Having to describe the terrible storm of 1859, by a bold stroke which relates him to the symbolist poets, Michelet describes it *from within*; but where he goes further still is that this "within" is not metaphorical, subjective, but literal, spatial: the whole description is made from inside the room where the storm keeps him confined; in other words, he describes *what he does not see*, not *as if he were seeing it* (this would be a banal instance of poetic clairvoyance), but as if the storm's reality were an unheard-of substance, coming from another world, perceptible to all our organs except that of sight. This is a veritably drugged perception, the economy of our five senses being disordered within it. Michelet, moreover, knew the *physiological* stake of his description: the storm provokes him to make an experiment *on his own body*, like any taker of hashish or mescaline: "I went on working, curious to see if this wild force would succeed in oppressing, fettering a free mind. I kept my thought active, self-controlled. I went on writing and observed myself. Only in the long run did fatigue and lack of sleep affect a power within me—the most delicate power a writer possesses, I believe—the sense of rhythm. My sentences became inharmonious. This was the first string of my instrument to be broken." Hallucination is not far off: "[The waves] . . . affected me as a dreadful mob, a horrible throng, not of men but of baying dogs, a million, a billion fierce or mad hounds . . . But what am I saying? dogs, hounds? That was no closer to the reality. These were hateful and nameless apparitions, beasts with neither eyes nor ears, only frothing gullets." If we say that it is Michelet's entire history which is hallucinated, it is not his historical sense which we depreciate but a modern language which we exalt; that intuition or that courage he has had to proceed *as if* our discourse passed through the world and time to infinity, as if yesterday's hallucinations were tomorrow's truths, and so on.

There are two means of demystifying a great man: by reducing him as an individual, or by dissolving him into historical generality, making him the determined product of a situation, of a moment, the delegate of a class. Michelet was not unaware of this second means; on several occasions he indicated the links between Bonaparte and Finance, a procedure which already moves in the direction of a Marxist critique; but the crux—or the obsession—of his demonstration is to depreciate Bonaparte *in his body*. The human body—it would be better to say the historical body, as Michelet sees it—exists, as we know, only in proportion to the affections and disgusts it provokes; it is at once an erotic body (implying desire or repulsion: pulsion) and a moral body (Michelet is *for* or *against*, according to avowed moral principles). It is, one might say, a body which altogether abides within the space of a metaphor: for instance, that of *nausea*, a physical spasm and a philosophical rejection. Rereading Michelet after a good number of years, I am struck once again by the *imperious* character of his portraits. Yet the portrait can easily become a tiresome genre, for it is not sufficient to describe a body in order to make it exist (desire); Balzac, for instance, never produces an erotic relation between himself (and therefore ourselves) and his characters; his portraits are deadly. Michelet, on the other hand, does not describe (at least in the portrait I am thinking of, that of Bonaparte): in the whole body (laboriously itemized by Balzac, organ after organ), he briskly checks off two or three sites and scrutinizes them; in Bonaparte (we should say *on* him), it is the hair: brown, but so heavily pomaded it looks black; the yellow, waxy face: *without eyebrows or lashes*; the eyes: gray as a pane of glass; and the extremely white teeth:

"But how dark he is, this Bonaparte! . . . He is dark, but what white teeth he has!" This portrait is striking, but what attests to Michelet's power (the excess of his text, its transcendence of any rhetoric) is that we cannot really say why; it is not that his art is ineffable, mysterious, inherent in a "brushstroke," a "*je ne sais quoi*," but rather that it is a kind of pulsional art which directly plugs the body (Bonaparte's *and* Michelet's) into language, without the intermediary of any rational relay (by which we might understand the subjection of the description to a grid, either anatomical—the kind observed by Balzac—or rhetorical—traditionally, the portrait derived from a strong code, that of prosopography). Now, it is never possible to speak directly with regard to pulsions; all one can do is to divine their locus; in Michelet, this locus can gradually be situated: in the broad sense—including states of substance, half visual, half tactile—it is *color*. Bonaparte's colors are sinister (black, white, gray, yellow); elsewhere—outside history, in Nature—color is jubilatory; consider the description of insects: ". . . charming creatures, bizarre creatures, admirable monsters, with wings of fire, encased in emerald, dressed in enamel of a hundred varieties, armed with strange devices, as brilliant as they are threatening, some in burnished steel frosted with gold, others with silky tassels, lined with black velvet; some with delicate pincers of russet silk against a deep mahogany ground; this one in garnet velvet dotted with gold; then certain rare metallic blues, heightened with velvety spots; elsewhere metallic stripes, alternating with matte velvet"; the pulsion of multiple color (as it is perceived behind closed eyelids), which reaches the point of a perceptual transgression: "I succumbed, I closed my eyes and asked for mercy; for my mind was benumbed, blinded, growing unconscious." And always that faculty of making the pulsion *signify* without ever severing it from the body; here, the motley refers to the inexhaustible profusion of the insects' generating nature; but elsewhere just the contrary occurs, the bold reduction to an obsessional color: the chain of the Pyrenees is—*green*: "In the Pyrenees, the singular water-greens of the torrents, certain emerald fields . . . the green marble . . ." We must not conclude that Michelet is a "painter": color goes far beyond painting (I refer here to the recent observations of J.-L. Schefer and Julia Kristeva); color belongs to the order of succulence, it belongs to the *deep body*; it affords Michelet's text certain zones, certain reaches available to a reading we might qualify as *nutritive.*

Yes, in Michelet the signifier is sumptuous. And yet Michelet is not read. Perhaps the signifier is too strong (a veritable poison), if we read Michelet as a historian or as a moralist—which was his public role until he fell into oblivion. Our languages are coded, we must not forget: society is forbidden, by a thousand means, to mingle them, to transgress their separation and their hierarchy; the discourse of History, that of moral ideology (or that of philosophy) are to be kept pure of desire: by not reading Michelet, it is his desire we censure. Thus, because he blurs the discriminatory law of "genres," Michelet fails first of all to be given his place: serious people—conformists—exclude him from their reading. But, by a second displacement, this prince of the signifier is acknowledged by no avant-garde (or more simply, by no "literature"). This second exclusion is more interesting, and more contemporary as well; we must say a word about it, for it is here that we can understand not only why Michelet is not read by active, productive readers (by the young, one might say) but also, more generally, what certain intolerances of contemporary reading might be.

What we do not tolerate is *pathos* (it remains to be seen if we do not have our own). Michelet's discourse is obviously filled with those apparently vague and sublime words, those noble and stirring phrases, those pompous and conformist thoughts, in which we no longer see anything but distant objects, the rather crude curiosities of French romanticism: a whole *vibrato* which no longer moves anything in us (*Action, Nature, Education, People*, etc.); how receive today a sentence (taken at random) like: "The Father is for the child a revelation of justice," etc.? This capitalized language no longer *passes*, for various reasons, which relate to history and to language at the same time (nothing is more important and less studied than fashions in words); and, no longer passing, this language accumulates in Michelet's discourse and constitutes a barrier: if the book does not fall from our hands—for the signifier is there to enliven it—at least we must continually decant it, *split* Michelet—and, worst of all, *make excuses for him.*

This pathetic fall from grace is very extreme in Michelet. Paradoxically, we might say this: what is sincerest ages fastest (the reason for this, of a psychoanalytic order, is that "sincerity" belongs to the realm of the image-repertoire: a realm where the unconscious is least acknowledged). Further, we must acknowledge the fact that no writer ever produces a *pure* discourse (one that is irreproachable, integrally incorruptible): work exfoliates and fragments under the action of time, like a limestone relief; there are always, in the greatest, the boldest writers, the ones we like the most, perfectly antipathetic sites of discourse. It is wisdom to accept the fact (or, less passively, more aggressively, it is the very plural of writing which obliges us to do so). We cannot, moreover, reconcile ourselves to this situation in Michelet's case with such simple liberalism, we must go further. These words, whose magic is dead for us, can be renewed.

First of all, these words had, in their time, a living meaning, sometimes even a fiercely combative one. Michelet used them with passion *against* other words, themselves active, oppressive (language always proceeds in this polemical direction). Here, a certain historical culture must come to the aid of our reading: we must divine what language's stake was at the time Michelet was writing. The historical meaning of a word (not in the narrow acceptation of philology, but in the much broader one of lexicology: I am thinking of the word *civilization* as studied by Lucien Febvre)—that meaning must always be evaluated *dialectically*: for historical recall sometimes encumbers and constrains our present reading, subjects it to an untimely equality, and therefore we must free ourselves from it quite summarily; sometimes, on the contrary, history serves to revivify a word and then we must rediscover this historical meaning as an enjoyable, not authoritarian element, witness of a truth, but free, plural, consumed in the very pleasure of a *fiction* (that of our reading). In short, dealing with a *text*, we must make use of the historical reference *with cynicism*: reject it if it reduces and diminishes our reading, accept it if it extends that reading and makes it more delectable.

The more a word has a magic use, the more mobile its function: it can be employed for everything. This word is something of a mana-word, a joker-word: it can be blank, it is true, but it also assumes, at the same time, *the highest rank*; and the word's justification is less its meaning than its rank, its relation to other words. The word lives only as a function of its context, and this context must be understood in an unlimited fashion: it is the writer's whole thematic and ideological system, and it is also our situation as reader, in all its scope and fragility. The word *Liberty* is eroded (by dint of having been employed by impostors)—but history can restore its terrible contemporaneity; we understand today that liberty, in the meaning this word has had since the French Revolution, was too abstract an entity to satisfy the concrete demands of a worker alienated in his labor and in his leisure; but such a crisis can make us fall back on the word's very abstraction; this abstraction will once again become a power, and Michelet once again be readable (the rise of certain "ecological" dangers may revivify the Micheletist word *Nature*: this process is already beginning). In short, words never die, because they are not "beings" but functions: they merely undergo avatars (in the strict sense), reincarnations (here again, Febvre's text, published just after the Nazi occupation, shows how in 1946 Michelet's work suddenly reechoed the sufferings of the French oppressed by foreign occupation and by fascism).

What separates us from Michelet is, obviously and chiefly, the intervention of Marxism: not only the accession of a new type of political analysis but also a whole implacable series of conceptual and verbal demystifications. Michelet would doubtless have understood little or nothing of Marxist rationality (I doubt if he ever had any awareness of such a thing, though he died in 1874); his ideology, in the strict sense of the word, was petit-bourgeois, but he has openly assumed the morality (even if the word is disagreeable) which is present, like an inevitable quantum, in any political choice: his work is effectively *political*, not by his paths of analysis—anything but realistic, dialectical—but by his *project*, which was pitilessly to recover the *intolerable* elements of history and of sociality. The word *People*, so important for him (it was a word of the Revolution), can no longer be analyzed today as in his time; we no longer speak of the People; but we still say—at least in French—"the popular forces, the masses"; and Michelet had a living relation, a true relation with the "*populaire*," for he could locate this relation at the very heart of his situation as a writer (i.e., of his métier). I offer as proof of this what today touches me most: not all his testimony as to the worker's condition (though this is not negligible), but this somber remark: "I am born of the people, I had the people in my heart . . . But their language, their language was inaccessible to me. I have not been able to make them speak." Michelet here posits our present burning problem of the social separation of languages. In his time, what he called the People were of course not devoid of language (which would be inconceivable), but that language of the People (in fact, what was it?) was located, for lack of mass communications, for lack of schools, outside the pressure of bourgeois and petit-bourgeois models; to attempt to speak in the "popular" idiom—even if one failed to do so—was to lay claim to a certain "spontaneity," an extra-ideological state of language (quite apparent in certain fine folk songs); today this romantic substance has been destroyed: the "popular" language is nothing but the bastardized, generalized, vulgarized bourgeois language, embalmed in a kind of shared meaning of which press, television, and radio are the means of diffusion, all social classes being amalgamated. For Michelet, the language-of-the-people was a promised land; for us, it is a purgatory we must traverse (whence, in some of us, the *revolutionary* refusal to make the crossing). There is nothing more tragic, more overwhelming, for Michelet and for us—so great are the difficulties it heralds—than this text which concludes a chapter of one of Michelet's books (*Nos Fils*, 1869), though full of *pathos*: "After the horrible and sinister affair of June 24, 1848, oppressed, overwhelmed with sufferings, I said to Béranger: 'Oh, who can speak to the people? . . . Unless we do so, we shall die.' That firm, cool mind replied: 'Patience! it is the people who will write their books.' Eighteen years have passed. And these books—where are they?"

Perhaps this problem, inherited from the old Michelet, is the problem of *tomorrow*.

L'Arc, 1972

Michelet's Modernity

Michelet is not in fashion, Michelet is not modern. The great historian has himself fallen through History's trapdoor. Why?

This is a severe, even a dramatic question, at least for someone who loves Michelet's work and yet wants to participate in the accession of those new values whose offensive constitutes what we expediently call the avant-garde. This "someone" therefore believes he is living in contradiction—what our civilization, since Socrates, regards as the most serious trauma a human subject can receive from others and from himself. And yet: what if it were not that "someone" who was contradictory, but Modernity itself? The evident censorship the avant-garde imposes on Michelet would then turn against Modernity as an illusion, a negative phantasmagoria which must be explained: can History—to which Modernity belongs—be unfair, even on occasion idiotic? It is Michelet himself who has taught us so.

Michelet's Modernity—I mean his effective, scandalous modernity, in whose name we would invite him to remain forever young in the history of French literature—blazes forth in at least three points.

The first concerns historians. Michelet, as we know, established what is still timidly called the ethnology of France: a way of apprehending the dead men of the past, not in a chronology or a Rationality, but in a network of carnal practices in a system of aliments, of garments, of everyday customs, of mythic representations, of amorous actions. Michelet reveals what we might call the sensual side of History: with him, the body becomes the very basis of knowledge and of discourse, of knowledge as discourse. It is the example of the body which unifies his entire oeuvre, from the medieval body—that body which tasted of tears—to the delicate body of the Witch: Nature itself—sea, mountain, animality—is never anything but the human body in expansion and, one might say, in contact. Michelet's work corresponds to an unknown level of perception which is still largely occulted by the so-called human sciences. This way of handling what is historically intelligible remains very odd, for it contradicts the belief which continues to tell us that in order to understand we must abstract and, in some sense, *disembody* knowledge.

Michelet's second modernity concerns epistemology. All of Michelet's oeuvre postulates—and often achieves—a truly new science, which is still being fought for. We do not yet call it the science of the unconscious, nor even more broadly a symbolics; let us call it by the very general name Freud gave it in his *Moses*: the *science of displacement*: *Entstellungswissenschaft*. How could we put this (without fear of neologism)? *Metabology?* It is of little consequence. No doubt certain operations of displacement, of substitution, metaphoric or metonymic, have permanently marked the human *logos*, even when this *logos* has become a positive science. But what gives Michelet his high standing in this new discourse of Science is that in his entire oeuvre—perhaps under the influence of Vico, who, we must not forget, long before contemporary structuralism, used the great figures of Rhetoric as ciphers of human History—substitution, symbolic equivalence is a systematic path of knowledge, or, if one prefers, knowledge is not separated from its means, from the very structure of language. When, for example, Michelet tells us, literally, that "*coffee is the alibi of sex*," he formulates a new logic which flourishes today in all knowledge: the Freudian, the structuralist, even the Marxist—all adherents of this science of substitution—should feel at home in Michelet's work.

Michelet's third modernity is the most difficult to perceive, perhaps even to acknowledge, for it presents itself under an absurd name: that of *bias*. Michelet is prejudiced—how many critics, how many historians, proudly installed in the comfort of objective science, have castigated him for it! In order to write, one might say, he takes sides: his entire discourse is openly the result of a choice, of an evaluation of the world, of substances, of bodies; no fact which is not preceded by its own value: the meaning and the fact are given at the same time, an outrageous proposition in the eyes of Science. One philosopher has assumed it: Nietzsche. Nietzsche and Michelet are separated by the most implacable of distances, that of style. Yet see how Michelet *evaluates* his age, the nineteenth century: under a figure familiar to Nietzsche, then to Bataille (a veteran reader of Michelet, we must not forget): that of Ennui, of the deflation of values. The astonishment of Michelet in his age, an age which he regarded in a sense as "extinguished," was that he stubbornly brandished Value as a kind of apocalyptic torch, for the most modern idea of all—an idea he shares specifically with Nietzsche and Bataille—is that we are at the end of History, and even today, which avant-garde would dare to espouse such a notion? It is a "burning" issue—it is dangerous.

Yet, as we have said, Michelet's modernity does not get through to us. Why is this? In Michelet, a certain language constitutes an obstacle, weighs like a dead hand upon his work, keeps it from spreading. In the battles of modernity, an author's historical strength is measured by the array of citations made from him. Now, Michelet "arrays" poorly, he is not cited.

This language is what we must call Michelet's *pathos*. Such pathos is not constant, for Michelet's style is fortunately heteroclite, even baroque (modernity would here have a further reason for recovering the Micheletist text), but it keeps recurring, it encloses Michelet in repetition, in failure. Now, what is it that is repeated in a language? The signature. Of course, Michelet sparkles incessantly, he is incessantly new, but the huge and continuous power of his writing is also incessantly signed by an ideological feature, and it is this feature, this signature, which modernity rejects. Michelet writes his ideology naïvely, and this is his downfall. Where Michelet believes he is being true, sincere, ardent, inspired, is just where today he appears dead, embalmed: *démodé* to the point of discard.

The present power of a past writer is measured by the *detours* he has managed to impose upon the ideology of his class. The writer can never destroy his ideology of origin, he can only cheat with it. Michelet could not, or would not, cheat with the language inherited from the Father: small-time printer, then manager of a rest home, Republican, Voltairean; in a word, petit-bourgeois. Now, petit-bourgeois ideology, nakedly expressed, in Michelet's case, is one of those which are not forgiven today, for it is still broadly our own, that of our institutions, of our schools; hence, it cannot be taken unseasonably, as can the "progressive" ideology of the eighteenth-century bourgeoisie. From a *modern* point of view, Diderot is readable, Michelet virtually no longer so. All of Michelet's pathos remains a consequence of his class ideology, of the idea—the fiction, one might say—that the goal of republican institutions was not to suppress the division between capital and the working class but to attenuate and in some sense to harmonize their antagonism. Whence, on the one hand, a whole unitary discourse (today we would say a *discourse of the signified*) which must alienate from Michelet any psychoanalytic reading, and on the other, an "organicist" conception of History which can only close to him a Marxist reading.

Then what is to be done? Nothing. Each of us must deal with Michelet's text as best he can. Obviously, we are not yet ready for a differential reading, which would agree to fragment, to distribute, to pluralize, to disconnect, to dissociate the text of an author according to the law of Pleasure. We are still theologians, not dialecticians. We prefer to throw out the baby with the bathwater, rather than get ourselves wet. We are not yet "educated" enough to read Michelet.

Revue d'histoire littéraire de la France, 1974

Brecht and Discourse: A Contribution to the Study of Discursivity

The third discourse

Poor B.B.: this is the title of a poem by Bertolt Brecht, written in 1921 (Brecht is twenty-three). These are not the initials of fame; this is the person reduced to two markers; these two letters (and repetitive ones at that) frame a void, and this void is the apocalypse of Weimar Germany; out of this void will rise (around 1928–30) Brechtian Marxism. Hence, there are two discourses in Brecht's oeuvre: first, an apocalyptic (anarchizing) discourse concerned to express and to produce destruction without trying to see what comes "*afterwards*," for "*afterwards*" is just as undesirable; this discourse generates Brecht's first plays (*Baal, Drums in the Night, In the Jungle of Cities*): then, an eschatological discourse: a critique constructed *with a view to* ending the fatality of social alienation (or the belief in this fatality): what does not go well with the world (war, exploitation) is *remediable*: a time of cure is conceivable; this second discourse generates all of Brecht's oeuvre after *The Threepenny Opera.*

A third discourse is missing: an apologetic discourse. There is no Marxist catechism in Brecht: no stereotype, no recourse to the vulgate. Doubtless, the theatrical form shielded him from this danger, since in the theater, as in any text, the origin of the speech-act cannot be located: impossible the—Sadean—collusion of subject and signified (this collusion produces a fanatic discourse), or the—hoaxing—collusion of sign and referent (which produces a dogmatic discourse); but even in his essays—I refer here to the French anthology *Ecrits sur la politique et la société*, published in 1970, a crucial work which has gone virtually unnoticed, as far as I know—Brecht never allows himself the facility of *signing* the origin of his discourse, of imprinting upon it the official stamp of the Marxist imperium: his language is not a coinage. In Marxism itself, Brecht is a permanent inventor; he reinvents quotations, accedes to the inter-text: "He thought in other heads; and in his own, others besides himself thought. This is true thinking." True thinking is more important than the (idealist) thought of truth. In other words, in the Marxist field, Brecht's discourse is never a priestly discourse.

The shock

All that we read and hear covers us like a layer, surrounds and envelops us like a medium: the logosphere. This logosphere is given to us by our period, our class, our métier: it is a "datum" of our subject. Now, to displace what is given can only be the result of a shock; we must shake up the balanced mass of words, pierce the layer, disturb the linked order of the sentences, break the structures of the language (every structure is an edifice of levels). Brecht's work seeks to elaborate a shock-practice (not a subversion: the shock is much more "realistic" than subversion); his critical art is one which opens a crisis: which lacerates, which crackles the smooth surface, which fissures the crust of languages, loosens and dissolves the stickiness of the logosphere; it is an *epic* art: one which discontinues the textures of words, distances representation without annulling it.

And what is this distancing, this discontinuity which provokes the Brechtian shock? It is merely a reading which detaches the sign from its effect. Have you ever seen a Japanese pin? It is a dressmaker's pin whose head is a tiny bell, so that you cannot forget it once the garment has been finished. Brecht remakes the logosphere by leaving the bell-headed pins in it, the signs furbished with their tiny jingle: thus, when we hear a certain language, we never forget where it comes from, how it was made: the shock is a *reproduction*: not an imitation, but a production that has been disconnected, displaced: *which makes noise.*

Hence, better than a semiology, what Brecht leaves us with is a seismology. Structurally, what is a shock? A moment difficult to sustain (and therefore antipathetic to the very notion of "structure"); Brecht does not want us to fall under the spell of another smooth surface, another language-"nature": no positive hero (the positive hero is always sticky), no hysterical practice of the shock: the shock is distinct, discrete (*and* discreet), swift, repeated if need be, but never *established* (this is not a theater of subversion: no great contestatory apparatus). For instance, if there is a field buried under the smooth layer of the quotidian logosphere, it is certainly that of class relations; now, Brecht does not subvert this field (this is not the role he assigns to his dramaturgy; moreover, how would a *discourse* subvert these relations?), he imprints a shock upon it, sticks in a bell-headed pin: for example, it is Puntila's drunkenness, a temporary and recurrent laceration, imposed upon the sociolect of the big landowner; contrary to so many scenes of bourgeois theater and cinema, Brecht never deals with drunkenness as such (the sticky tedium of boozer's scenes): drunkenness is never anything but the agent which modifies a relation, and consequently *offers it to be read* (a relation can be read only *retrospectively* when somewhere, at some point, however remote or tenuous, this relation has altered). Alongside so exact a treatment (exact because kept to its strictest economy), how absurd seem most films about "narcotics"! Using the alibi of the *underground*, it is drugs "as such" which are always represented, their evil effects, their ecstasies, their style, in short their "attributes," not their functions: does this representation permit a critical reading of some supposedly "natural" configuration of human relations? Where is the reading-shock?

Rehearse softly

In his political texts, Brecht gives us a reading exercise: he reads us a Nazi speech (by Hess) and suggests the rules for a proper reading of this kind of text.

Thus, Brecht joins the group of Exercise-Givers, of "Regulators"; those who give not regulations but regulated means for achieving a goal; in the same way, Sade gave rules for pleasure (it is a veritable exercise that Juliette imposes upon the lovely Countess de Donis), Fourier those for happiness, Loyola those for communication with the Divine. The rules taught by Brecht aim at reestablishing the truth of a text: not its metaphysical (or philological) truth, but its historical truth: the truth of a governmental script in a fascist country: an action-truth, a truth *produced* and not asserted.

The exercise consists in saturating the mendacious text by intercalating between its sentences the critical complement which demystifies each one of them: "Legitimately proud of the spirit of sacrifice . . ." Hess pompously began, in the name of "Germany"; and Brecht softly completes: "Proud of the generosity of those possessors who have sacrificed a little of what the non-possessors had sacrificed to them . . ."—and so forth. Each sentence is reversed because it is supplemented: the critique does not diminish, does not suppress, it adds.

In order to produce the proper supplement, Brecht recommends *rehearsing* the text, the exercise, *softly*. The critique is first produced in a kind of clandestinity: what is read is the text *for oneself,* not *in itself*; the low voice is *the one that concerns me*: a reflexive (and sometimes erotic) voice, producing what is intelligible, the original voice of reading. To repeat the exercise (to read the text several times) is gradually to liberate its "supplements"; thus, the haiku compensates for its conspicuous brevity by repetition: the tiny poem is murmured three times, in echoes; this practice is so well coded that the amplitude of the supplements (the "length of the resonance") bears a name: *hibiki*; as for the infinity of links liberated by repetition, this is called *utsuri*.

What is astonishing, at the endurable limit of the paradox, is that this refined practice, closely linked to an erotics of the text, is applied by Brecht to the reading of a hateful text. The destruction of monstrous discourse is here conducted according to an erotic technique; it mobilizes not the reductive weapons of demystification but rather the caressses, the amplifications, the ancestral subtleties of a literary mandarinate, as if there were not, on one side, the vengeful rigor of Marxist science (the science which knows the reality of fascist speeches) and, on the other, the complacencies of the man of letters; but rather as if it were natural *to take pleasure in the truth,* as if one had the simple right, the *immoral* right to submit the bourgeois text to a critique itself formed by the reading techniques of a certain bourgeois past; and indeed where would the critique of bourgeois discourse come from if not from that discourse itself? Discursivity is, till now, without alternative.

Concatenation

Because they are concatenated, Brecht says, errors produce an illusion of truth; Hess's speech may seem true, insofar as it is *successive.* Brecht questions concatenation, questions successive discourse; all the pseudo-logic of the discourse—links, transitions, the patina of elocution, in short the continuity of speech—releases a kind of force, engenders an illusion of assurance: concatenated discourse is indestructible, triumphant. The first attack is therefore to make it discontinuous—to discontinue it: literally to dismember the erroneous text is a polemical act. "To unveil" is not so much to draw back the veil as to cut it to pieces; in the veil, one ordinarily comments upon only the image of that which conceals, but the other meaning of the image is also important: the *smooth,* the *sustained,* the *successive*; to attack the mendacious text is to separate the fabric, to tear apart the folds of the veil.

The critique of the *continuum* (here applied to discourse) is a constant one in Brecht. One of his first plays, *In the Jungle of Cities,* still seems enigmatic to many critics because in it two partners take part in a duel incomprehensible not on the level of each of its peripeties but on the level of the whole, i.e., according to a continuous reading: Brecht's theater is henceforth a series (not a consequence) of cut-up fragments deprived of what in music is called the Zeigarnik effect (when the final resolution of a musical sequence retroactively gives it its meaning). Discontinuity of discourse keeps the final meaning from "taking": critical production does not wait—it will be instantaneous and repeated: this is the very definition of epic theater according to Brecht. Epic is what cuts (shears) the veil, disaggregates the stickiness of mystification (see the preface to *Mahagonny*).

The maxim

Brecht's praise of the fragment (of the scene presented "for its own sake") is not that of the maxim. The maxim is not a fragment; first of all, because the maxim is generally the point of departure of an implicit reasoning, the outset of a continuity surreptitiously developing in the docile inter-text which inhabits the reader; then, because the Brechtian fragment never generalizes—it is not "concise," it does not "assemble"; it can be loose, relaxed, fed on contingencies, specifications, dialectical *données*; whereas the maxim is a statement minus History: it remains a bluff of "Nature."

Hence, Brecht's unceasing supervision of the maxim. The Hero is doomed, one might say, because the maxim is his "natural" language ("Wherever you find great virtues, you can be sure that something is going wrong"); the same applies to widespread Custom, for it is based on gnomic truths: "He who takes the first step must also take the second": who says this, and in this form? The cultural code, whose false logic is abusive, for he who takes the first step does not necessarily have to take the second. To break the custom is, first of all, to break the maxim, the stereotype: under the rule, discover the abuse; under the maxim, discover the concatenation; under Nature, discover History.

Metonymy

In his speech, Hess constantly speaks of Germany. But Germany, here, is only the German "possessors." The Whole is given, abusively, for the part. Synecdoche is totalitarian: it is an act of force. "The whole for the part"—this definition of metonymy means: one part *against* another part, the German possessors *against* the rest of Germany. The predicate ("German") becomes the subject ("the Germans"): there occurs a kind of local *Putsch*: metonymy becomes a class weapon.

How to combat metonymy? How, *on the level of discourse,* to restore the sum to its parts, how to undo the abusive Name? This is a very Brechtian problem. In the theater, the undoing of the Name is easy enough, for it is inevitably only bodies that are represented there. If we must speak of the "People" on the stage (for this word itself can be metonymic, can engender abuses), we must divide up the concept: in *The Trial of Lucullus,* the "People" is the meeting of a peasant, a slave, a schoolmaster, a fishmonger, a baker, a prostitute. Brecht says somewhere that Reason is never what the totality of reasonable people think: the (invariably abusive?) concept is reduced to a summation of historical bodies.

However, de-nomination—or ex-nomination—because *infinitely subversive,* is difficult to sustain. It is tempting to exculpate a Cause, to excuse the errors and stupidities of its partisans, separating the excellence of the Name from the imbecilities of its subjects. Berdyaev once wrote a brochure entitled *On the Dignity of Christianity and the Indignity of Christians* . . . Ah, if we could similarly purify Marxist discourse of the dogmatism of Marxists, the Revolution of the hysteria of revolutionaries, and in a general way the Idea from the neurosis of its supporters!

But in vain: political discourse is fundamentally metonymic, for it can only be established by the power of language, and this power is metonymy itself. Thus, there recurs in discourse the major religious figure, that of Contagion, of Fault, of Terror, i.e., in all these cases, the subjection by violence of the part to the whole, of the body to the Name; religious discourse is indeed the model of all political discourse: no theology could acknowledge that Faith is merely the entirety of those who believe. Now, from the viewpoint of Marxist "custom," Brecht is very heretical: he resists all metonymies; there is a kind of Brechtian individualism: the "People" is a collection of individuals assembled on the stage; the "Bourgeoisie" is here a landlord, there a rich man, etc. The theater compels undoing the Name. I can readily imagine some theoretician, ultimately disgusted with Names yet reluctant to abandon all language—I can imagine this Brechtian epigone renouncing his past speeches and resolving henceforth to write only novels.

The sign

Yes, Brecht's theater is a theater of the Sign. But if we want to understand how and whereby this semiology can be, more profoundly, a seismology, we must always remember that the originality of the Brechtian sign is that it is *to be read twice over:* what Brecht gives us to read is, by a kind of disengagement, the reader's gaze, not directly the object of his reading; for this object reaches us only by the act of intellection (an alienated act) of a first reader who is already on the stage. The best example of this "turn," paradoxically, I should borrow not from Brecht but from my personal experience (a copy is readily more exemplary than the original; "Brecht-like" can be more Brechtian than "Brecht").

Here then is a "street scene" of which I was a witness. The public beach of Tangier, in summer, is carefully supervised; one is not permitted to undress there—not out of modesty, no doubt, but rather to compel bathers to rent the cabanas which line the promenade—i.e., to keep the "poor" (this category exists in Morocco) off the beach, thereby reserved for the bourgeois and the tourists. On the promenade, an adolescent boy, solitary, sad, and poverty-stricken (signs *for me,* I confess, deriving from a *simple* reading, which is not yet Brechtian), is walking along; a policeman (almost as filthy as the boy) passes him and looks him up and down, I *see* his scrutiny, I see it reach and linger over the *shoes*; then the cop orders the boy off the beach.

This scene invites two commentaries. The first will accommodate our indignation provoked by the barricading of the beach, the grim subjection of the boy, the arbitrary action of the police, the segregation of money, the Moroccan regime; now, this commentary would not be Brecht's (though this would certainly be his "reaction"). The second commentary will establish the mirror action of the signs; it will note first of all that there is a feature in the boy's garments which is the major sign of poverty: the shoe; it is here that the social sign explodes in all its violence (there used to be, not so long ago, in the days when we had "the poor," a mythology of the cast-off shoe: if the intellectual rots from his head down, like fish, the poor man rots from the feet up—which is why Fourier, seeking to invert the civilized order, imagines a corps of flamboyant cobblers); and, in the realm of the shoe, the extreme point of poverty is the old slipper, without laces, the upper flattened beneath the heel, precisely in the fashion exhibited by the boy. But what this second commentary would especially note is that this sign is read by the cop himself: it is when his gaze, descending the body's length, perceives the wretched shoe, that the policeman, with a single impulse, by a veritable paradigmatic leap, classifies the boy among those to be expelled: we understand that he has understood—and why he has understood. The action may not stop here: the cop himself is almost as ragged as his victim: except, precisely, for his shoes! Round, shiny, solid, old-fashioned, like all policemen's shoes. Whence we can read *two alienations confronting one another* (a situation sketched in a scene from a neglected play by Sartre, *Nékrassov*). Our exteriority is not simple: it establishes a dialectical (and not a Manichaeist) critique. "Truth-as-action" would be to awaken the boy, but also to awaken the cop.

Pleasure

The theater must give pleasure, Brecht has said a thousand times: the great critical tasks (liquidation, theoretization, problematization) do not exclude pleasure.

Brechtian pleasure is chiefly a sensualism; there is nothing orgiastic about it, it is more oral than erotic, it is "good-to-be-alive" (rather than "good-living"), it is "eating-well," not in the French sense, but in the rural, woodsman, Bavarian sense. In most of Brecht's plays, food is served (let us note that food is at the intersection of Need and Desire; hence it is, alternatively, a realistic theme and a utopian theme); the most complex Brechtian hero (hence no "hero" at all), Galileo, is a sensual man: having abdicated everything, alone upstage, he eats his goose and lentils, while down front, apart from him, his books are feverishly packed up—they will cross frontiers and spread the anti-theological scientific spirit.

Brechtian sensualism does not stand in opposition to intellectualism; there is a kind of circulation from one to the other: "For a vigorous thought, I would give any woman, almost any. There are many fewer thoughts than women. Politics is good only when there are enough thoughts (here, too, the blanks are boring!) . . ." The dialectic is a kind of delight. It is therefore possible to conceive, *revolutionarily*, a culture of pleasure; apprenticeship to "taste" is "progressive"; Paul Vlassov, the Mother's militant son, differs from his father in this (according to his mother): he reads books and he is picky about his soup. In the 1954 *Propositions on Peace,* Brecht outlines the program for a School of Aesthetics: ordinary objects (utensils) must be the sites of beauty, it is licit to recuperate old styles (no "progressive" reward for "modern" furnishing). In other words, aesthetics is absorbed into an art of living: "All the arts contribute to the greatest of all: the art of living"; hence, it is less a matter of making pictures than furniture, clothes, tablecloths, which will have distilled all the juice of the "fine" arts; the socialist future of art will therefore not be the work (except as a productive game) but the object of use, the site of an *ambiguous* flowering (half functional, half ludic) of the signifier. The cigar is a capitalist emblem, so be it; but *if it gives pleasure*? Are we no longer to smoke cigars, to enter into the metonymy of the social Fault, to refuse to compromise ourselves in the Sign? It would be hardly dialectical to think so: it would be to throw out the baby with the bathwater. One of the tasks of a critical age is precisely to pluralize the object, to separate pleasure from the sign; we must de-semanticize the object (which does not mean de-symbolize it), give the sign a shock: let the sign *fall*, like a shed skin. This shock is the very fruit of dialectical freedom: the freedom which judges everything in terms of reality, and takes signs conjointly for operators of analysis and for games, never for laws.

L'Autre Scène, 1975

TWO

F.B.*

1. Splinters of language

Though F.B.'s texts may well be the premonitory signs of a *concerted*, large-scale work, the author puts his reader under no obligation, and what each of these texts has to tell us is its fulfillment. What is fulfilled, here, is writing. Of all the work's substances, only writing, as a matter of fact, can be divided without ceasing to be total: a fragment of writing is still an essence of writing. This is why, willy-nilly, every fragment is finished, from the moment it is written; this is why, too, we cannot compare a broken work to a sustained one; this is why, lastly, no one can deny the greatness of fragmentary works: the greatness not of ruin or of promise, but the greatness of the silence which follows any fulfillment (only scholarship, which is the contrary of reading, can regard Pascal's *Pensées* as an uncompleted work). Because they are *written*, F.B.'s texts are neither sketches nor notations nor raw materials nor exercises; they suggest neither the notebook nor the diary: they are *splinters of language*. Poe once claimed there was no such thing as a long poem; for example, he saw *Paradise Lost* as "a succession of

* Unpublished, this text was written as a footnote to fragments by a young writer who seems not to have pursued a literary vocation and who published nothing. A marginal text, then, intended for the person whose enterprise it examines. Here tone and address are distinctly ludic, which does not prevent this text—quite the contrary—from constituting a system of acute propositions on a new type of fictive writing. We can recognize *in nucleo*, as early as 1964, certain features of Barthes's final manner.—Ed.

poetical excitements interspersed, *inevitably*, with corresponding depressions. . . ." F.B. manages to eliminate these depressions; his writing is of a luxuriance without loss, i.e., *without duration;* it is the writing itself, and not the story, which ceases, here, to be uneven, hence boring, hence periodically ugly, as happens in so many beautiful works: everything is referred to writing, but this delegation has nothing to do with the effort of form; artisanry is no longer the necessary condition of style; Stendhal scoffed at Chateaubriand and virtually never "corrected." Here the writer gives his effort not to the verbal substance but to the decision to write: everything happens *before* writing. The least of F.B.'s texts bespeaks this anterior "transumption"; the tender and sumptuous luxury of an *absolutely free* writing, in which there is not an atom of death, invulnerable by dint of grace, expresses the initial decision which makes language into the fragile salvation of a *certain* suffering.

2. Incidents

The power of writing: these texts are also, in their way, splinters of a novel. F.B.'s texts show two indestructible signs of the novel: first, the uncertainty of the narrative consciousness, which never clearly says *he* or *I*; then a cursive manner, i.e., a continuity which relates writing to the sustained forms of nature (water, plant, tune); you "sample" nothing from a novel, rather a novel is "devoured" (which means that the sustained nature of novelistic reading derives not from the care you might take in reading anything but, quite the contrary, from the rapid trajectory which makes you *forget* certain parts of the itinerary; writing's continuity is a matter of *speed*, and this speed is perhaps ultimately no more than that of the hand). Thus with F.B.'s texts: they, too, are "devoured": a very small space of words encloses here (the paradox of writing) an essence of continuity. F.B.'s writing, once it is completed (always too soon), nonetheless has *already* flowed past: light, profound, luminescent as the sea it often speaks of, it leads us, gives us at once the idea of a goal and of a detour; it is never enclosed, never *set* (a word which refers to ice, to a wound, to stupefaction, all things alien to F.B.'s writing); physically subtle, it participates in the fictive essence because its end (in the double sense of the word) is never aphoristic; its (material) brevity intimates no gnomism; a paradoxical situation for brief texts, they observe, they do not judge: they have the novel's profound *amorality*; in them reigns the fundamental tense of free literatures, language's last conquest (according to its prehistory): the *indicative*. For this reason, we might call F.B.'s texts not fragments but *incidents*, things that *fall*, without a jolt yet with a movement which is not infinite: the discontinuous continuity of the snowflake. One might say this in another way: the function of the maxim's brevity is to induce in us a certain ambiguity and reversibility of meaning, its figure is the ellipsis; F.B.'s texts are the contrary of this system of writing: they are not "brief," turned in upon themselves; they have the *development* of the infinite metaphor (as one says the *development of a wheel*), they have the length and the élan of the line (that vestimentary notion); the author can halt them very rapidly, they *already* have the respiration of time: refusing the novel's time, this is still a writing *which has time*. What prevails here is not ambiguity, it is mystery.

3. The description

The novel's "descriptions" are necessary and thereby intractable; they are "services" or, better still, servitudes; the anecdote obliges the author to present certain items of information as to persons and places; communicating a status, these are kinds of "halts," and we often read them with tedium. Abjuring the novel, F.B. nonetheless takes the dead parts of the novel and makes an active substance out of them. Thus, in one of his finest texts, F.B. describes a boy walking in the streets of Rome; we do not know, we shall never know, where this boy is coming from, where he is going, and why he is here—he is attached to no narrative logic; yet his creator gives him a *suspense*; the more accurately the boy is described, the more curious we are about his essence, the more we are focused on *something we must understand.* F.B. thus substitutes for the grammar of the anecdote a new intelligibility: that of desire. Desire itself becomes story and intelligence, there is, finally, coincidence of description and suspense. In a novelistic description, if it isn't too bad, the story remotely penetrates every detail, making each contribute to a general meaning (the poverty of a dwelling, the austerity of a character); here, in the same way, desire makes description "profound," or, one might say, *alienated*: desire becomes *ratio, logos*: a power it cannot derive from its satisfaction, but only from speech, whereby all of literature is justified. Just as the anecdote always overflows toward a certain meaning, which has long been called *destiny*, so desire, once recounted, mysteriously loses its contingency: embarrassment, sadness, lucidity, sleep, the city, the sea become the names of desire. Whence this new literature which works at once by metaphor and by narrative, by the variation of being and by the concatenation of acts: something like a new La Bruyère or Theophrastus—*Characters* not of manners but of bodies.

4. Sublimation

Thereby, F.B. silences not only narrative's morality but also its logic (which is perhaps the same thing); his descriptions are subversions, they do not lead on, they detach and "exceed." How? Each text *starts* like a novel, each text is a simulacrum of a novel: there are objects, characters, a situation, a narrator, in short a realistic instance; but very quickly (i.e., both instantly and imperceptibly, as if we were leaving the ground), this whole familiarity of the novel begins to move *elsewhere*: we are lifted toward another meaning (what will be given of this meaning is nothing more than this: it is *other*; a pure alterity, which is the sufficient definition of the strange): a character arrives at a railroad station; the station is described, then suddenly it *is* the site, or better still, the triumph of desire; now, this identity is immediate: the station does not *become* other than itself, there is no metaphor, no transport of vision; by a special illogicality, we receive the succession and the coincidence of the two sites. This very special montage effaces something which has been very difficult for literature to get rid of: the astonishment of its own notations; F.B.'s writing is never to any degree accessory to the effect it produces: it is a writing without complicity. Another text begins like an adventure story: a man makes his way into an airplane hangar and knocks out the pilot sleeping there; very quickly, an "excessively" amorous description of the young pilot (everything is in this "excess") alienates this classical start; the hallucination "takes," and without leaving the framework of the traditional narrative, the scene of escape changes its nature and *finds itself* an erotic scene. For F.B. the novel is *at discretion*; it lends desire its inceptions; the narration is like a launching pad; but what happens at the end no longer belongs to the order of the successibility of events, in other words of suspense, but to the order of essences. In the (real) novel, desire is strong by its acts, its effects, the situations it produces; it is always treated according to a causal logic (which moralizes it at every turn); in the simulated novels of F.B., everything stops at desire, everything glorifies it (theologically, glorification is the manifestation of essence); the novel yields like a curtain parting in order to show desire in its "glory." A truth of reversals: desire sublimates reason.

5. Eros

Of course, desire prowls through all literature, ever since language, having become sovereign, useless, began *saying* something which has been called *beauty*; but this written desire has never hitherto been anything more than an element of moral, psychological, theological algebra: literature once served to comprehend desire, in the name of a larger whole; all literature thus tended to morality, i.e., to an economy of good and evil, of light and dark: an Eros recounted means something else than

Eros. In F.B.'s texts, the movement is reversed: it is Eros which "comprehends"; here there is nothing which does not proceed from Eros: boy-love forms a perfect circle outside of which nothing is left; all transcendence is concentrated; yet this circle is a formal one: its closure does not come from society, or even from an existential choice, as in other works with the same object: it is only *writing* which traces that circle; the desire for boys is never, here, "culturalized," it has the naturalness of what is without cause and without effect, it is both without freedom and without fatality. This naturalness has major consequences for writing (unless, of course, it derives from writing): what is written does not appeal to *something else;* both soft and rich, writing is nonetheless *matte*; conforming in this to the newest languages of today, but without their coldness, it denies itself and us any *induction*; because there is no ellipsis in them, we can infer nothing from these texts. Now, the value of an art, in a crowded world, is defined by the privative operations it has the audacity to invoke: not in order to satisfy an aesthetic of constraint (the classical model), but in order to subjugate meaning fully, to deprive it of any secondary outlet. We might say that, coming at the end of a very heavy tradition, a literature of desire is the most difficult thing of all; F.B.'s does not derive its erotic essence from the realism of figures, but from an unconditional submission to Eros, chosen as the sole god of the work (Satan is eliminated, and hence God). This regnum assured, nothing would seem more *out of place* than an erotic repertoire of gestures. F.B.'s texts are therefore not in the erotic tradition (in the current meaning of the term), precisely to the degree that Eros here is not a collection and a nomination (of "postures"), but a sovereign principle of writing. Hence, we must set in opposition to traditional *erotics* a new *eroticism*; in the former case, the writer must work up the description of "what happened" until he has found in Eros a transcendence—God, Satan or the Unnamed—whereas in F.B.'s "incidents," Eros being the ultimate intelligence, there can be no paroxysm. Another difference: traditional *erotics* are heavy, or tense; here *eroticism* is light (writing runs over the surface of the encounters without completing them) and profound (writing is the *thought* of things); it is an air, a space, one might say a geometry, since we now have geometries which subtilize the cosmos; it is *present*, without provocation and without complicity: not naïve, for Eros knows everything, it is *wise*; and perhaps this is the extreme note of this writing, that in it desire is a figure of *sophrosyne*. Grace and wisdom: it is this *impossibility* which the Ancients hold to be perfection, representing it in the lovely myth of the *puer senilis*, the adolescent master of every human age. How long it has been that our literature, in the best of cases, could transport but not seduce; such a *charm*, then, is a new thing.

6. General, individual, particular

The tremor of romantic *Sehnsucht*, consisting of a dreamy confusion of the sensitive and the sensual, and yet a deep metaphysical silence: F.B. takes from language—that category of the general—only the extreme, particular edge, never intimating a judgment, a maxim, never summarizing the description under that lyric or moral discourse which the old rhetoric had recognized as *epiphoneme*: in F.B.'s writing, nothing ever comes *over* what is written: a silky and inductile metal. F.B. occupies, among our various writing, a *dangerous* situation. Language being general (and therefore moral), literature is doomed to the universal; everything that happens in literature is originally cultural: its pulsions are always born clad in an anterior language; the generality with which the writer has been credited for centuries, endlessly congratulated for making the individual into the human, is in reality a terrible servitude: how can one be praised for a constraint imposed by the very nature of language? The writer's problem, on the contrary, is to find an ultimate particularity despite the general and moral instrument he is *given*. This is the problem which is *treated* (but not argued) in F.B.'s texts; here the author teaches himself (and us) that *the particular is not the individual*; quite the contrary, it is, so to speak, the impersonal and uncollective share of ourselves; hence, we shall not find in these texts anything dealing with a *formed* person, i.e., with a history, a life, a character; but we shall also not find here any mirror of humanity. In other words, the substance of this writing is not *experience* (*experience*, "what has been lived," is banal—it is precisely what the writer must combat), but it is also not *reason* (a general category adopted under various pretexts by all ready-made literatures); this famous conflict, so apparently irreducible in some people's eyes that it keeps them from writing, is one whose terms F.B. rejects, and it is by this *innocent* rejection that he is likely to fulfill the utopia of a particular language. This action has a great critical consequence: though F.B.'s texts can be described as *being*, nothing in the world can keep them from *becoming*: achieved in *writing*, the particular struggles here with the *work* which every society, being moral, demands of *the one who writes*.

7. Technique

Literature's substance is the general category of language; in order to create itself, not only must it kill what has engendered it, but even, in order to commit this murder, it can use no other instrument than this very language it must destroy. This *almost* impossible reversal constitutes F.B.'s texts: it is that *almost* which is the narrow space in which the author writes. This cannot be done without a *technique*, which is not necessarily an apprenticeship, but according to Aristotle's definition, the faculty of producing that which can be or not be. The goal of this technique is to describe a world chosen, not as a desirable world, but as the desirable itself; desire is here not the attribute of a creation which preexists it, it is immediately a substance; in other words, again, the author does not discover (by the action of a privileged subjectivity) that the world is desirable, he determines it desirable; hence, it is the time of judgment, psychological time, which is eluded here: particular, but not individual, the author does not recount what he sees, what he feels, he does not reel off the precious epithets he has the fortune of finding, he does not act as a psychologist who uses a felicitous language in order to enumerate the original attributes of his vision, rather he acts *immediately* as a writer; he does not make bodies desirable, he makes desire corporeal, inverting substance and attribute by the very paradox of writing: everything is shifted to objects, in order to express not what they are (what are they?) but the essence of the desire which constitutes them, exactly as luminescence constitutes phosphorus; in F.B.'s texts, there is never any *undesirable* object. Thus, the author creates a vast metonymy of desire: a *contagious* writing which transfers to its reader the very desire out of which it has formed things.

8. *Signum facere*

The old rhetoric distinguished *disposition* from *elocution*. Disposition (*taxis*) accounts for the work's major units, its general arrangement, its "development"; elocution (*lexis*) accounted for the figures, the turns of speech, what we should call today the writing [*écriture*], i.e., a class (and not an epitome) of "details." F.B.'s texts are fully (at least for the moment) texts of *elocution*. The unit of elocution has a very ancient name: it is the *song*. The song is not a euphony or a quality of images; according to the Orphic myth, it is a way of *keeping* the world under one's language. What sings here is not directly the words, it is that second writing, that mental writing which forms itself and advances between the things and the words—a kind of anterior song (as Baudelaire speaks of a *vie antérieure*, a previous existence). Vico at one point mentions certain *universals of the imagination*: that is the space where F.B. forms a *particular* writing, without tradition and without provocation; neither "noble" nor "natural," this writing eludes all the models without ever assuming the heavy signaletics of originality. Whence, perhaps, its naked friendliness, severed from any humanism. To read F.B. is constantly to form in oneself certain adjectives: fresh, simple, silky, light, sensitive, accurate, intelligent, desirable, strong, rich

(Valéry: *"After all, the artist's—sole—object comes down to securing an epithet"*), but ultimately these adjectives dislodge each other, truth is only in the whole and the whole cannot support any definition; the very function of this writing is to say what we could never say about it: if we could, it would no longer be justified. F.B. stands at the precise point of a double postulation: on the one hand, his writing *makes meaning,* whereby we cannot name it, for this meaning is infinitely more remote than ourselves; and on the other, it *makes a sign. Signum facere,* such might be the motto of these texts: these sentences, this entirety of sentences floats in the mind like a future memory, predetermining the discourse of the latest modernity.

1964

The Baroque Side

French culture has always attached, it appears, a very powerful privilege to "ideas," or, to speak more neutrally, to the content of messages. What matters to the Frenchman is having "something to say," what we nowadays designate by a phonically ambiguous word with monetary, commercial, and literary applications: *le fond* (or *le fonds* or *les fonds*). With regard to the signifier (a word we hope can henceforth be used without apologies), French culture has known for centuries only the labor of style, the constraints of Aristotelio-Jesuit rhetoric, the values of "writing well," themselves centered, moreover, with an obstinate iteration, upon the transparency and distinction of the *"fond."* We had to wait till Mallarmé for our literature to conceive a free signifier no longer burdened by the censure of the false signified, and to attempt writing finally rid of the historical repression in which the privileges of "thought" imprison it. Even the Mallarmean project—so stubborn is the resistance—can only be, here and there, "varied," i.e., repeated, in infrequent works which are all works of combat: suppressed twice in our history—at the moment of the baroque impetus and of Mallarmean poetics—French writing is still in a situation of repression.

Here is a book to remind us that besides cases of transitive or ethical communication (*Pass the cheese* or *We sincerely desire peace in Vietnam*), there is a pleasure of language, of similar fabric, similar silk as erotic pleasure, and that this pleasure of language is its truth. This book comes not from Cuba (no question of folklore, even Castrist) but from the language of Cuba, from that Cuban text (cities, words, drinks, garments, bodies, odors, etc.), which is itself an inscription of diverse cultures and periods. Here something is happening which matters to us as Frenchmen: transported into *our* language, this Cuban language subverts its landscape: here is one of the very rare occasions when a translation manages to displace its language of origin instead of merely joining it. If the verbal baroque is historically Spanish (Gongoresque or Quevedian), and if that history is present in Severo Sarduy's text, national and "maternal" like any language, this text also reveals to us the baroque side of the French idiom, thereby suggesting that writing can do anything with a language, and in the first place give it its freedom.

This baroque side (baroque is a temporarily useful word, in that it allows us to provoke the inveterate classicism of French literature), to the degree that it manifests the signifier's ubiquity, present at all levels of the text and not, as is commonly said, on its surface alone, modifies the very identity of what we call a narrative, without the tale's pleasure ever being lost. *Ecrit en dansant* consists of three episodes, three *gestes*—an old French word which here recuperates the title of Severo Sarduy's first book and which corresponds as well to the word's masculine sense (gesture) as its feminine (exploit)—but in it will be found none of those narrative prostheses (personality of the protagonists, situation of the locales and of the weather, complicity of the narrator, and God, who sees into the hearts of the characters) by which we usually mark the abusive (and, moreover, illusory) right of reality over language. Severo Sarduy is a good narrator of "something," which draws us to its end and makes for the death of writing, but this something is freely displaced, "seduced" by that *sovereignty* of language, which Plato in fact sought to challenge in Gorgias, inaugurating that repression of writing which marks our Western culture. Thus, we find deployed in *Ecrit en dansant*, a hedonist text and thereby a revolutionary one, the great theme proper to the signifier, sole predicate of essence it can actually support, *metamorphosis*: Cubans, Chinese, Spaniards, Catholics, addicts, pagans, performers, traveling from caravelles to cafeterias and from one sex to the other, Severo

Sarduy's creatures pass back and forth through the pane of refined prattle which they fob off on the author, thereby demonstrating that this pane does not exist, that there is nothing to see *behind* language, and that discourse, far from being the final attribute and the last touch of the human statue, as the misleading myth of Pygmalion suggests, is never anything but its irreducible scope.

However, let humanists be reassured, at least partially. The allegiance given to writing by any subject, the one who writes and the one who reads, an act which has no relation with what classical repression, by a self-seeking ignorance, calls "verbalism" or more nobly "poetry," suppresses none of reading's "pleasures," provided we agree to find its correct rhythm. Severo Sarduy's text deserves all the adjectives which constitute the lexicon of literary value: it is a brilliant, lively, sensitive, funny, inventive text, unexpected yet clear, cultural even, and continuously affectionate. Yet I fear that, in order to be received without difficulty in literary good society, it lacks that suspicion of remorse, that touch of transgression, that shadow of the signified which transforms writing into a sermon and thus ransoms it under the name of "fine work," like a piece of merchandise useful to the economy of the "human." Perhaps this text does have one thing in excess, which will embarrass: the energy of speech, which suffices for the writer to be reassured.

La Quinzaine littéraire, 1967

What Becomes of the Signifier

Eden, Eden, Eden is a free text: free of any subject, of any object, of any symbol: it is written in that recess (that abyss or that blind spot) where the traditional constituents of discourse (he who speaks, what he tells, how he expresses himself) are *de trop*. The immediate consequence is that criticism, since it can speak neither of the author nor of his subject nor of his style, can do nothing with this text: one must "enter" Guyotat's language; not believe in it, be the accomplice of an illusion, participate in a hallucination, but write this language with him, in his place, sign it at the same time as P. Guyotat himself.

To be *in language* (as we say: *to be in on the deal*): this is possible because Guyotat produces not a manner, a genre, a literary object, but a new element (why not add it to the four Elements of the cosmogony?); this element is a sentence: substance of speech which has the special nature of a fabric, or a foodstuff, a single sentence which never ends, whose beauty derives not from its "report" (the reality to which it is presumed to refer) but from its respiration, interrupted, repeated, as if it were the author's business to represent for us not imagined scenes but the scene of language, so that the model of this new *mimesis* is no longer the adventure of a hero but the adventure of the signifier itself: what becomes of it.

Eden, Eden, Eden constitutes (or should constitute) a kind of upsurge, of historic shock: a whole anterior action, apparently twofold, but whose coincidence we see more and more clearly, from Sade to Genet, from Mallarmé to Artaud, is collected, displaced, purified of its period circumstances; there is no longer either Narrative or Transgression (no doubt one and the same), there is nothing left but desire and language, not the latter expressing the former, but placed in a reciprocal, indissoluble metonymy.

The strength of this metonymy, sovereign in Guyotat's text, suggests that a strong censorship is likely—a censorship which will find united here its two habitual quarries, language and sex; but also such censorship, which can take many forms, will be immediately unmasked by its very strength: doomed to be excessive if it censors sex and language *at the same time*, doomed to be hypocritical if it claims to censor only the subject and not the form, or conversely: in both cases, doomed to reveal its essence as censorship.

However, whatever the institutional peripeties may be, the publication of this text is important: all critical, theoretical work will be advanced by it, without the text ever ceasing to be seductive: at once unclassifiable and indubitable, a new reference and a departure for writing.

Preface to P. Guyotat's *Eden, Eden, Eden* (Gallimard), 1970

Outcomes of the Text

Here is a text by Georges Bataille "The Big Toe."*

I shall not explicate this text; I shall merely produce a number of fragments which will be, in a sense, *outcomes* of the text. These fragments will be in a more or less emphatic state of severance with each other: I shall not attempt to link, to organize these "outcomes"; and in order to be sure of frustrating any liaison (any systematizing of the commentary), in order to avoid any rhetoric of "development," of the developed subject, I have titled each of these fragments, and I have put these titles in alphabetical order—which is, of course, both an order and a disorder, an order stripped of meaning, the degree zero of order. It will be a kind of dictionary (Bataille supplies one at the end of *Documents*) which will deal obliquely with the sustaining text.

Aplatissement des valeurs / Deflation of values

There is, in Nietzsche and in Bataille, one theme in common: that of regret. A certain form of the present is disparaged, a certain form of the past is exalted; neither this present nor this past is actually historical; they are both read according to the formal, ambiguous movement of a *decadence*. Thus is born the possibility of a non-reactionary regret, a *progressive* regret. *Decadence* is not read, contrary to the word's accepted connotation, as a sophisticated, hypercultural condition, but on the

* First published in *Documents* in 1929; reprinted in the first volume of Bataille's *Oeuvres complètes*, 1970. Translated in 1985 by Allan Stoekl as "The Big Toe," in *Visions of Excess: Selected Writings of Georges Bataille, 1927–1939* (Minnesota University Press).

contrary as a *deflation of values*: return of tragedy as farce (Marx), clandestinity of festal expenditure in bourgeois society (Bataille), critique of Germany, disease, exhaustion of Europe, theme of the *last man*, of the vermin "that diminishes everything" (Nietzsche). We might add Michelet's diatribes against the nineteenth century—his own—the century of Boredom. In all, the same disgust provoked by bourgeois deflation: bourgeois man does not destroy value, he *deflates* it, diminishes it, establishes a system of the paltry. This is a theme at once historical and ethical: fall of the world out of the tragic, rise of the petite-bourgeoisie, written as an *advent*: the Revolution (Marx) and the *Übermensch* (Nietzsche) are vital shocks applied to deflation; all of Bataille's heterology is of the same order: electric. In this apocalyptic history of value, "The Big Toe" refers to two time frames: an ethnological time (marked in the text by verbs in the present tense), the time "of men," "of peoples" who anthropologically disparage the low and exalt the high, and a historical time (marked by episodes in the past tense), which is the time of Christianity and of its quintessence, Spain, for which the low is purely and scrupulously censured (modesty). Such is the dialectic of value: when it is anthropological, rejection of the foot designates the very site of a seduction: seduction is where one *savagely* conceals, value is in the savage transgression of the forbidden; but when it is historical, sublimated in the figure of modesty, condemnation of the foot becomes a repressed, deflated value which invites the denial of *Laughter*.

Codes du savoir / Codes of knowledge

In Bataille's text, there are many "poetic" codes: thematic (high / low, noble / ignoble, light / muddy), amphibological (the word *erection*, for instance), metaphorical ("man is a tree"); there are also codes of knowledge: anatomical, zoological, ethnological, historical. Of course, the text *exceeds* knowledge—by value; but even within the field of knowledge, there are differences of pressure, of "seriousness," and these differences produce a heterology. Bataille stages two knowledges. An endoxal knowledge: this is the knowledge of Salomon Reinach and of the members of the editorial committee of *Documents* (the periodical from which the text under consideration is taken); citational, referential, reverential knowledge. And a remoter knowledge, produced by Bataille (by his personal culture). The code of this knowledge is ethnological; it corresponds to what was once called *Le Magasin pittoreque,* a collection of linguistic, ethnographic "curiosities"; in the discourse of this second knowledge there is a double reference: that of the *strange* (of *elsewhere*) and that of the *detail*; thus is produced an incipient collapse of knowledge (of its law) by its futilization, its miniaturization; at the end of this code, there is *astonishment* ("wide-eyed"); such knowledge is paradoxical in that it astonishes, de-naturalizes itself, unsettles the formula "it is self-evident . . ." This search for ethnological fact is certainly very close to the novelistic search: the novel in fact is a faded *mathesis*, tending to *circumvent* knowledge. This interference of codes—diverse in origin, in style—is contrary to the monology of knowledge, which consecrates "specialists" and disdains polygraphs (amateurs). In short, there occurs a burlesque, *heteroclite* knowledge (etymologically: leaning to one side and the other): this is already an operation of writing (what we have elsewhere called *écrivance* or inauthentic writing imposes the separation of knowledges—as we say: the separation of genres); proceeding from the mixture of knowledges, writing holds in check "the scientific arrogances" (as Bataille calls them in *Documents*) and at the same time sustains an apparent readability: a dialectical discourse which might be that of journalism, if journalism were not deflated by the ideology of mass communications.

Commencement / Beginning

The "beginning" is a rhetorician's notion: How to begin a discourse? For centuries, the problem has been argued. Bataille raises the question of the beginning where it had never been raised: *Where does the human body begin?* The animal begins by the mouth: "the mouth is the beginning, or, if one prefers, the *prow* of animals . . . But man does not have a simple architecture like beasts, and it is not even possible to say where he begins" (from "Mouth," in *Visions of Excess*): This raises the question of the body's meaning (let us not forget that in French—a precious ambiguity—*sens* means both *meaning* and *vectorization*). Let us give three states of this question.

1. In the animal body, only one element is marked, the *beginning*, the mouth (gullet, muzzle, mandibles, organ of predation); being the only notable (noted) one, *this element cannot be a term* (a *relatum*): thus, there is no paradigm, and consequently no meaning. The animal is in a sense provided with a mythological beginning: there is, one might say, ontogenesis starting from a being, the being of manducation.

2. When the human body is the subject of psychoanalytic discourse, there is semanticization ("meaning"), because there is paradigm, opposition of two "terms": mouth, anus. These two permit two trajectories, two "narratives"; on the one hand, the trajectory of food, which proceeds from succulence to excrement: meaning here is born of a temporality, that of alimentary transformation (food serves as an external reference); on the other, the trajectory of libidinal genesis; a syntagmatic extension is superimposed on the (semantic) opposition of oral and anal: the anal stage follows the oral stage; it is then a different history which gives its meaning to the human body, a phylogenetic history: as species, anthropological reality, the body acquires a meaning by developing.

3. Bataille does not exclude psychoanalysis, but it is not his reference; a text on the foot, like the one we are considering, would naturally require a vast reference to fetishism. Yet here there is merely a swift allusion to "classical fetishism." For Bataille, the body begins nowhere, it is the space of *anywhere*; a meaning cannot be recognized in it except at the price of a violent operation: *subjective-collective*; meaning appears thanks

to the intrusion of a *value*: *noble* and *ignoble* (top and bottom, hand and foot).

Déjouer / Baffling

Bataille's text teaches us how to deal with knowledge. We need not reject it. We must even, occasionally, pretend to place it in the forefront. It did not at all trouble Bataille that the editorial committee of *Documents* consisted of professors, scholars, librarians. Knowledge must be made to appear where it is not expected. As has been said, this text, which concerns a part of the human body, discreetly but stubbornly avoids psychoanalysis; the (discursive) play of knowledge is capricious, cunning: "high heels" appear on the text's stage, yet Bataille eludes the expected stereotype of the heel-as-phallus; and yet again, by a third turn, Bataille immediately afterwards invokes sexuality, bringing it on stage by a transition ("furthermore") that seems deceptively naïve. Knowledge is fragmented, pluralized, as if the *one* of knowledge were ceaselessly made to divide in two: synthesis is faked, *baffled*; knowledge is there, not destroyed but displaced; its new place is—in Nietzsche's word—that of a *fiction*: meaning precedes and predetermines fact, value precedes and predetermines knowledge. Nietzsche: "No fact exists in itself. What occurs is a set of phenomena selected and grouped by a being who interprets them . . . There is no such thing as a state of fact; on the contrary, a meaning must be introduced before there can be a fact." Knowledge, in short, would be an interpretative fiction. Thus, Bataille assures the baffling of knowledge by a fragmentation of the codes, but more particularly by an outburst of value (*noble* and *ignoble, seductive* and *deflated*). The role of value is not a role of destruction, nor yet of dialectization, nor even of subjectivization, it is perhaps, quite simply, a role of *rest* . . . "it suffices for me to know that truth possesses a great *power*. But it must be able to do *battle*, and it must have an opposition, and from time to time one must *rest* from it in the non-true. Otherwise, truth would become tedious for us, without savor and without strength, and we would become so as well" (Nietzsche). In short, knowledge is retained as power, but it is opposed as tedium; value is not what despises, relativizes, or rejects knowledge, but what keeps it from being tedious, what *rests* us from it; value is not opposed to knowledge according to a polemical perspective but according to a structural meaning; there is an alternation of knowledge and value, *rest* from one in the other, according to a kind of *amorous rhythm.* And here, in short, is what writing is, and singularly the writing of essays (we are speaking of Bataille): the amorous rhythm of science and value: heterology, delight.

Habillé / Dressed

In ancient Chinese cultures, a husband must not see his wife's bare feet: "The Turks of Central Asia consider it immoral to show their bare feet, and even go to bed in stockings." We should extend the little ethnographic dossier constituted by Bataille—add North American petting parties; the custom of certain Arab populations where the women do not undress when making love; the habit—reported by a contemporary author—of certain hustlers who remove every garment except their socks. All of which would lead us to discuss the relation of clothes and erotic conduct; this is not at all the—abundantly documented—problem of striptease; for our society, which regards itself as "erotic," never speaks of the real practices of love, of the body in a state of love: this is what we know least about each other—not, perhaps, by ethical taboo, but by a taboo of futility. In short, we must—and this would not be so banal as it seems—we must rethink *nudity*. As it happens, for us *the nude* is a plastic value, or even erotico-plastic; in other words, *the nude* is always in a position of *figuration* (this is the very example of striptease); closely linked to the ideology of representation, *the nude* is the figure par excellence, the figure of the figure. To rethink *the nude* would therefore mean, on the one hand, to conceive of nudity as a historical, cultural, Occidental (Greek?) concept, and on the other, to transfer it from the *Tableau* of bodies to an order of erotic *practices*. Now, once we begin to glimpse the complicity of *the nude* and representation, we are led to suspect its power of delight [*jouissance*]. The nude is a cultural object (linked perhaps to an order of *pleasure*, but not to that of loss, of delight), and consequently, in conclusion, a moral object: the nude is not perverse.

Idiomatique / Idiomatic

How to make the body talk? We can transfer the codes of knowledge (of that knowledge which deals with the body) into the text; we can also take into account the *doxa*, the opinion of people about the body (what they say about it). There is a third means, to which Bataille systematically resorts (and which is interesting from the viewpoint of contemporary work on the text): this is to articulate the body not on discourse (that of others, that of knowledge, or even my own) but on *language*: to let idiomatic expressions intervene, to explore them, to unfold them, to represent their "letter" (i.e., their significance); *mouth* will lead us to "fire-mouth" (cannibal expression for cannon), "close-mouthed" ("lovely as a strongbox"); *eye* will provoke a complete exploration of all the idioms in which this word occurs; the same for *foot* ("flat-footed," "stupid as a foot," etc.). By this means, the body develops on the level of language: idiomatism and etymologism are the signifier's two great *resources* (proof *a contrario: écrivance,* which is not writing [*écriture*], but its inauthentic form, ordinarily censures the work of what, in language, is both its center and its excess; have you ever seen a metaphor in a sociological study or in an article of *Le Monde*?). Bataille engages in textual work of the same type, of the same productive energy we see in operation, on stage, in Philippe Sollers's *Lois*.

Orteil / Toe

We must recall, before going any further—for here, already, is a wealth of possibilities—the word's lexicography. *Orteil* is the French word for toe, any of them; it derives from *articulus*, little member or limb; i.e., *das Kleines,* the little thing, the infantile phallus. In the expression *le gros orteil* (the big toe), the significance is reinforced: on the one hand, *gros* is repulsive in a way that *grand* is not; and on the other, the diminutive (*articulus*) can also be repulsive (dwarfism is disconcerting): the toe is seductive-repulsive; fascinating as a contradiction: that of the tumescent and miniaturized phallus.

Paradigme / Paradigm

We have spoken of *value*. This word has been taken in a Nietzschean sense; value is the fatality of an intractable paradigm: *noble / base.* Now, in Bataille, value—which rules the entire discourse—rests on a special paradigm, one that is anomic because ternary. There are, so to speak, three poles: *noble / ignoble / low*. Let us give the terminological coinage of these three terms (the examples are taken from our text and from "The Notion of Expenditure").

1. "*Noble*" pole: "large and free social forms; generous, orgiastic, excessive; excessive light, growing splendor; generosity; nobility."

2. "*Ignoble*" pole: "disease, exhaustion. Shame. Petty hypocrisy. Darkness. Shameful eructations. Timorous manner. Depressing conventions filled with tedium. Degrading. Tiresome bitterness. Grimaces. Rotten society. Petty bragging. A grim businessman and his ancient wife, even grimmer. Inadmissible favors. Lethargy and low idiocy. Pure and superficial."

3. "*Low*" pole: "Spittle. Mud. Blood streaming. Fury. Terrors and obsessions. The violent discord of the organs. Proud and boastful. Hideously cadaverous. The bellowing waves of the viscera."

Bataille's heterology consists in this: there is a contradiction, a simple, canonical paradigm between the first two terms: *noble* and *ignoble* ("the fundamental division of the classes of men into noble and ignoble"); *but* the third term is not regular: *low* is not the neutral term (neither noble nor ignoble), nor is it the mixed term (noble and ignoble). It is an independent term, concrete, eccentric, irreducible: the term of seduction *outside the* (structural) *law.*

The *low* in fact is a value on two accounts: on the one hand, it is what is outside the mimicry of authority;* on the other, it is caught up in the paradigm *high / low,* i.e., in the simulation of a meaning, of a form, and hence it baffles the nature of matter *in itself*: ". . . contemporary materialism, by which I mean a materialism not implying that matter is the thing in itself." In short, the true paradigm is one which confronts two positive values (*noble / low*) in the very field of materialism; and it is the normally contradictory term (*ignoble*) which becomes neutral, mediocre (the negative value, whose negation is not contrariety but deflation). Nietzsche once again: "What is it that is mediocre in the average man? He does not understand that the *wrong side of things* is necessary." In other words, once again: meaning's apparatus is not destroyed (prattle is avoided), but it is made *eccentric,* it is made insecure, wobbly (the etymological meaning of "scandalous"). This process is assured by two operations: on the one hand, the subject (of writing) deflects *in extremis* the paradigm: *modesty,* for example, is not denied in favor of its anticipated statutory and structural contrary (*exhibitionism*); a third term appears: *Laughter,* which baffles Modesty, the *meaning* of Modesty; and on the other hand, language itself is audaciously

* "For above all one must not submit oneself and one's reason to anything higher, to anything which might give my being, and to the reason which arms that being, a borrowed authority. My being and its reason can only submit, in fact, to what is *lower,* to what in any case cannot serve to ape a conventional authority. Low matter is external and alien to ideal human aspirations and refuses to allow itself to be reduced to the great ontological machinery resulting from these aspirations."—*Documents*

distended: *low* [*bas*] is used as a positive, approbative value ("the low materialism of gnosis"), but its correlative adverb, which according to language should have the same value as the original adjective, is employed negatively, disparagingly ("the *basely* idealistic orientation of Surrealism"): it is the theme of deflation which separates—like a violent, severing value—the root word and its derivative.

Quoi et qui? / What and who?

Knowledge says of each thing: "What is it?" What is the big toe? What is this text? Who is Bataille? But value, according to the Nietzschean watchword, prolongs the question: *What is it for me?*

In a Nietzschean way, Bataille's text answers the question: *What is the big toe for me, Bataille?* And by displacement: What is this text, *for me, the reader*? (Answer: It is the text I would want to write.)

Hence it is necessary—and perhaps urgent—to come out in favor of a certain subjectivity: the subjectivity of the non-subject, opposed both to the subjectivity of the subject (impressionism) and to the non-subjectivity of the subject (objectivism). We can conceive such revision in two forms: first of all, to come out in favor of the *for-me* which is in every "What is it?", to demand and to protect the intrusion of value in the discourse of knowledge. Second, to attack the *who*, the subject of interpretation; here again, Nietzsche: "We have no right to ask *who* is interpreting. It is interpretation itself, a form of the will to power, which exists (not as a 'being,' but as a process, a becoming) as a passion . . ." "No subject but an activity, a creative invention, neither 'causes' nor 'effects.' "

Vocables / Vocables

Value appears in certain words, certain terms, certain *vocables* ("vocable" is good, for it means both: appellation and patronage of a Saint: as it happens, we are concerned with *numen-words,* with sign-words, with judgment-words). These vocables erupt in the discourse of knowledge: the vocable is that mark which discriminates writing [*écriture*] from its inauthentic version [*écrivance*] (as in an expression like "the most revolting filth," which no "scientific" discourse would tolerate). Doubtless, we ought to have—and someday shall have—a theory of value-words (of vocables). We may note, meanwhile: vocables are sensuous, subtle, amorous words, denoting seductions or repulsions; another morpheme of value is sometimes italics or quotation marks; quotation marks serve to frame the code (to denaturalize, to demystify the word); italics, on the contrary, are the trace of the subjective pressure imposed upon the word, of an insistence which substitutes for its semantic consistency (italicized words are very frequent in Nietzsche). Bataille himself seems to have had a theoretic consciousness of this opposition between knowledge words and value words (names and vocables). But in his discussion there is a terminological crisscross: "word" is the element of philosophical analysis, of ontological system, "denoting properties which permit an external action," while "aspect" (our "vocable") is what "introduces the decisive values of things," derives "from the decisive moments of nature."

Thus, there is in the text (by Bataille and according to Bataille) a whole fabric of value (by vocables, "graphisms"), an entire "verbal display". Linguistically, these vocables are what? (Of course, linguistics does not know and does not wish to know; linguistics is adiaphorous, indifferent.) I merely indicate some hypotheses:

1. Contrary to a whole modernistic prejudice which attends only to syntax, as if language could emancipate itself (enter the avant-garde) only on this level, we must acknowledge a certain "erratism" of words: some behave, in the sentence, like erratic stones; the role of the word (in writing) can be to interrupt the sentence by its brilliance, by its difference, its fissuring, separating power, by its fetish-situation. "Style" is more palpable than is supposed.

2. Bataille used to say: "A dictionary begins once it gives, not

the meaning, but the *tasks* of words." This is a very linguistic notion (Bloomfield, Wittgenstein); but *task* goes further (moreover, it is a value-word); we shift from the word's *use*, its utilization (functional notions), to its work, to its delight [*jouissance*]: how the word "rummages" in the inter-text, in connotation, acts by working on itself, in short, the word's task is the word's Nietzschean *for-me.*

3. The fabric of value-words constitutes a terminological apparatus, rather as one says "apparatus of power": the word has a molesting force; the word belongs to a war of idioms.

4. Why not (someday) conceive of a "linguistics" of value—no longer in the Saussurian meaning (*valid-for,* element of a system of exchange), but in the quasi-moral, martial, or even erotic meaning? Value-words (vocables) put desire in the text (in the fabric of the speech-act)—and cause it to emerge: desire is not in the text by the words which "represent" it, which recount it, but by words sufficiently characterized, sufficiently brilliant, triumphant, to make themselves loved, in the manner of fetishes.

Colloquium at Cerisy-la-Salle, 1972

Reading Brillat-Savarin

Degrees

Brillat-Savarin (whom we shall henceforth call B.-S.) observes that champagne is stimulating in its initial effects and stupefying in those which follow (I am not so sure of this: for my part, I should say this was more likely to be the case with whiskey). Here we find posited, apropos of a trifle (but taste implies a philosophy of trifles), one of the most important formal categories of modernity: that of the *sequence* of phenomena. What we have is a form of time, less well known than rhythm, but present in so many human productions that we might even risk a neologism to designate it: let us call this "sequential" disposition of champagne a *bathmology*. A Bathmology is the field of discourses subject to the action of *degrees*. Certain idioms, certain languages are like champagne: they develop a meaning subsequent to their first reception, and it is in this withdrawal of meaning that literature is born. The sequence of champagne's effects is crude, entirely physiological, leading from stimulation to lethargy; but it is certainly this same principle of (refined) displacement which controls the quality of *taste*: taste is that very meaning which knows and practices certain multiple and successive apprehensions: entrances, returns, overlappings, a whole counterpoint to sensation: to *perspective* in vision (in the great panoramic pleasures) corresponds *sequence* in taste. B.-S. thus decomposes *in time* (for he does not undertake a simple analysis) the gustative sensation: (1) *direct* (when flavor still affects the front part of the tongue); (2) *complete* (when flavor shifts to the rear of the mouth); (3) *reflected* (at the final moment of judgment). The entire *luxury* of taste is in this sequence; the submission of the gustative sensation to time actually permits it to develop somewhat in the manner of a narrative, or of a language: temporalized, taste knows surprises and subtleties; these are the perfumes and fragrances, constituted in advance, so to speak, like memories: nothing would have kept Proust's madeleine from being analyzed by B.-S.

Need / desire

If B.-S. had written his book today, he would surely have included among the perversions this taste (specifically, of food) which he defended and illustrated. Perversion is, one might say, the exercise of a desire which serves no purpose, like the exercise of the body which gives itself up to love with no intention of procreation. Now, in the schema of food, B.-S. always marked the distinction between need and desire: "The pleasure of eating requires, if not hunger, at least appetite; the pleasure of the table is generally independent of both." At a period when the bourgeoisie knew no social culpability, B.-S. sets up a cynical opposition: on one side, *natural appetite*, which is of the order of need; and on the other, *appetite for luxury*, which is of the order of desire. Everything is here, of course: the species *needs* to procreate in order to survive, the individual *needs* to eat in order to subsist; yet the satisfaction of these two needs does not suffice man: he must bring on stage, so to speak, the *luxury* of desire, erotic or gastronomic: an enigmatic, useless supplement, the desired food—the kind that B.-S. describes—is an unconditional waste or loss, a kind of ethnographic ceremony by which man celebrates his power, his freedom to consume his energy "for nothing." In this sense, B.-S.'s book is altogether the book of the "strictly human," for it is desire (insofar as it is spoken) which distinguishes man. This anthropological basis gives a paradoxical cachet to *The Physiology of Taste*: for what is expressed through the turns of style, the worldly tone of the anecdotes, and the graceful futility of the descriptions is the great adventure of desire. The question, however, remains unbroached as to why the social subject (at least in our societies) must assume *sexual* perversion in a crude, fierce, "criminal" style, as the purest of transgressions, while *gastronomic* perversion, as described by B.-S. (and on the whole it could hardly be described better), always implies a kind of affable and accommodating acknowledgment which never departs from the tone of *good breeding*.

The gastronome's body

Food provokes an *internal* pleasure, interior to the body, enclosed within it, not even beneath the skin, but in that deep, central zone, all the more original for being soft, confused, permeable, which is called, in the most general sense, the bowels; although taste is one of man's five acknowledged, classified senses, and although this sense is localized (on the tongue and, as B.-S. describes so well, in the whole mouth), gustative delight is diffuse, extensive to the entire secret lining of the mucous membranes; it derives from what we should probably consider our sixth sense—if B.-S., precisely, did not reserve that place for the genetic sense—and which is *cenesthesia*, the total sensation of our internal body. B.-S., of course, acknowledges this diffuse arrangement of the pleasure of food as the sense of *well-being* which follows good meals; but, oddly enough, he does not analyze, he does not scrutinize, he does not "poeticize" this internal sensation; when he wants to grasp the voluptuous effects of food, he will seek them out on the adverse body; these effects are in a sense signs, received during an interlocution: the other's pleasure is deciphered; sometimes, indeed, if a woman is involved, it is spied on, it is *surprised* as if we were dealing with a minor erotic rape; conviviality, the pleasure of dining together, is thus a less innocent value than it appears; in the "staging" of a good meal there is more than the exercise of a worldly code, even if that code has a venerable historical origin; around the table prowls a vague scopic pulsion: we observe in the Other the effects of food, we grasp how the body works on itself from within; like those sadists who delight in the signs of emotion on their partner's face, we observe the changes in the body which is dining well. The index of this pleasure is, according to B.-S., a very specific thematic quality: *shininess*, the physiognomy brightens, coloring is heightened, the eyes gleam, while the mind is refreshed and a gentle warmth penetrates the entire body. Shininess is evidently an erotic attribute: it refers to the state of a substance which is at once ignited and moistened, desire giving the body its sparkle, ecstasy its radiance (the word is B.-S.'s), and pleasure its lubrification. The gourmand's body is thus seen as a glowing painting, illuminated from *within*. This sublimity nonetheless includes a subtle texture of triviality; we perceive this unexpected supplement in the scene of the *belle gourmande*: she has shining eyes, glistening lips, and she bites her partridge wing; for all the affable hedonism, which is the usual genre of descriptions of conviviality, we must read another index in such shininess: that of carnivorous aggression, exemplified here, paradoxically, by woman; woman does not devour food, she bites, and this bite radiates; perhaps, in this rather brutal illumination, we may perceive an anthropological notion: in spasms, desire reverts to its origins and turns back into need, *gourmandise* into appetite (transferred to the erotic order, this reversal would lead humanity back to the simple practice of coupling). The strange thing is that, in the excessively civilized range of gastronomic customs which B.-S. continually provides, the strident note of Nature is sounded by woman. We know that in the vast mythology men have elaborated around the feminine ideal, food is systematically neglected; we commonly see woman in a state of love or of innocence; we never see her eating: hers is a glorious body, purified of any need. Mythologically, food is men's business; woman takes part in it only as a cook or as a servant; she is the one who prepares or serves but does not eat. With a light touch, B.-S. subverts two taboos: that of a woman pure of any digestive activity and that of a gastronomy of pure repletion: he puts food in Woman, and in Woman appetite (the appetites).

The anti-drug

Baudelaire rebuked B.-S. for not speaking well of wine. For Baudelaire, wine is memory and forgetting, joy and melancholy; it is what permits the subject to be transported outside himself, to make his ego's consistency yield to certain alienated states; it is a path of deviance; in short, a drug.

Now, for B.-S., wine is not at all a conductor of ecstasy. The reason for which is clear: wine is part of food, and food, for B.-S., is essentially convivial; wine cannot therefore proceed from a solitary protocol: one drinks at the same time one eats, and one always eats with others; a narrow sociality governs the pleasures of food; of course, dope smokers can gather in groups, like the guests at a fine table; but in principle this is so that each can withdraw into his own singular dream; now, this gap is forbidden to the gastronome, for in eating he submits to a rigorous communal practice: conversation. Conversation (among several people) is in a sense the law which protects culinary pleasure from any psychotic risk and maintains the gourmand in a "healthy" rationality: talking—chatting about one thing and another—while he eats, the guest confirms his ego and protects himself against any subjective leakage, by the image-repertoire of discourse. Wine, for B.-S., has no special privilege: like food, and with it, wine slightly amplifies the body (renders it "brilliant") but does not mute it. It is an anti-drug.

Cosmogonies

Bearing on transformable substances, culinary practice quite naturally leads the writer who speaks of it to deal with a general thematics of matter. Just as ancient philosophies attributed great importance to the fundamental states of matter (water, fire, air, earth) and from these states derived various generic attributes (the aerial, the liquid, the ardent, etc.) which could pass into all forms of discourse, beginning with poetic discourse, in the same way food, by the treatment of its substances, assumes a cosmogonic dimension. The *true* state of food, the one which determines the *human* future of nutriment, B.-S. believes, is the liquid: taste results from a chemical operation which always occurs by means of moisture, and "there is nothing sapid but that which is already dissolved or imminently soluble." Food, quite naturally, here joins the great maternal and thalassal theme: water *fosters*; fundamentally, food is an interior bath, and this bath—a detail on which B.-S. insists—is not only vital, it is also euphoric, paradisal; for on it depends taste, i.e., the felicity of eating.

Liquidity is the anterior or posterior state of the ailment, its total history, and thus its truth. But in its solid state, dry, alimentary substance knows differences of value. Take coffee beans: you can grind them in a mortar or mill them. B.-S. greatly prefers the first method of reduction, which he attributes to the Turks (does one not pay a good price for the wooden mortar and pestle which have long served to triturate the beans?). Of the superiority of the one operation over the other, B.-S., playing the scientist, gives experimental and theoretical proofs. But it is not difficult to divine the "poetics" of this difference: the *milled* derives from a mechanism; the hand is applied to the mill as a force, and not as an art (as is proved by the fact that the hand mill has quite naturally been converted into an electric mill); what the mill thus produces—abstractly, one might say—is a coffee *dust*, a dry and depersonalized substance; on the contrary, the *pounded* results from a set of bodily gestures (to press, to turn in various ways), and these gestures are directly transmitted by the noblest, the most human of substances, wood; what comes out of the mortar is no longer mere dust, but a *powder*, a substance whose alchemical vocation (attested to by a whole mythology) is to ally itself with water in order to produce magic brews: the coffee powder is, so to speak, irrigable, therefore closer to the major state of alimentary substance, which is *the liquid*. In this little conflict which opposes the pounded to the milled, we can therefore read a reflection of the great myth operative today, more than ever, among a technological humanity: the excellence of the tool (as opposed to the machine), the preeminence of the artisanal over the industrial, in a word the nostalgia for the Natural.

The search for essence

Scientifically, by the end of the eighteenth century, the mechanism of digestion is more or less understood: it is known how the most varied and heteroclite roster of foodstuffs (all those which humanity, since the origins of life, has been able to discover and ingest) produces one and the same vital substance, by which man survives. With a slight historical delay, starting in 1825, chemistry discovers the elements. All of B.-S.'s culinary ideology is armed with a notion at once medical, chemical, and metaphysical: that of a simple essence, the nutritive (or gustative—since, for B.-S., there is in fact no food until it is *tasted*) *ichor*. The completed state of nutriment is thus the juice—the liquid and rarified essence of a piece of food. The reduction to essence, or quintessence, the old alchemist's dream, greatly impresses B.-S.: he delights in it as in an astonishing spectacle; the Prince de Soubise's cook, like a magician out of the Arabian Nights, actually conceived enclosing fifty hams in a crystal flask no larger than one's thumb! Miraculous equations: the ham's Being is in its juice, and this juice itself can be reduced to an essence—of which only crystal is worthy. The alimentary essence, thus projected, assumes a divine aura, as is proved by the fact that, like the Promethean fire, outside of human laws, it can be stolen: an Englishman having ordered a leg of lamb at an inn, B.-S. steals its juice (for an egg dish); he incises the meat turning on its spit and makes away with its quintessence by theft (adding, moreover, a touch of Anglophobia).

Ethics

It has been possible to reveal the physical nature of erotic pleasure (tension / release), but gustative pleasure escapes any such reduction, and consequently any science (as is proved by the heteroclite nature of tastes—and disgusts—down through history and around the world). B.-S. speaks as a scholar, and his book is a physiology; but his science (does he know this?) is merely an irony of science. All gustative delight inheres in the opposition of two values: the *agreeable* and the *disagreeable*, and these values are quite simply tautological: the *agreeable* is what agrees and the *disagreeable* what disagrees. B.-S. can go no further: taste comes from an "appreciative power," just as, in Molière, sleep comes from a dormitive virtue. The science of taste thus reverts to being an ethic (this is the habitual fate of science). B.-S. immediately associates his physiology (what else can he do, if he wants to continue his discourse?) with certain moral qualities. There are two principles here. The first is statutory, castrating: it is *exactitude* ("of all the virtues of a cook, the most indispensable is exactitude"); here we encounter the classical rule: no art without constraint, no pleasure without order; the second is well known to the ethics of Transgression: it is *discernment*, which permits the separation of Good from Evil; there is a casuistry of taste: taste must always be alert, must train itself to be subtle, to be scrupulous; B.-S. respectfully cites the gourmands of Rome who could distinguish the taste of fish caught between the various bridges of the City from those taken from the Tiber downstream; or those hunters who manage to perceive the special flavor of the leg on which the partridge has rested in its sleep.

Language

Cadmus, who brought writing to Greece, had been the King of Sidon's cook. Let us take this mythological feature as apologue to the relation which unites language and gastronomy. Do not these two powers employ the same organ? And more broadly, the same apparatus, productive or appreciative: the cheeks, the palate, and nostrils, whose gustative role B.-S. remarks and which are responsible for fine singing? To eat, to speak, to sing (need we add: to kiss?) are operations which have the same site of the body for origin: cut off the tongue, and there will be neither taste nor speech.

Plato had compared (it is true, invidiously) rhetoric and cooking. B.-S. does not explicitly invoke this precedent: for him, there is no philosophy of language. Since the symbolic is not his strong point, it is in certain empirical remarks that we must seek this gastronome's interest in language, or, more exactly, in tongues. This interest is very great. B.-S., as he reminds us, knows five languages; thus, he possesses an enormous repertoire of words from every source, which he takes for his own use, in different compartments of his mind, quite shamelessly. In this, B.-S. is very modern: he is convinced that the French language is poor, and that it is therefore licit to borrow or steal words elsewhere; in the same way, he appreciates the charm of marginal languages, such as the language of "the people"; he transcribes and quotes with pleasure the patois of his region, the Bugey. Finally, each time he has occasion to do so, however remote from his own gastrosophic discourse, he notes this or that linguistic curiosity: "to make arms" means: to play the piano with exaggerated elbow movements, as if one were smothered by feeling; "to make eyes" means: to look up to heaven as if one were about to swoon; "to make brioches" (a metaphor which must have pleased him) means: to miss a note, an intonation. His attention to language is meticulous, as the cook's art must be.

Yet we must go further than these contingent proofs of interest. B.-S. is certainly linked to language—as he was to food—by an amorous relation: he desires words, in their very materiality. He comes up with an astonishing classification of the tongue's movements as it participates in manducation: there are, among other oddly learned words, *spication* (when the tongue takes the shape of a stalk of wheat) and *verrition* (when it sweeps). A twofold delight? B.-S. becomes a linguist, he deals with food the way a phonetician would (and subsequently will) deal with vocality, and he sustains this learned discourse in a radically—might one say insolently—neological style. Neologisms (or very rare words) abound in B.-S.; he employs them without restraint, and each of these unexpected words (*irrorator, garrulity, esculent, gulturation, comessation*, etc.) is the trace of a profound pleasure which refers to the tongue's desire: B.-S. desires the word as he desires truffles, a tuna omelette, a fish stew; like any neologist, he has a fetishistic relation to the individual word, haloed by its very singularity. And since these fetishized words are utilized within a very pure syntax, which restores to neological pleasure the framework of a classical art, consisting of constraints, of protocols, we can say that B.-S.'s language is literally *gourmand*: greedy for the words it wields and for the dishes to which it refers; a fusion or ambiguity to which B.-S. himself points when he sympathetically alludes to those gourmands whose passion and proficiency are identifiable merely by the way they pronounce the word "*bon*."

We know how insistent modernity has become in revealing the sexuality concealed in the exercise of language: to speak under certain constraints or certain alibis (including that of pure "communication") is an erotic act; a new concept has permitted this extension of the sexual to the verbal: the concept of *orality*. B.-S. here furnishes what his brother-in-law Fourier would have called a *transition*: that of taste, oral as language, libidinal as Eros.

Death

And Death? How does it come into the discourse of an author whose subject and style designate him as the very model of the "*bon vivant*"? As one might suspect: in an entirely trivial fashion. Beginning with the household fact that sugar enables certain foods to be preserved, B.-S. wonders why sugar is not used in the embalmer's art: *cadavre exquis*, preserved, candied, bottled! (Preposterous speculation, reminiscent of Fourier.)

(Whereas love's delight is ceaselessly associated—by how many mythologies—with death, nothing of the kind is instanced with the delight of food; metaphysically—or anthropologically—it is a matte delight.)

Obesity

A weekly paper entices its readers: a doctor has just discovered the secret of losing weight, in any part of the body, at will. This announcement would have interested B.-S., who describes himself, good-humoredly enough, as afflicted with a truncal obesity "confined to the belly" and which does not exist in women; this is what B.-S. calls *gastrophoria*; those who suffer from it are gastrophores (they seem, in effect, to bear their stomachs before them): "I am of their number," B.-S. says, "but though the bearer of a somewhat protuberant belly, my thighs are still slender, and my member as ready as an Arab steed's."

We know the vast success of this theme in our mass culture: not a week passes when there is not some article in the press about the necessity and the means of reducing. This passion for slenderness dates back, probably, to the end of the eighteenth century; under the influence of Rousseau and the Swiss physicians Tronchin and Tissot, a new notion of hygiene is formed: its principle is *reduction* (and no longer repletion); abstinence replaces the ubiquitous bleeding; the ideal diet consists of milk, fruit, cold water. When B.-S. devotes a chapter of his book to obesity and the means of combating it, he is therefore following the lead of this mythological History whose importance we are beginning to realize. Nonetheless, as a gastronome, B.-S. cannot emphasize the naturalistic aspect of the myth: how could he defend at the same time a rural nature (milk and fruit) and the culinary art which produces truffled quail and pyramids of vanilla meringue? The philosophic alibi—of Rousseauistic origin—yields to a strictly aesthetic reason: of course, we are not yet at the historical moment (our own) when it is *self-evident* that being thin is preferable to being stout (a proposition whose relativity is attested by history and ethnology as well); the aesthetic of the body evoked by B.-S. is not directly erotic; it is pictorial: obesity's main misdeed is to "fill cavities which nature had intended to produce shadows," and to "render virtually insignificant certain highly attractive physiognomies": the model of the body is, in short, the genre drawing, and dietetics a sort of *art plastique*.

What is B.-S.'s notion of a reducing diet? Virtually our own. He is quite familiar, in all essentials, with the differences in caloric status of various foods; he knows that fish, and above all shellfish, oysters, are not at all caloric, and that starchy and farinacious foods are very much so; he advises against soup, sweet pastry, beer; he recommends green vegetables, veal, chicken (but also chocolate!); he advises regular weighing, eating small amounts, sleeping little, taking a good deal of exercise, and in passing corrects certain prejudices (such as the one which led a young girl to her death because she believed that by drinking a great deal of vinegar she would become slender); add to this an anti-obesic belt and quinine water.

B.-S.'s participation in the myth of reducing that is so powerful today is not inconsiderable; he sketched out a very modern synthesis of dietetics and gastronomy, postulating that the prestige of a complicated art could be preserved for cookery, while at the same time conceiving it according to a more functional view; this synthesis is somewhat specious, for the reducing diet remains a true ascesis (and it is at this psychological price that it succeeds); at least a literature has been founded: that of cookbooks elaborated according to a certain *rationale* of the body.

Osmazome

We know that in the Middle Ages culinary technique required boiling meat (which was of poor quality) before frying it. This technique would have disgusted B.-S.; first of all, because he has, one might say, a high opinion of frying, whose secret—and therefore whose thematic meaning—is to surprise (by intense heat) the aliment submitted to it: what we enjoy in the crispness of fried food is, in a sense, the rape to which substance has been subjected; second, and especially, because B.-S. condemns boiling (but not bouillon): boiled meat loses (according to the period's chemistry) a precious substance (precious for its sapidity), naturally attached to red meat. This substance is *osmazome.*

Faithful to his philosophy of essences, B.-S. attributes to osmazome a kind of spiritual power; it is the very absolute of taste: a sort of alcohol of meat; like a universal (demoniac?) principle, it assumes various and seductive appearances; it is osmazome which produces the roux of meats, the "browning" of roasts, the bouquet of venison; above all, it is osmazome which makes juice and bouillon, direct forms of quintessence (the word's etymology refers to the combined notion of odor and bouillon).

Chemically, osmazome is a meat principle; but the symbolic realm does not respect chemical identity; by metonymy, osmazome lends its value to everything that is browned, caramelized, grilled: to coffee, for instance. B.-S.'s chemistry (however dated) allows us to understand the present vogue of grilled food: aside from the functionalist alibi (rapid preparation), there is a philosophical reason for the popularity of grilled food, which unites two mythic principles, that of fire and that of rawness, both transcended in the figure of the *grilled,* solid form of the vital juice.

Pleasure

Here is what B.-S. writes about pleasure: "It was only a few months ago that I experienced, while sleeping, an altogether extraordinary sensation of pleasure. It consisted in a kind of delicious thrill of every particle composing my being. It was a kind of magical tingling which, from the soles of my feet to the top of my head, racked me to the marrow of my bones. I seemed to see a violet flame that played around my forehead."

This lyrical description accounts nicely for the ambiguity of the notion of pleasure. Ordinarily, gastronomic pleasure is described by B.-S. as a refined and rational sense of well-being; of course, it gives the body a luster (*shininess*), but it does not depersonalize this body: neither food nor wine has a narcotic power. On the other hand, there is a kind of limit alleged; pleasure is close to toppling over into delight, into ecstasy: it changes the body, which feels itself in a state of electrical dispersion. Doubtless, this excess is laid to the account of dreams; yet it designates something very important: the incommensurable character of pleasure. Henceforth, it is enough to socialize pleasure's unknown quality in order to produce a utopia (here again we meet Fourier). B.-S. puts it very well: "The limits of pleasure are not yet known or posited, nor do we know at what point our body can be beatified." A surprising remark in an old author, whose style of thought is generally Epicurean: it introduces into this philosophy a sentiment of the historical limitlessness of sensation, of an unsuspected plasticity of the human body, which we find only in very marginal philosophies: it postulates a kind of mysticism of pleasure.

Questions

The object alluded to by a sign is called a referent. Each time I speak of food, I emit (linguistic) signs which relate to an aliment or to an alimentary quality. This banal situation has unfamiliar implications when the object alluded to by my speech-act is a desirable one. This is obviously the case with *The Physiology of Taste.* B.-S. speaks and I desire what he speaks about (especially if I am in a state of appetite). The gastronomic statement, because the desire it mobilizes is apparently simple, presents the power of language in all its ambiguity: the sign calls up the pleasures of its referent just when it traces its absence (which we know each word does, ever since Mallarmé said so of the flower, "missing from every bouquet"). Language provokes and excludes. Whereupon the gastronomic style presents us with a whole series of questions: What does it mean to represent? to figure? to project? to say? What is it to desire? What is it to desire and to speak at the same time?

The first hour

Like every hedonist subject, B.-S. seems to have an intense experience of boredom. And as always, boredom, linked to what philosophy and psychoanalysis have denoted as *repetition*, implies, by a contrary means (which is that of the opposition of meaning), the excellence of novelty. Everything deriving from a primary temporality is endowed with a kind of enchantment; the first moment, the first time, the freshness of a dish, of a rite, in short the *beginning*, refers to a kind of pure state of pleasure: where all the determinations of a felicity combine. Thus with the pleasure of the table: "The table," B.-S. says, "is the only place where one is not bored during the first hour." This first hour is marked here by the appearance of new dishes, the discovery of their originality, the élan of conversations, in short, by a word which B.-S. applies to the excellence of the best fried food: *surprise*.

Dreams

Appetite relates to dreaming, for it is both memory and hallucination, which is why, moreover, it might be better to say that it relates to hallucinations. When I have an appetite for food, do I not imagine myself eating it? And, in this predictive imagination, is there not the entire memory of previous pleasures? I am the constituted subject of a scene to come, in which I am the only actor.

B.-S. has reflected on dreams, then, "a life apart, a kind of extended fiction." He has grasped the paradox of dreams, which can be intense pleasure yet exempt from real sensuality: in dreams, neither odor nor taste. Dreams are memories or combinations of memories: "Dreams are only the memory of the senses." Like a language which is elaborated only on the basis of certain signs, isolated vestiges of another language, dreams are a decrepit narrative, consisting of the ruins of memory. B.-S. compares them to a reminiscence of melody, of which one might play only a few notes, without adding harmony to it. The discontinuity of dreams is opposed to sleep's consecution, and this opposition is reflected in the very organization of foodstuffs; some are somniferous: milk, fowl, lettuce, orange blossoms, pippin apples (eaten before going to bed); others produce dreams: dark meats, hare, asparagus, celery, truffles, vanilla; these are strong foods, perfumed or aphrodisiac. B.-S. discerns the dream as a marked, one might almost say a *virile* state.

Science

"Thirst," B.-S. says, "is the internal sentiment of the need to drink." Certainly, the interest of such sentences is not in the formation they provide (here, none at all). By such tautologies, evidently, B.-S. tries his hand at science, or at least at scientific discourse; he produces statements without surprise, which have no other *value* than to present a pure image of the scientific proposition (definition, postulate, axiom, equation): and is there a more rigorous science than the kind which defines the same by the same? Here, no risk of error; B.-S. is protected from that malign power which wrecks science: paradox. His audacity is one of style: to use a learned tone in order to speak of a sense reputed to be trivial (because banally sensual): taste.

Science is the great Superego of *The Physiology of Taste.* The book, it is said, was written in consultation with an official biologist, and B.-S. strews his discourse with scientific solemnities. Thus, he imagines he is submitting the desire for food to experimental measures: "Each time a dish of distinguished and well-known flavor is served, observe the guests closely, and you will note as unworthy all those whose physiognomy does not betray pleasure." By his "gastronomic assays," B.-S., however preposterous the notion, takes into account two very serious and very modern factors: sociality and language; the dishes he presents to his subjects for experiment vary according to the social class (income) of these subjects: a fillet of veal or eggs *à la neige* if one is poor; a fillet of beef or a turbot *au naturel* if one is well-off; truffle, quails, vanilla meringues if one is rich, etc.—which is to imply that taste is modeled by culture, i.e., by social class; and then, a surprising method, in order *to read* gustatory pleasure (since this is the goal of the experiment), B.-S. suggests interrogating, not the (probably universal) gestures and facial expressions of the diners, but their *language*, a socialized object if ever there was one: the expression of assent changes according to the speaker's social class: in front of his eggs *à la neige* the poor man will exclaim "Damnation!", while ortolans *provençale* will wring from the rich man: "My lord, your chef is an admirable man!"

These witticisms, which include several true intuitions, nicely express how B.-S. took science: in a fashion at once serious and ironical; his project of establishing a science of taste, of stripping culinary pleasure of its habitual signs of triviality, was certainly close to his heart; but he performs it rhetorically, i.e., with irony; he is like a writer who puts quotation marks around the truths he utters, not out of scientific prudence, but for fear of appearing naïve (whereby we can see that irony is always timid).

Sex

There are, it is said, five senses. From the first page of his book, B.-S. postulates a sixth: the *genesic*, or physical love. This sense cannot be reduced to touch; it implies a complete apparatus of sensations. "Let us give to the genesic," B.-S. says, "the *sensual* place we cannot deny it, and let us bequeath to our nephews the task of assigning its rank" (we the nephews have evidently not shrunk from the task). It is obviously B.-S.'s intention to suggest a kind of metonymic exchange between the first of delights (even if it is censored) and the sense whose defense and illustration he has undertaken, i.e., taste; from the point of view of sensuality, it signifies taste to put it in the same roster with erotic pleasure. B.-S. insists then, when he can, on the aphrodisiac power of certain foods: truffles, for example, or fish, which provokes his astonishment (a slight anti-clerical irony here) that this should be the food eaten during Lent by monks, dedicated to chastity. Yet try as he will, he can find little analogy between lust and gastronomy; between the two pleasures, a crucial difference: orgasm, i.e., the very rhythm of excitation and its release. Pleasures of the table include neither ravishments nor transports nor ecstasies—nor aggressions; bliss, if there is such a thing here, is not paroxystic: no mounting of pleasure, no culmination, no crisis; nothing but a duration; as if the only critical element of gastronomic joy were its expectation; once satisfaction begins, the body enters into the insignificance of repletion (even if this assumes the demeanor of a gluttonous compunction).

Sociality

Doubtless, a general ethnology could easily show that eating is in all places and at all times a social act. We eat together, that is the universal law. This alimentary sociality can assume many forms, many alibis, many nuances, according to societies, according to periods. For B.-S., the gastronomic collectivity is essentially worldly, and its ritual figure is conversation. The table is in a sense the geometric locus of all the subjects discussed; it is as if alimentary pleasure vivified them, brought them to a kind of rebirth; the celebration of food is laicized in the form of a new kind of gathering (and participation): the *convivium.* Added to the good food, the convivium produces what Fourier (whom we always find close to B.-S.) called a *composite* pleasure. The vigilant hedonism of the two brothers-in-law inspired them with this thought, that pleasure must be *overdetermined,* that it must have several simultaneous causes, among which there is no way of distinguishing which one causes delight; for the composite pleasure does not derive from a simple bookkeeping of excitations: it figures a complex space in which the subject no longer knows where he comes from and what he wants—except to have his voluptuous pleasure—*jouir*. The convivium—so important in B.-S.'s ethic—is therefore not only a sociological fact; it prompts us to consider (as the human sciences have so rarely done hitherto) communication as a delight, a *jouissance*—and no longer as a function.

Social classes

We have seen that, in the game of gastronomic experiments, B.-S. linked difference in tastes to difference in incomes. The originality here is not to recognize classes of money (want, comfort, wealth) but to conceive that taste itself (i.e., culture) is socialized: if there is an affinity between eggs *à la neige* and a modest income, it is not only because this dish costs relatively little to make; it is also, it seems, by reason of a social formation of taste, whose values are established not in the absolute but in a determined field. Hence, it is always by the relay of culture—and not by that of needs—that B.-S. socializes food. So when he turns from incomes to professional classes (to what was called the "states" or "conditions"), establishing that society's great gourmands are chiefly financiers, physicians, men of letters and the Church, what he considers is a certain profile of customs and habits, in short a social psychology: gastronomic taste seems to him linked by privilege either to a positivism of profession (financiers, physicians) or to a special aptitude to displace, to sublimate, or to intimize pleasure (men of letters, of the Church).

In this culinary sociology, modest as it is, the purely social is nonetheless present: precisely where it is missing from discourse. It is in what he does not say (in what he occults) that B.-S. most clearly registers the social condition in all its nakedness: and what is repressed, quite pitilessly, is the food of the people. What did such food chiefly consist of? Bread and, in the country, gruels, the cook using for these a grain she pounded herself in a mortar and pestle, which spared her having to submit to the monopoly of mills and communal ovens; no sugar, but honey.

The essential food of the poor was potatoes; these were sold, boiled or roasted, in the street (as they are still in Morocco), as chestnuts are today; long despised by people "of a certain rank," who relegated them to "animals and the very poor," potatoes owe nothing of their social elevation to Parmentier, an army physician whose main interest was in substituting starch for flour in making bread. In B.-S.'s own time, potatoes, while beginning their redemption, remain marked by the discredit attached, socially, to anything "boiled." Consider the menus of the period: nothing but discreet, separated dishes: the combined and the thickened are found only in sauces.

Topic

B.-S. has understood that, as a subject of discourse, food was a sort of grid (a *topic*, the old rhetoric would have said), through which he could successfully introduce all the sciences we nowadays call social and human. His book tends toward the encyclopedic, however summarily. In other words, its discourse is likely to treat food under several pertinences; in short, it is a total social phenomenon, around which can be convoked various meta-languages: those of physiology, of chemistry, of geography, of history, of economy, of sociology, and of politics. It is this encyclopedism—this "humanism"—which, for B.-S., is suggested by the name *gastronomy*: "Gastronomy is the knowledge of all that relates to man, insofar as he subsists on food." This "scientific" opening nicely corresponds to what B.-S. was in his own life; essentially, a polymorphous subject: jurist, diplomat, musician, man of fashion, he was quite familiar with both foreign parts and the provinces, so food was not an obsession for him but rather a kind of universal operator of discourse.

Perhaps, to conclude, we should glance at some dates. B.-S. lived from 1755 to 1826. He was (for instance) a contemporary of Goethe (1742–1832). Goethe and Brillat-Savarin: these two names, set side by side, constitute a riddle. Of course, Werther was not above ordering peas cooked in butter in his Wahlheim retreat; but do we see him interested in the aphrodisiac virtues of truffles and in the flashes of desire which cross the countenance of *les belles gourmandes*? This is because the nineteenth century is setting out on its twofold journey, positivist and romantic (and perhaps *this* because of *that*). Around 1825, the year *The Physiology of Taste* was published, begins a double postulation of History, or at the very least of Ideology, from which it is not certain that we have emerged: on the one hand, a kind of rehabilitation of earthly joys, a sensualism linked to the "progressive" meaning of History; and on the other, a grandiose explosion of the *mal de vivre,* linked to an entire new culture of the symbol. Western humanity thereby establishes a double repertoire of its conquests, of its values: on one side, chemical discoveries (responsible for the development of industry and for a social transformation); and on the other, a very great symbolic adventure: 1825, B.-S.'s year, is also the year Schubert composes his quartet *Death and the Maiden.* B.-S., who teaches us the concomitance of sensual pleasures, also represents for us, indirectly, as a good witness should, the importance—still undervalued—of *composite* cultures and histories.

Preface to Brillat-Savarin's *Physiologie du goût* (C. Hermann), 1975

An Idea of Research

In the little Balbec train, a solitary lady is reading the *Revue des deux mondes;* she is ugly and vulgar; the Narrator takes her for the madam of a brothel; but on his next journey the little clan, having invaded the train, informs the Narrator that his lady is Princess Sherbatoff, a woman of high birth, the pearl of the Verdurin salon.

This pattern, which conjoins two absolutely antipathetic states in one and the same object and radically reverses an appearance into its contrary, is frequent in Proust's novel. Here are a few examples, noted while reading the first volumes: 1. Of the two Guermantes cousins, the more affable is in reality the more disdainful (the duke); the colder, the more sincere (the prince). 2. Odette Swann, a superior woman in the judgment of her circle, is regarded as stupid by the Verdurin clan. 3. Norpois, pontificating to the point of intimidating the Narrator's parents and of persuading them that their son has no talent, is utterly destroyed by Bergotte's single phrase ("But he's an old fool"). 4. The same Norpois, a monarchist aristocrat, is entrusted with extraordinary diplomatic missions by radical cabinets "which even a reactionary bourgeois would have refused to serve and whose suspicions should have been aroused by Monsieur de Norpois's past, his connections, and his opinions." 5. Swann and Odette pamper the Narrator; yet there was a time when Swann did not even deign to answer Marcel's "persuasive and detailed" letter; the concierge in the Swanns' apartment building is transformed into a benevolent Eumenid. 6. Monsieur Verdurin speaks of Cottard in two ways: if he believes the professor is little known to his interlocutor, he glorifes him, but follows the converse procedure and speaks of Cottard's medical genius quite simply if Cottard is recognized. 7. Having just read in a great scholar's book that perspiration is harmful to the kidneys, the Narrator encounters Dr. E., who informs him: "The advantage of these hot days we're having, when one perspires so abundantly, is that the kidney is greatly relieved." And so forth.

These notations are so frequent, they are applied so consistently to such different objects, situations, and languages, that we may identify in them a form of discourse whose very obsessiveness is enigmatic. Let us call this form, at least provisionally, *inversion*, and let us anticipate (without presently being able to do so) inventorying its occurrences, analyzing its modes of expression, the devices which constitute it, and situating the considerable extensions it seems capable of at very different levels in Proust's work. This would propose "an idea of research"—though without allowing us to entertain any positivist ambition: Proust's novel is one of those great cosmogonies endemic to the nineteenth century (Balzac, Wagner, Dickens, Zola), whose character, at once statutory and historical, is that they are infinitely explorable spaces (galaxies); thereby, our critical work is shifted (from any illusion of "result") toward the simple production of a supplemental writing whose tutelary text (Proust's novel), if we write up our "research," would be only a pre-text.

Here, then, are two identities of one and the same body: on one side, the madam of a brothel; and, on the other, Princess Sherbatoff, lady-in-waiting to the Grand Duchess Eudoxia. We may be tempted to see this figure as the banal interplay of appearance and reality: the Russian princess, ornament of the Verdurin salon, *is only* a woman of the coarsest vulgarity. Such an interpretation is strictly *moralistic* (the "*is only*" syntactic form is constantly used by La Rochefoucauld, for instance); we would thereby recognize (as has occasionally been the case) the Proustian oeuvre as an alethic project, an energy of decipherment, a search for essences, whose first effort is to rid human truth of the contrary appearances which superimpose upon it vanity, worldliness, snobbery. Yet, by reading the Proustian inversion as a simple reduction, we sacrifice the efflorescences of form and risk distorting the text. There are three such efflorescences (truth of the discourse and not truth of the project): 1. *Temporality*, or more exactly, an effect of time; the two terms of the contradiction are separated by a period of time, an adventure: it is not, literally, the *same* Narrator who reads the madam of the brothel and the great Russian lady: two trains separate them. 2. *Climax*: the inversion is effected according to an exact figure, as if a god—a *fatum*—were maliciously presiding over the trajectory which leads the princess to coincide with her geometrically determined absolute contrary; like one of those riddles Proust was so fond of: What is a madam's apotheosis? To be a lady-in-waiting to the Grand Duchess Eudoxia—or vice versa. 3. *Surprise*: the reversal of appearances—let us no longer say of appearance into reality—always affords the Narrator a delicious astonishment: essence of surprise—to which we shall return—and not essence of truth, veritable jubilation, so complete, so pure, so triumphant (as is proved by the success of its expression), that this mode of inversion can only derive from an erotics (of discourse), as if its occasion was the very moment in which Proust took his delight in writing: studded all through the great continuum of the search, inversion is the *supplement-bliss* of narrative, of language.

Pleasure once found, the subject knows no rest until he can repeat it. Inversion—as *form*—invades the entire structure of *La Recherche.* It inaugurates the narrative itself: the first scene—from which will emerge, through Swann, the entire novel—is articulated around the reversal of a despair (that of having to go to sleep without the mother's kiss) into a delight (that of spending the night in the mother's company); here, in fact, are inscribed the characteristics of Proustian inversion: not only will the mother, finally (temporality), come to embrace her son against all expectation (*surprise*) but, moreover (*climax*), out of the darkest despair, the most overwhelming joy will appear, the stern Father unexpectedly turning into the kindly Father (". . . and tell Françoise to make the big bed for you, and sleep with him tonight"). Reversal does not remain limited to the thousand notations of detail of which we have given a few examples; it structures the very development of the main characters, subject to "exact" elevations and falls: from the height of aristocratic grandeur, Charlus falls, in the Verdurin salon, to the rank of petit-bourgeois; Swann, habitual companion of princes, is for the Narrator's great-aunts a colorless figure of no particular status; the cocotte Odette becomes Mme Swann; Mme Verdurin ends as the Princess de Guermantes, etc. An incessant permutation animates, overturns the social interplay (Proust's work is much more sociological than is acknowledged: it describes with great exactitude the grammar of promotion, of class mobility), to the point where worldliness can be defined by a form: reversal (of situations, opinions, values, feelings, languages).

In this regard, sexual inversion is exemplary (but not necessarily primary), since it enables us to read one and the same body as the super-impression of two absolute contraries, Man and Woman (contraries which Proust defined biologically and not symbolically: a period feature, no doubt; in order to rehabilitate homosexuality, Gide proposes examples of pigeons and dogs); the scene of the hornet, during which the Narrator discovers the Woman in the Baron de Charlus, is theoretically valid for any reading of the interplay of contraries; whence, in the whole work, homosexuality develops what we might call its enantiology (or discourse of reversal); on the one hand, it gives rise in the world to a thousand paradoxical situations, misunderstandings, surprises, climaxes, and tricks, which the novel scrupulously collects; and on the other, as exemplary reversal, it is animated by an irresistible movement of expansion; by a broad sweep which takes up the entire work, a patient but infallible curve, the novel's population, heterosexual at the outset, is ultimately discovered in exactly the converse position—i.e., homosexual (like Saint-Loup, the Prince de Guermantes, etc.): there is a pandemia of inversion, of reversal.

Reversal is a law. Every feature is required to reverse itself, by an implacable movement of rotation: endowed with an aristocratic language, Swann can only, at a certain moment, invert it into bourgeois language. This constraint is so statutory that it renders futile, Proust says, any observation of manners: one can readily *deduce* them from the law of inversion. A reading of reversal is therefore equivalent to knowledge. But we must be careful: such knowledge does not reveal content, or at least does not stop there: what is notable (statutory) is not that the great Russian lady is vulgar or that M. Verdurin adapts his description of Cottard to his interlocutor; it is the form of this reading, the logic of inversion which structures the world, i.e., worldliness; this inversion itself has no meaning, we cannot retain it, one of the permuted terms is not "truer" than the other: Cottard is neither "great" nor "small"; his truth, if he has one, is a truth of discourse, extensive with the entire oscillation to which the Other's speech (in this case, M. Verdurin's) subjects him. For classical syntax, which would tell us that the Princess Sherbatoff *is only* a madam, Proust substitutes a concomitant syntax: the princess is *also* a madam; a new syntax we should call metaphorical because metaphor, contrary to what rhetoric has long supposed, is a labor of language deprived of any vectorization: it moves from one term to another only in a circular and infinite fashion. Thus, we understand why the *ethos* of Proustian inversion is Surprise; it is the astonishment of a *return*, of a *junction*, of a *recognition* (and of a reduction): to *utter* the contraries is finally to *unite* them in the very unity of the text, of writing's journey. It follows, then, that the great opposition which seems at the outset to animate both the Combray excursions and the divisions of the novel (*Swann's Way / The Guermantes' Way*) is, if not fallacious (we are not within the order of truth), at least revocable: the Narrator discovers with stupefaction (the same stupefaction he experiences when he realizes that the Baron de Charlus is a Woman, the Princess Sherbatoff a madam, etc.) that the two paths which diverge from the family house will converge, and that Swann's world and that of Guermantes, through a thousand anastomoses, ultimately coincide in the person of Gilberte, Swann's daughter and the wife of Robert de Saint-Loup.

Yet there is a moment in the novel when the great inverting form no longer functions. What keeps it from doing so? Nothing less than Death. We know that all of Proust's characters come together in the last volume of the work (*Time Regained*); in what condition? Not in the least inverted (as would have been warranted by the great lapse of time at whose end they are collected at the Princess de Guermantes's luncheon), but on the contrary prolonged, paralyzed (even more than aged), *preserved,* and—the neologism is warranted—"*persevered.*" In reprieved life, inversion no longer "takes": the narrative has nothing left to do but come to an end—the book has nothing left to do but begin.

Paragone, 1971

Longtemps, je me suis couché de bonne heure . . .

Some of you will have recognized my title, and the passage it initiates: "Time was, I went to bed early. Some evenings, my candle was no sooner out than my eyes would close so quickly I had no time to think: 'I'm falling asleep.' And half an hour later, the thought that it was time to go to sleep would waken me . . .": it is the opening of *In Search of Lost Time.* Does this mean I am offering you a lecture "on" Proust? Yes and no. My subject will be, if you like, *Proust and I.* How pretentious! Nietzsche spared no irony about the Germans' use of that conjunction: "Schopenhauer *and* Hartmann," he jeered. "Proust and I" is worse still. Let me suggest that, paradoxically, the pretentiousness subsides once I myself take the stand, and not some witness: by setting Proust and myself on one and the same line, I am not in the least comparing myself to this great writer but, quite differently, *identifying myself with him:* an association of practice, not of value. Let me explain: in figurative language, in the novel, for instance, it seems to me that one more or less identifies oneself with one of the characters represented; this projection, I believe, is the very wellspring of literature; but in certain marginal cases, once the reader himself wants to write a work, he no longer identifies himself merely with this or that fictive character but also and especially with the actual author of the book he has read, insofar as that author wanted to write this book and succeeded in doing so; now, Proust is the privileged site of this special identification, insofar as his *Search . . .* is the narrative of a desire to write: I am not identifying myself with the prestigious author of a monumental work but with the worker—now tormented, now exalted, in any case modest—who wanted to undertake a task upon which, from the very start of his project, he conferred an absolute character.

1

Therefore, first of all, Proust . . .

In Search of Lost Time was preceded by many writings: a book, translations, articles. The great work was not really launched, it seems, until the summer of 1909; and from that point on, as we know, a stubborn race was run against death and incompletion. Apparently there was, in that year (even if it is futile to try dating the inception of a work with any specificity), a crucial period of hesitation. Certainly, Proust seems to be at the intersection of two paths, two genres, torn between two "ways" he does not yet know could converge, any more than the Narrator knows, for a very long time—until Gilberte's marriage to Saint-Loup—that Swann's Way meets the Guermantes' Way: the way of the Essay (of Criticism) and the way of the Novel. At the time of his mother's death, in 1905, Proust passes through a period of despondency, but also of sterile agitation; he wants to write, to create a work, but which? Or rather, which form? Proust writes to Mme de Noailles, in December 1908: "I'd like, sick as I am, to write on Sainte-Beuve [incarnation of the aesthetic values he abhors]. The thing has taken shape in my mind in two different ways, between which I must choose. Now, I am totally without will, and without any power to see my way."

I should point out that Proust's hesitation—to which, quite naturally, he gives a psychological form—corresponds to a structural alternation: the two "ways" he hesitates between are the two terms of an opposition articulated by Jakobson: that of Metaphor and Metonymy. Metaphor sustains any discourse which asks: "What is it? What does it mean?"—the real question of any Essay. Metonymy, on the contrary, asks another question: "What can follow what I say? What can be engendered by the episode I am telling?"; this is the Novel's question. Jakobson cited the experiment conducted in a classroom, where schoolchildren were asked to react to the word *hut*; some said that a hut was a little cabin (metaphor), others that it had burned down (metonymy); Proust is a divided subject, like Jakobson's class; he knows that each incident in life can give rise either to a commentary (an interpretation) or to an affabulation which produces or imagines the narrative *before* and *after*: to interpret is to take the Critical path, to argue theory (siding against Sainte-Beuve); to think incidents and impressions, to describe their developments, is on the contrary to weave a Narrative, however loosely, however gradually.

Proust's indecision is profound, insofar as Proust is no novice (in 1909, he is thirty-eight); he has already written, and what he has written (especially on the level of certain fragments) often derives from a mixed, uncertain, hesitant form, both fictive and intellectual; for example, in order to express his ideas about Sainte-Beuve (realm of the Essay, of Metaphor), Proust writes a fictive dialogue between himself and his mother (realm of the Narrative, of Metonymy). Not only is this indecision profound, it is even, perhaps, *cherished*: Proust loves and admires certain writers who, he remarks, have also practiced a certain indecision of genres: Nerval, Baudelaire . . .

We must recover the *pathos* of this debate. Proust is seeking a form which will accommodate suffering (he has just experienced it in an absolute form through his mother's death) and transcend it; now, "intelligence" (a Proustian word), indicted by Proust beginning with *Contre Sainte-Beuve,* if we follow the romantic tradition, is a power which traumatizes or desiccates affect; Novalis called poetry "that which heals the wounds of intellect"; the Novel can do this too, but not just any novel: a novel which is not written according to Sainte-Beuve's notions.

We do not know by what determination Proust emerged from this hesitation, and why (if indeed there was a circumstantial cause), after having given up his *Contre Sainte-Beuve* (rejected by *Le Figaro* in August 1909), he flung himself so deeply into his *Search . . .* ; but we do know the form he chose: it is the very form of his *Search . . .* : novel? essay? Neither one, or both at once: what I should call *a third form.* Let us question this third genre a moment.

If I began these reflections with the first sentence of Proust's *Search . . .* , it is because it opens an episode of some fifty pages which, like a Tibetan *mandala,* collects together within its view the entire Proustian oeuvre. What does this episode discuss? Sleep. Proustian sleep has an inceptive value: it organizes what is original (and "typical") in the novel (but this organization, as we shall see, is in fact a disorganization).

Of course, there is a good sleep and a bad. The good kind is the one begun, inaugurated, permitted, consecrated by the mother's evening kiss; it is the right sleep, in accord with Nature (to sleep by night, to act by day). The bad kind is the sleep far from the mother: the son sleeps by day, while the mother is up; they see each other only at the brief intersection of the right time and the inverted time: awakening for one, bedtime for the other; this bad sleep (under Veronal) can only be justified, redeemed by the entire novel, since it is at the painful price of this inversion that Proust's *Search . . .* , night after night, will be written.

And what is this good sleep (of childhood)? It is a "half waking" ("I have tried to wrap my first chapter in the impressions of half waking.") Although Proust speaks on one occasion of the "depths of our unconscious," this sleep has nothing Freudian about it; it is not oneiric (there are few real dreams in Proust's work); rather, it is constituted by the depths of consciousness *as disorder.* A paradox defines it nicely: it is a sleep which can be written, because it is a consciousness of sleep; the whole episode (and, consequently, I believe, the whole work which emerges from it) is thus held suspended in a sort of grammatical scandal: to say "I'm asleep" is in effect, literally, as impossible as to say "I'm dead"; writing is precisely that activity which tampers with language—the impossibilities of language—to the advantage of discourse.

What does this sleep (or this half waking) do? It leads to a "false consciousness": a consciousness out of order, vacillating, intermittent; the logical carapace of Time is attacked; there is no longer a chrono-logy (if we may separate the two parts of the word): "A man who is asleep [read: that Proustian sleep which is a half waking] holds in a circle around him the course of the hours, the order of years and worlds . . . but *their ranks can mingle, can break*" [italics mine]. Sleep establishes another logic, a logic of Vacillation, of Decompartmentalization, and it is this new logic which Proust discovers in the episode of the madeleine, or rather of the biscuit, as it is recounted in *Contre Sainte-Beuve* (i.e., before his *Search* . . .): "I remained motionless . . . when suddenly the shaken partitions of my memory gave way." Naturally, such a logical revolution can only provoke a reaction of stupidity: Humblot, the reader for Editions Ollendorf, receiving the manuscript of *Swann's Way,* declared: "I don't know if I've gone completely blind and deaf, but I can't see any interest in reading thirty pages [*precisely our mandala*] on how a Gentleman tosses and turns in bed before falling asleep." The interest, however, is crucial: it will open the floodgates of *Time*: once chrono-logy is shaken, intellectual or narrative fragments will form a series shielded from the ancestral law of Narrative or of Rationality, and this series will spontaneously produce the *third form,* neither Essay nor Novel. The structure of this work will be, strictly speaking, *rhapsodic,* i.e. (etymologically), *sewn*; moreover, this is a Proustian metaphor: the work is produced like a gown; the rhapsodic text implies an original art, like that of the couturiere: pieces, fragments are subject to certain correspondences, arrangements, reappearances: a dress is not a patchwork, any more than is *A la Recherde du temps perdu.*

Emerging from sleep, the work (*the third form*) rests on a provocative principle: the *disorganization* of Time (of chronology). Now, this is a very modern principle. Bachelard calls *rhythm* that force which aims to "rid the soul of the false permanence of ill-made durations," and this definition applies very nicely to Proust's novel, whose every sumptuous effort is to subtract Time Remembered from the false permanence of biography. Nietzsche, more lapidarily, says that "we must reduce the universe to crumbs, lose respect for the whole," and John Cage, prophesying the new musical work, announces: "In any case, the whole will constitute a disorganization." This vacillation is not an aleatory anarchy of associations of ideas: "I see," Proust says with a certain bitterness, "readers supposing that I am writing, by trusting to arbitrary and fortuitous associations of ideas, the story of my life." In fact, if we adopt Bachelard's word, what we are dealing with is a *rhythm*, and a highly complex one: "systems of moments" (Bachelard again) succeed each other, but also correspond to each other. For what the principle of vacillation disorganizes is not Time's intelligibility but biography's illusory logic, insofar as it traditionally follows the purely mathematical order of the years.

This disorganization of biography is not its destruction. In the work, many elements of personal life are retained, in an identifiable fashion, but these elements are in a sense *shifted*. I shall indicate two of these shifts, insofar as they turn not on details (of which biographies of Proust are full) but on major creative options.

The first shift is that of the discoursing person (in the grammatical sense of the word *person*). The Proustian oeuvre brings on stage (or into writing) an "I" (the Narrator); but this "I," one may say, is not quite a self (subject and object of traditional autobiography): "I" is not the one who remembers, confides, confesses, he is the one who discourses; the person this "I" brings on stage is a writing self whose links with the self of civil life are uncertain, displaced. Proust himself has explained this well: Sainte-Beuve's method fails to realize that "a book is the product of a different 'self' from the one we manifest in our habits, in society, in our vices." The result of this dialectic is that it is vain to wonder if the book's Narrator is Proust (in the civil meaning of the patronymic): it is simply *another* Proust, often unknown to himself.

The second shift is more flagrant (easier to define): in Proust's novel, there is certainly "narrative" (it is not an essay), but this narrative is not that of a life which the Narrator apprehends at birth and follows from year to year until the moment he takes up his pen to tell the story. What Proust *recounts*, what he puts into narration, is not his life but *his desire to write:* Time weighs heavily on his desire, maintains it in a chronology; it (the steeples of Martinville, Bergotte's phrase) encounters trials, discouragements (the verdict of Monsieur de Norpois, the incomparable prestige of the Goncourts' *Journal*), and ultimately triumphs when the Narrator, arriving at the Guermantes' party, discovers *what he must write:* Time regained, and thereby assures himself that he is going to be able to write: *In Search of Lost Time* (though it is already written).

As we see, what passes into the work is certainly the author's life, but a life *disoriented*. George Painter, Proust's biographer, has accurately seen that the novel is constituted by what he has called a "symbolic biography," or again, "a symbolic story of Proust's life": Proust understood (and this is genius) that he did not have to "recount" his life, but that his life nonetheless had the signification of a work of art. "A man's life of any worth is a continual Allegory," says Keats, quoted by Painter. Posterity proves Proust increasingly right: his work is not only read as a monument of universal literature but as the impassioned expression of an absolutely personal subject who ceaselessly returns to his own life, not as to a curriculum vitae, but as to a constellation of circumstances and figures. More and more, we find ourselves loving not "Proust" (civil name of an author filed away in the histories of literature) but "Marcel," a singular being, at once child and adult, *puer senilis,* impassioned yet wise, victim of eccentric manias and the site of a sovereign reflection on the world, love, art, time, death. I have proposed calling this very special interest readers take in the life of Marcel Proust "Marcelism" in order to distinguish it from "Proustism," which would be merely a preference for a certain work or a certain literary manner.

If I have emphasized in Proust's work-as-life the theme of a new logic which permits one—in any case, permitted Proust—

to abolish the contradiction between Novel and Essay, it is because this theme concerns me personally. Why? That is what I want to explain now. Hence I shall be speaking of "myself." "Myself" is to be understood here in the full sense: not the asepticized substitute of a general reader (any substitution is an asepsis); I shall be speaking of the one for whom no one else can be substituted, for better and for worse. It is the *intimate* which seeks utterance in me, seeks to make its cry heard, confronting generality, confronting science.

2

Dante (another famous opening, another overwhelming allusion) begins his poem *"Nel mezzo del camin di nostra vita . . ."* In 1300, Dante was thirty-five (he was to die twenty-one years later). I am much older than that, and the time I have left to live will never be half the length of my life so far. For the "middle of our life" is obviously not an arithmetical point: how, at the moment of writing, could I know my life's total duration so precisely that I could divide it into two equal parts? It is a semantic point, the perhaps belated moment when there occurs in my life the summons of a new meaning, the desire for a mutation: to change lives, to break off and to begin, to submit myself to an initiation, as Dante made his way into the *selva oscura,* led by a great initiator, Virgil (and for me, at least during this text, the initiator is Proust). Age, need we be reminded?—but yes, we do, so indifferently do we experience each other's age—age is only very partially a chronological datum, a garland of years; there are classes, compartments of age: we pass through life from lock to lock; at certain points there are thresholds, gradients, shocks; age is not gradual and progressive, it is mutative: to consider one's age, if that age is what we French call *un certain age,* is not a coquetry intended to bring forth kindly protestations; rather, it is an active task: what are the real forces which my age implies and seeks to mobilize? That is the question, appearing quite lately, which it seems to me has made the present moment the "middle of the journey of my life."

Why today?

There comes a time (and this is a problem of consciousness) when "our days are numbered": there begins a backwards count, vague yet irreversible. You *knew* you were mortal (everyone has told you so, ever since you had ears to hear); suddenly you *feel* mortal (this is not a natural feeling; the natural one is to believe yourself immortal; whence so many accidents due to carelessness). This evidence, once it is experienced, transforms the landscape: I must, imperatively, lodge my work in a compartment which has uncertain contours but which I know (new consciousness) are *finite*: the last compartment. Or rather, because the compartment is designated, because there are no longer any "outside-instances," the work I am going to lodge there assumes a kind of formality, a solemn instance. Like Proust ill, threatened by death (or believing himself so), we come back to the phrase of St. John quoted, approximately, in *Contre Sainte-Beuve:* "Work, while you still have the light."

And then a time also comes (the same time) when what you have done, worked, written, appears doomed to repetition: What! Until my death, to be writing articles, giving courses, lectures, on "subjects" which alone will vary, and so little! (It's that "on" which bothers me.) This feeling is a cruel one; for it confronts me with the foreclosure of anything New or even of any Adventure (that which "advenes"—which befalls me); I see my future, until death, as a series: when I've finished this text, this lecture, I'll have nothing else to do but start again with another . . . Can this be all? No, Sisyphus is not happy: he is alienated, not by the effort of his labor, or even by its vanity, but by its repetition.

Finally, an event (and no longer only a consciousness) can supervene which will mark, incise, articulate this gradual silting up of work, and determine that mutation, that transformation of the landscape which I have called the "middle of life." Rancé, hero of the Fronde, a worldly dandy, comes from his travels and discovers the body of his mistress, decapitated by an accident: he withdraws from the world and founds the Trappist Order. For Proust, the "middle of life's journey" was certainly his mother's death (1905), even if the mutation of existence, the inauguration of the new work, occurred only a few years later. A cruel bereavement, a unique and somehow irreducible bereavement can constitute for me that "pinnacle of the particular" Proust spoke of; though belated, this bereavement will be for me the middle of my life; for the "middle of life" is perhaps never anything but the moment when you discover that death is real, and no longer merely dreadful.

Journeying thus, there occurs all of a sudden this obvious situation: on the one hand, I no longer have time to try several lives: I must choose my last life, my new life, "*Vita Nova*," Michelet said, marrying at fifty-one a girl of twenty and preparing to write new books of natural history; and on the other hand, I must emerge from that shadowy state (medieval theory called it *acedie*) to which the attrition of repeated tasks and mourning dispose me. Now, for the subject who writes, who has chosen to write, there can be no "new life," it seems to me, except in the discovery of a new practice of writing. To change doctrine, theory, philosophy, method, belief, spectacular though this seems, is in fact quite banal: one does such things the way one breathes; one invests, one lays aside, one reinvests: intellectual conversions are the very pulsion of the intelligence, once it is attentive to the world's surprises; but the search, the discovery, the practice of a new form—this, I believe, is equivalent to that *Vita Nova* whose determinations I have described.

It is here, in this middle of my journey, at this pinnacle of my particularity, that I come back to two readings (in truth, so often repeated that I cannot date them). The first is that of a great novel: *War and Peace.* I am not speaking here of a work but of a disruption, one that for me culminates at the death of old Prince Bolkonsky, in the last words he addresses to his daughter, Maria, in the explosion of tenderness which, under the impulsion of his death, lacerates these two beings who love each other without ever engaging in the discourse (the verbiage) of love. My second reading is that of an episode in Proust's novel (this work intervenes here at quite a different level than at the beginning of this text: I am now identifying myself with the Narrator, not with the writer), the grandmother's death; this is a narrative of absolute purity; I mean that here grief is pure, insofar as it is not commented upon (contrary to other episodes of the *Search* . . .), one in which the cruelty of the death which supervenes, which will separate forever, is expressed only through indirect objects and incidents: the rest room in the Pavilion of the Champs-Elysées, the pathetic head which sways under the comb wielded by Françoise.

From these two readings, from the emotion they constantly reawaken in me, I have learned two lessons. First of all, that I received these episodes as "moments of truth" (I find no other expression): suddenly literature (for it is literature which matters here) coincides absolutely with an emotional landslide, a "cry"; in the body of the reader who suffers, by memory or anticipation, the remote separation of the beloved person, a transcendence is posited: What Lucifer created *at the same time* love and death? The "moment of truth" has nothing to do with "realism" (moreover, it is absent from every theory of the novel). The "moment of truth," supposing an analytic notion of such a thing could be produced, implies a recognition of *pathos* in the simple, non-pejorative sense of the term, and literary science, strangely enough, has difficulty acknowledging *pathos* as a force of our reading; Nietzsche, no doubt, could help us establish the notion, but we are still far from a "pathetic" theory or from a "pathetic" history of the Novel; for in order even to sketch such a thing, we should have to disperse the "whole" of the novelistic universe, no longer to place a book's essence in its structure, but on the contrary acknowledge that the work moves, lives, germinates, through a kind of "collapse" which leaves only certain moments standing, moments which are strictly speaking its summits, our vital, concerned reading following only a "skyline": moments of truth are the *plus-value* points of the anecdote.

The second lesson, I should say the second courage I derived from this scalding contact with the Novel, is that one must acknowledge that the work to be written (since I am defining myself as "the subject who wants to write") actively represents, *without saying so,* a sentiment of which I was sure, but which I now have great difficulty naming, for I cannot emerge from a circle of worn-out words, dubious by dint of having been used without rigor. What I can say, what I cannot help but say, is that this sentiment which must animate the work has something to do with love: what then—kindess? generosity? charity? Perhaps, simply because Rousseau has given it the dignity of a "philosopheme": pity (or compassion).

One of these days I should like to develop this power of the novel—this loving or amorous power (certain mystics do not dissociate *Agape* from *Eros*)—either by means of an Essay (I have spoken of a Pathetic History of Literature) or by means of a Novel, it being understood that for convenience's sake this is what I am calling any Form which is new in relation to my past practice, to my past discourse. Such a form I cannot subject in advance to the Novel's structural rules—I can only ask it to fulfill, in my own eyes, three missions. The first would permit me to *say* whom I love (Sade, yes, Sade used to say that the novel consists in painting those one loves), and not to say *to* them that I love them (which would be a strictly lyrical project); I expect from the novel a kind of transcendence of egotism, insofar as to say whom one loves is to testify that they have not lived (and frequently suffered) "for nothing": say, through sovereign writing, the illness of Proust's mother, the death of old Prince Bolkonsky, the grief of his daughter, Maria (members of Tolstoy's own family), the anguish of Madeleine Gide (in *Et nunc manet in te*) do not fall into History's nothingness: these lives, these sufferings are gathered up, pondered, justified (this is how we must understand the theme of Resurrection in Michelet's History). The second mission entrusted to this (fantasized and probably impossible) Novel would permit me, fully but indirectly, the representation of an affective order. I read almost everywhere that it is characteristic of a "moden" sensibility to "conceal its tenderness" (beneath the stratagems of writing); but why? Is it "truer," is it more valuable because one struggles to conceal it? An entire ethic, today, scorns and condemns the expression of *pathos* (in the simple sense I intend), with regard to either political or pulsional (sexual) rationality; the Novel, as I read or desire it, is precisely that Form which, by delegating the discourse of affect to characters, permits saying that affect openly: here *the pathetic* can be said, for the Novel, since it is representation and not expression, can never be for the subject who writes it a discourse of bad faith. Finally and perhaps especially, the Novel (I still mean by the Novel that uncertain, quite uncanonical Form, insofar as I do not conceive it but only remember or desire it), since its writing is mediate (it presents ideas and feelings only by intermediaries)—the Novel, then, exerts no pressure upon the other (the reader); its power is the truth of affects, not of ideas: hence, it is never arrogant, terrorist: according to Nietzsche's typology, it aligns itself with Art, not with Priesthood.

Does all this mean I am going to write a novel? How should I know? I don't know if it will be possible still to call a "novel" the work I desire and which I expect to break with the uniformly intellectual nature of my previous writings (even if a number of fictive elements taint their rigor). It is important for me to act *as if* I were to write this utopian novel. And here I regain, to conclude, a method. I put myself in the position of the subject who *makes* something, and no longer of the subject who speaks *about* something: I am not studying a product, I assume a production; I abolish the discourse on discourse; the world no longer comes to me as an object, but as a writing, i.e., a practice: I proceed to another type of knowledge (that of the Amateur), and it is in this that I am methodical. "As if": is not this formula the very expression of scientific procedure, as we see it in mathematics? I venture a hypothesis and I explore, I discover the wealth of what follows from it; I postulate a novel to be written, whereby I can expect to learn more about the novel than by merely considering it as object already written by others. Perhaps it is finally at the heart of this subjectivity, of this very intimacy which I have invoked, perhaps it is at the "pinnacle of my particularity" that I am scientific without knowing it, vaguely oriented toward that *Scienza Nuova* Vico spoke of: should it not express at once the world's brilliance and the world's suffering, all that beguiles and offends me?

Lecture given at the Collège de France, 1978

Preface to Renaud Camus's *Tricks*

Why have you agreed to write a preface to this book by Renaud Camus?

Because Renaud Camus is a writer, because his text belongs to literature, because he cannot say so himself, and because someone else, therefore, must say so in his place.

If it is literary, the text must show as much for itself.

It shows as much, or you can hear as much, from the first turn of phrase, from a certain way of saying "I," of conducting the narrative. But since this book seems to speak, and bluntly, about sex, about homosexuality, some readers may forget about literature.

Then, for you, asserting the literary nature of a text is a way of taking it out of quarantine, sublimating or purifying it, giving it a kind of dignity which, according to you, sex doesn't have?

Not in the least. Literature is here to afford more pleasure, not more propriety.

Get on with it then, but make it short.

Homosexuality shocks less, but continues to be interesting; it is still at that stage of excitation where it provokes what might be called feats of discourse. Speaking of homosexuality permits those who "aren't" to show how open, liberal, and modern they are, and those who "are" to bear witness, to assure responsibility, to militate. Everyone gets busy, in different ways, whipping it up.

Yet, to proclaim yourself something is always to speak at the behest of a vengeful Other, to enter into his discourse, to argue with him, to seek from him a scrap of identity: "You are . . ." "Yes, I am . . ." Ultimately, the attribute is of no importance; what society will not tolerate is that I should be . . . *nothing*, or, more precisely, that the *something* I am should be openly expressed as provisional, revocable, insignificant, inessential, in a word irrelevant. Just say "I am," and you will be socially saved.

To reject the social injunction can be accomplished by means of that form of silence which consists in saying things *simply*. Speaking *simply* belongs to a higher art: writing. Take the spontaneous utterances, the spoken testimony then transcribed, as increasingly utilized by the press and by publishers. Whatever their "human" interest, something rings false in them (at least to my ears): perhaps, paradoxically, an excess of style (trying to sound "spontaneous," "lively," "spoken"). What happens, in fact, is a double impasse: the accurate transcription sounds made-up; for it to seem true, it has to become a text, to pass through the cultural artifices of writing. Testimony runs away with itself, calling nature, men, and justice to witness; the text goes slowly, silently, stubbornly—and arrives faster. Reality is fiction, writing is truth: such is the ruse of language.

Renaud Camus's *Tricks* are simple. This means that they speak homosexuality, but never speak about it: at no moment do they invoke it (that is simplicity: never to invoke, not to let Names into language—Names, the source of dispute, of arrogance, and of moralizing).

Our period interprets a great deal, but Renaud Camus's narratives are neutral, they do not participate in the game of interpretation. They are surfaces without shadows, *without ulterior motives*. And once again, only writing allows this purity, this priority of utterance, unknown to speech, which is always a cunning tangle of concealed intentions. If it weren't for their extent and their subject, these *Tricks* might be haikus; for the haiku combines an asceticism of form (which cuts short the desire to interpret) and a hedonism so serene that all we can say about pleasure is that *it is there* (which is also the contrary of Interpretation).

Sexual practices are banal, impoverished, doomed to repetition, and this impoverishment is disproportionate to the wonder of the pleasure they afford. Now, since this wonder cannot be said (being of an ecstatic order), all that remains for language to do is to figure or, better still, to cipher, as economically as possible, a series of actions which, in any case, elude it. Erotic scenes must be described sparingly. The economy here is that of the sentence. The good writer is the one who utilizes syntax so as to link several actions within the briefest linguistic space (we find, in Sade, a whole art of subordinate clauses); the sentence's function is somehow to scour the carnal operation of its tediums and its efforts, of its noises and its adventitious thoughts. In this regard, the final scenes of the various *Tricks* remain entirely within the domain of *writing.*

But what I like best of all in *Tricks* are the preparations: the cruising, the alert, the signals, the approach, the conversation, the departure for the bedroom, the household order (or disorder) of the place. Realism finds a new site; it is not the *love scene* which is realistic (or at least its realism is not pertinent), it is the *social scene.* Two young men who do not know each other but who know that they are about to become partners in a specific act risk between them that fragment of language to which they are compelled by the trajectory they must cover together in order to reach their goal. The *Trick* then abandons pornography (before having really approached it) and joins the novel. The suspense (for these *Tricks,* I believe, will be read eagerly) affects not behavior (which is anticipated, to say the least) but the characters: Who are they? How do they differ from each other? What delights me, in *Tricks,* is this juxtaposition: the scenes, certainly, are anything but chaste, yet the remarks are just that: they say sotto voce that the real object of such modesty is not the Thing ("*La Chose, toujours la Chose,*" Charcot used to say, as quoted by Freud) but the person. It is this *passage* from sex to discourse that I find so successfully achieved in *Tricks.*

This is a form of subtlety quite unknown to the pornographic product, which plays on desires, not on fantasies. For what excites fantasy is not only sex, it is sex plus "the soul." Impossible to account for falling in love or even for infatuations, simple attractions or Wertherian raptures, without admitting that what is sought in the other is something we shall call, for lack of a better word and at the cost of great ambiguity, the person. To the person is attached a kind of homing device that causes this particular image, among thousands of others, to seek out and capture me. Bodies can be classified into a finite number of types ("That's just my type"), but the person is absolutely individual. Renaud Camus's *Tricks* always begin with an encounter with the longed-for type (perfectly encoded; the type could figure in a catalogue or in a page of personal want ads); but once language appears, the type is transformed into a person, and the relation becomes inimitable, whatever the banality of the first remarks. The person is gradually revealed, and lightly, without psychologizing, in clothing, in discourse, in accent, in setting, in what might be called the individual's "domesticity," which transcends his anatomy, yet over which he has control. All of which gradually enriches or retards desire. The *trick* is therefore homogeneous to the amorous progression; it is a *virtual* love, deliberately stopped short on each side, by contract; a submission to the cultural code which identifies cruising with Don Juanism.

The *Tricks* repeat themselves; the subject is on a treadmill. Repetition is an ambiguous form; sometimes it denotes failure, impotence; sometimes it can be read as an aspiration, the stubborn movement of a quest which is not to be discouraged; we might very well take the cruising narrative as the metaphor of a mystical experience (perhaps this has even been done; for in literature everything exists: the problem is to know *where*). Neither one of these interpretations, apparently, suits *Tricks*: neither alienation nor sublimation; yet something like the methodical conquest of happiness (specifically designated, carefully boundaried: discontinuous). The flesh is not sad (but it is quite an art to convey as much).

Renaud Camus's *Tricks* have an inimitable tone. It derives from the fact that the writing here imitates an ethic of dialogue. This ethic is that of Good Will, which is surely the virtue most contrary to the amorous pursuit, and hence the rarest. Whereas ordinarily a kind of harpy presides over the erotic contract, leaving each party within a chilly solitude, here it is the goddess Eunoia, the Eumenid, the Kindly One, who accompanies the two partners; certainly, in literary terms, it must be very agreeable to be "tricked" by Renaud Camus, even if his companions do not always seem aware of this privilege (but we, the readers, are the third ear in these dialogues: thanks to us, this bit of Good Will has not been vouchsafed in vain). Moreover, this goddess has her retinue: Politeness, Kindness, Humor, Generous Impulse, like the one which seizes the narrator (while tricking with an American) and causes his wits to wander so amiably with regard to the author of this preface.

Trick—the encounter which takes place only once: more than cruising, less than love: an intensity, which passes without regret. Consequently, for me, *Trick* becomes the metaphor for many adventures which are not sexual; the encounter of a glance, a gaze, an idea, an image, ephemeral and forceful association, which consents to dissolve so lightly, a faithless benevolence: a way of not getting stuck in desire, though without evading it; all in all, a kind of wisdom.

Preface to Renaud Camus's *Tricks* (Persona), 1979

One Always Fails in Speaking of What One Loves*

A few weeks ago, I made a short trip to Italy. The first evening, in the Milan station, it was cold, dark, dirty. A train was leaving; on each car hung a yellow placard bearing the words *Milano-Lecce*. I began dreaming: to take that train, to travel all night and wake up in the warmth, the light, the peace of a faraway town. At least that was my fantasy, and it doesn't matter what Lecce (which I have never seen) is really like. Parodying Stendhal (my references throughout will be to *Rome, Naples, Florence, The Life of Henri Brulard, The Charterhouse of Parma,* and *On Love*), I might have exclaimed: "At last I shall see *la bella Italia!* A madman still, and at my age!" For lovely Italy is always farther away . . . elsewhere.

Stendhal's Italy is indeed a fantasy, even if he partially realized it. (But did he? I shall end by saying how.) The phantasmatic image burst into his life—it was love at first sight. This explosion assumed the countenance of a soprano singing in Cimarosa's *Matrimonio segreto* at Ivrea; the singer had a broken front tooth, but love at first sight is never affected by such things: Werther fell in love with Charlotte glimpsed through an open door as she was slicing bread-and-butter for her little brothers, and this first glimpse, trivial as it was, would lead him to the most powerful of passions and to suicide. We know that, for Stendhal, Italy was the object of a veritable transference, and we also know that what characterizes transference is its gratuitousness:

* Probably the last text Barthes wrote—given here as he left it, largely unrevised.—Ed.

it occurs without any apparent reason. Music, for Stendhal, is the *symptom* of the mysterious action by which he inaugurated his transference—the symptom, i.e., the thing which simultaneously produces and masks passion's irrationality. For once the opening scene is established, Stendhal constantly reproduces it, like a lover trying to regain that crucial thing which rules so large a share of our actions: the first pleasure. "I arrive at seven in the evening, tormented with fatigue; I run to La Scala. My journey was justified," etc.: like some madman disembarking in a city favorable to his passion and rushing that very evening to the haunts of pleasure he has already located.

The signs of a true passion are always somewhat incongruous, the objects of transference always tending to become tenuous, trivial, unforeseen . . . I once knew someone who loved Japan the way Stendhal loved Italy; and I recognized the same passion in him by the fact that he loved, among other things, the red-painted fireplugs in the Tokyo streets, just as Stendhal was mad for the cornstalks of the "luxuriant" Milanese campagna, for the sound of the Duomo's eight bells, "perfectly *intonate*," or for the pan-fried cutlets that reminded him of Milan. In this erotic promotion of what is commonly taken for an insignificant detail, we recognize a constitutive element of transference (or of passion): partiality. In the love of a foreign country there is a kind of reverse racism: one is delighted by Difference, one is tired of the Same, one exalts the Other; passion is Manichaean for Stendhal, the wrong side is France, i.e., *la patrie*—for it is the site of the Father—and the right side is Italy, i.e., *la matrie*, the space in which "the Women" are assembled (not forgetting that it was the child's Aunt Elisabeth, the maternal grandfather's sister, who pointed her finger toward a country lovelier than Provence, where according to her the "good" side of the family, the Gagnon branch, originated). This opposition is virtually physical: Italy is the *natural* habitat, where Nature is recovered under the sponsorship of Women, "who listen to the natural genius of the country," contrary to the men, who are "spoiled by the pedants"; France, on the contrary, is a place repugnant "to the point of physical disgust." All of us who have known Stendhal's passion for a foreign country (this was also my case for Italy, which I discovered belatedly, in Milan, at the end of the nineteen-fifties—then for Japan) are familiar with the intolerable annoyance of encountering a compatriot in the adored country: "I must confess, though it goes against the national honor, that finding a Frenchman in Italy can destroy my happiness in a moment"; Stendhal is visibly a specialist in such inversions: no sooner has he crossed the Bidassoa than he is charmed by the Spanish soldiers and customs officers; he has that rare passion, the passion for *the other*—or to put it more subtly: the passion for that other which is in himself.

Thus, Stendhal is in love with Italy: this is not a sentence to be taken metaphorically, as I shall try to show. "It is like love," he says: "and yet I am not in love with anyone." This passion is not in the least vague; it is invested, as I have said, in specific details; but it remains *plural*. What is loved and indeed what is enjoyed are collections, concomitances: contrary to the romantic project of *Amour fou*, it is not Woman who is adorable in Italy, but always Women; it is not *a* pleasure which Italy affords, it is a simultaneity, an overdetermination of pleasures: La Scala, the veritable eidetic locus of Italian delights, is not a theater in the word's banally functional sense (to see what is represented); it is a polyphony of pleasures: the opera itself, the ballet, the conversation, the gossip, love, and ices (*gelati, crepe*, and *pezzi duri*). This amorous plural, analogous to that enjoyed today by someone "cruising," is evidently a Stendhalian principle: it involves an implicit theory of *irregular discontinuity* which can be said to be simultaneously aesthetic, psychological, and metaphysical; plural passion, as a matter of fact—once its excellence has been acknowledged—necessitates leaping from one object to another, as chance presents them, without experiencing the slightest sentiment of guilt with regard to the disorder such a procedure involves. This conduct is so conscious in Stendhal that he comes to recognize in Italian music—which he loves—a principle of irregularity quite homologous to that of *dispersed love*: in performing their music, Italians do not observe *tempo; tempo* occurs among Germans; on one side, the German *noise*, the uproar of German music, beating out an implacable measure ("the first *tempisti* in the world"); on the other, Italian opera, *summa* of discontinuous and untamed pleasures: this is the *natural*, guaranteed by a civilization of women.

In Stendhal's Italian system, Music has a privileged place because it can replace everything else: it is the degree zero of this system: according to the needs of enthusiasm, it replaces and signifies journeys, Women, the other arts, and in a general manner any sensation. Its signifying status, precious above all others, is to produce effects without our having to inquire as to their causes, since these causes are inaccessible. Music constitutes a kind of *primal state* of pleasure: it produces a pleasure one always tries to recapture but never to explain; hence, it is the site of the pure effect, a central notion of the Stendhalian aesthetic. Now, what is a pure effect? An effect severed from and somehow purified of any explicative reason, i.e., ultimately, of any *responsible* reason. Italy is the country where Stendhal, being neither entirely a traveler (a tourist) nor entirely a native, is voluptuously delivered from the responsibility of the *citizen*; if Stendhal were an Italian citizen, he would die "poisoned by melancholy": whereas, a Milanese by affection rather than civil status, he need merely harvest the brilliant effects of a civilization for which he is not responsible. I have been able to experience the convenience of this devious dialectic myself: I used to love Morocco, I often visited the country as a tourist, even spending rather long vacations there; therefore, it occurred to me to spend a year there as a professor: the magic vanished; confronted by administrative and professional problems, I plunged into the ungrateful world of causes and allegiances, I surrendered Festivity for Duty (this is doubtless what happened to Stendhal as consul: Civitavecchia was no longer Italy). I believe we must include within Stendhal's Italian sentiment this fragile status of innocence: Milanese Italy (and its Holy of Holies, La Scala) is literally a Paradise, a place without Evil, or again—let us put matters positively—the Sovereign Good: "When I am with the Milanese and speak their dialect, I forget that men are wicked, and the whole wicked aspect of my own soul instantly falls asleep."

This Sovereign Good, however, must express itself: hence, it must confront a power which is not at all innocent, language. This is necessary, first of all, because the Good has a natural force of expansion, it constantly opens out toward expression, seeks at all costs to communicate itself, to be shared; then, because Stendhal is a writer and because for him there is no fulfillment from which the word is absent (and in this his Italian delight has nothing mystical about it). Now, paradoxical as it seems, Stendhal is uncertain how to express Italy: or rather, he speaks it, he sings it, he does not *represent* it; he proclaims his love, but he cannot express it, or, as we say nowadays (a metaphor from driving), he cannot negotiate it. This he knows, this he suffers from, this he complains of; he constantly observes that he cannot "render his thought," and that to explain the difference his passion proposes between Milan and Paris "is the height of difficulty." Hence, fiasco lies in wait for lyric desire as well. All his accounts of Italian travels are strewn with declarations of love and of failures of expression. The fiasco of style has a name: platitude; Stendhal has at his disposal only one empty word: beautiful (*"beau," "belle"*): "In all my life, I have never seen so many beautiful women together; their beauty made me lower my eyes." "The most beautiful eyes I have ever encountered I saw that evening; such eyes are as beautiful and their expression as celestial as those of Mme Tealdi . . ." And in order to vivify this litany, he has only the emptiest of figures, the superlative: "The women's heads, on the contrary, often reveal the most impassioned finesse, uniting the rarest beauty," etc. This "etc." which I am adding, but which emerges from our reading, is important, for it yields up the secret of this impotence or perhaps, despite Stendhal's complaints, of this indifference to variation: the monotony of Italian travel is quite simply *algebraic*: the word, the syntax, in their platitude, refer expeditiously to a different order of signifiers; once this reference is suggested, Stendhal moves on to something else, i.e., repeats the operation: "This is as beautiful as Haydn's liveliest symphonies." "The men's faces at the ball that night would have afforded magnificent models to sculptors of busts like Danneker or Chantrey." Stendhal does not describe the thing, he does not even describe the effect; he simply says: *there*, there is an effect; I am intoxicated, transported, touched, dazzled, etc. In other words, the platitudinous word is a cipher, it refers to a system of sensations; we must read Stendhal's Italian discourse like a figured bass. Sade employs the same procedure: he describes beauty very poorly, platitudinously and rhetorically; this is because beauty is merely the element of an algorithm whose goal is to construct a system of practices.

What Stendhal wants to construct is, so to speak, a nonsystematic set, a perpetual flow of sensations: that Italy, he says, "which is in truth merely an occasion for sensations." From the point of view of discourse, then, there is an initial evaporation of the thing: "I am not claiming to say what things *are*, I am describing the *sensation* they produce upon me." Does he really describe it? Not really; he says it, indicates it, and asserts it without describing it. For it is just here, with sensation, that the difficulty of language begins; it is not easy to "render" a sensation: you recall that famous scene in Jules Romains's play *Knock* in which the old peasant woman, ordered by the implacable doctor to say how she feels, hesitates in her confusion between "it tickles" and "it itches" [*ça me chatouille / ça me gratouille*]. Any sensation, if we want to respect its vivacity and its acuity, leads to aphasia. Now Stendhal must go quickly, that is the constraint of his system; for what he wants to note is "the sensation of the moment"; and the moments, as we have seen apropos of *tempo*, occur irregularly, refractory to *measure*. Hence, it is by fidelity to his system, fidelity to the very nature of his Italy, "a country of sensations," that Stendhal seeks a rapid writing: in order to proceed quickly, sensation is subjected to an elementary stenography, to a kind of expedient grammar of discourse in which he tirelessly combines two stereotypes: the beautiful and its superlative; for nothing is faster than the stereotype, precisely because it is identified, alas and invariably, with the spontaneous. We must go still deeper into the economy of Stendhal's Italian discourse: if Stendhalian sensation lends itself so well to an algebraic treatment, if the discourse it feeds is continuously inflamed and continuously platitudinous, this is because that sensation, strangely enough, is *not sensual*; Stendhal, whose philosophy is sensualistic, is perhaps the least sensual of our authors, which is doubtless why it is difficult to apply to him a thematic critique. Nietzsche, for instance—I am deliberately choosing an extreme contrary—when he speaks of Italy, is much more sensual than Stendhal: he can thematically describe the food of Piedmont, the only cooking in the world he enjoyed.

If I am insisting on this difficulty in expressing Italy, despite so many pages which describe Stendhal's "promenades," it is because I see in them a kind of suspicion attached to language itself. Stendhal's two loves, Music and Italy, are, one may say, spaces *outside of language;* music is so by status, for it escapes any description, lets itself be described, as we have seen, only by its effect; and Italy joins the status of the art with which it is identified; not only because the Italian language, Stendhal says in *On Love*, "being much more apt to be sung than spoken, will be supported against the invading French clarity only by music"; but also, for two stranger reasons: the first is that to Stendhal's ears Italian conversation constantly tends to that limit of articulated language which is exclamation: "At a Milanese soirée," Stendhal notes admiringly, "the conversation consists entirely of exclamations. For three quarters of an hour, reckoned by my watch, there was not a single completed sentence"; the sentence, completed armature of language, is the enemy (we need merely recall Stendhal's antipathy for the author of the most beautiful sentences in the French language, Chateaubriand). The second reason, which preciously withdraws Italy from language, from what I should call the militant language of culture, is precisely its lack of culture: Italy doesn't read, doesn't talk, Italy exclaims,

Italy sings. This is its genius, its "naturalness," and this is why Italy is adorable. Such delicious suspension of articulated, civilized language recurs for Stendhal in everything that for him constitutes Italy: in "the profound idleness enjoyed under a splendid sky [I am quoting from *On Love*] . . . ; it is the absence of novel reading, and of virtually all reading, which leaves still more to the inspiration of the moment; it is the passion for music which excites within the soul a movement so similar to that of love."

Thus, a certain suspicion attached to language joins the kind of aphasia which is generated by the excess of love: before Italy and Women, and Music, Stendhal is, literally, *speechless, interloqué,* i.e., ceaselessly interrupted in his locution. This interruption is indeed an intermittence: Stendhal speaks of Italy by an almost daily but enduring intermittence. He himself explains it very well (as always): "What choice to make? How to paint such insane happiness? My word, I cannot continue, the subject exceeds all expression. My hand can no longer write the words, I shall resume tomorrow. I am like a painter who no longer has the courage to fill in a corner of his picture. In order not to spoil the rest, he sketches in *alla meglio* what he cannot paint . . ." This painting of Italy *alla meglio,* which occupies every account of Stendhal's Italian journeys, is a kind of daubing, a scribbling, one might say, which expresses both love and the impotence to express love, because this love suffocates by its very vivacity. Such a dialectic of extreme love and difficult expression resembles what the very young child experiences—still *infans,* deprived of adult speech—when he plays with what Winnicott calls a *transitional object*; the space which separates and at the same time links the mother and her baby is the very space of the child's play and of the mother's counterplay: it is the still-shapeless space of fantasy, of the imagination, of creation. Such is, it seems to me, Stendhal's Italy: a kind of transitional object whose manipulation, being ludic, produces these *squiggles* which Winnicott notes and which are here any number of travel journals.

To keep to these Journals, which betoken a love of Italy but do not communicate it (at least, such is the judgment of my own reading), we are entitled to repeat mournfully (or tragically) that *one always fails in speaking of what one loves.* Yet, twenty years later, by a kind of after-the-fact which also constitutes part of the devious logic of love, Stendhal writes certain triumphant pages about Italy which, this time, fire up the reader (this reader—but I don't suppose I'm the only one) with that jubilation, with that *irradiation* which the private journals claimed but did not communicate. These admirable pages are the ones which form the beginning of *The Charterhouse of Parma.* Here there is a kind of miraculous harmony between "the mass of happiness and pleasure which explodes" in Milan with the arrival of the French and our own delight in reading: the effect described finally coincides with the effect produced. Why this reversal? Because Stendhal, shifting from the Journal to the Novel, from the Album to the Book (to adopt one of Mallarmé's distinctions), has abandoned sensation, a vivid but inconstruable fragment, to undertake that great mediating form which is Narrative, or better still Myth. What is required to make a Myth? We must have the action of two forces: first of all, a hero, a great liberating figure: this is Bonaparte, who enters Milan, penetrates Italy, as Stendhal did, more humbly, from the Saint-Bernard pass; then an opposition, an antithesis—a paradigm, in short—which stages the combat of Good and Evil and thereby produces what is lacking in the Album and belongs to the Book, i.e., a meaning: on one side, in these first pages of *The Charterhouse,* boredom, wealth, avarice, Austria, the Police, Ascanio, Grianta; on the other, intoxication, heroism, poverty, the Republic, Fabrizio, Milan; and above all, on the one side, the Father; on the other, Women. By abandoning himself to the Myth, by entrusting himself to the Book, Stendhal gloriously regains what he had somehow failed to achieve in his albums: the expression of an effect. This effect—the Italian effect—finally has a name, which is no longer the platitudinous one of Beauty: it is festivity. Italy is a feast, that is what is ultimately conveyed by the Milanese preamble of *The Charterhouse,* which Stendhal was quite right to retain, despite Balzac's reservations: festivity, i.e., the very transcendence of egotism.

In short, what has happened—what has transpired—between the travel journals and *The Charterhouse,* is writing. Writing—which is what? A power, probable fruit of a long initiation, which annuls the sterile immobility of the amorous image-repertoire and gives its adventure a symbolic generality. When he was young, in the days of *Rome, Naples, Florence,* Stendhal could write: ". . . when I tell lies, I am like M. de Goury, I am bored"; he did not yet know that there existed a lie, the lie of novels, which would be—miraculously—both the detour of truth and the finally triumphant expression of his Italian passion.

Tel Quel, 1980

7
ENVIRONS OF THE IMAGE

Writers, Intellectuals, Teachers

What follows depends on the idea that there is a basic link between teaching and speech. This is a very old observation (has not the whole of our teaching emerged from Rhetoric?), but we can frame it differently, nowadays, from the way we used to; first of all, because there is a (political) crisis in teaching; then, because (Lacanian) psychoanalysis has exposed the twists and turns of *la parole vide*; finally, because the opposition between speech and writing has become so obvious that we must begin deducing its effects.

As opposed to the teacher, who is on the side of speech, let us call any operator of language on the side of writing a *writer*; between the two, the intellectual: the subject who prints and publishes his speech. There is virtually no incompatibility between the teacher's language and the intellectual's (they frequently coexist in one and the same individual); but the writer is alone, separate: writing begins at the point where speech becomes *impossible* (as the word is used about a child).

Two constraints

Speech is irreversible: a word cannot be retraced except precisely by saying that one retracts it. Here, to cancel is to add; if I want to erase what I have just said, I can do so only by showing the eraser itself (I must say: "*or rather . . . ,*" "*I expressed myself badly . . .*"); paradoxically, it is ephemeral speech which is indelible, not monumental writing. There is nothing to be done with speech but add on more. The corrective and perfective movement of speech is a stammer, a fabric that frays out as it knits itself together, a chain of augmentative corrections which is the chosen abode of the unconscious part of our discourse (it is no accident that psychoanalysis is linked to speech, not to writing: a dream is not written): the eponymous figure of the speaker is Penelope.

Nor is this all: we cannot make ourselves understood (properly or poorly) unless we maintain, as we speak, a certain *speed* of delivery. We are like a bicyclist or a film—doomed to keep riding or turning if we are to avoid falling or jamming; silence and hesitation are both denied us: articulatory speed subjugates each point of the sentence to what immediately precedes or follows it (impossible to "venture" the word in the direction of odd or alien paradigms); context is a structural datum not of language but of speech; now, context by its very status is reductive of meaning, the spoken word is "clear"; such clarity, the banishment of polysemy, serves the Law: *all speech is on the side of the Law.*

Anyone preparing to speak (in a teaching situation) must become conscious of the *staging* imposed by the use of speech, by the simple effect of a *natural* determination (which derives from its physical nature: that of ariculatory breathing). This staging develops in the following way. Either the speaker chooses the role of Authority in all good faith, in which case it is sufficient to "speak well," i.e., to speak in accordance with the Law inherent in all speech: without stammering, at the right speed; or again *clearly* (this is what is asked of good pedagogical discourse: clarity, authority); the distinct sentence is a sentence indeed, *sententia,* a penal speech. Or else the speaker is hampered by the Law which his speech will introduce into what he wants to say; of course, he cannot spoil his delivery (which condemns him to "clarity"), but he can *apologize* for speaking (for laying down the Law): in this case he uses the irreversibility of speech to breach its legality; he corrects himself, adds on, stammers, enters into the infinitude of language, superimposes upon the simple message expected of him a new message which spoils the very notion of message, and by the shimmer of blemishes and mistakes with which he accompanies his speech line, he asks us to believe with him that language is not reduced to communication. By all these operations, which bring his stammering closer to the Text, the imperfect orator hopes to attenuate the ungrateful role which makes every speaker a kind of policeman. Yet, at the end of this effort to "speak badly," there is still a role which is imposed upon him: for the audience (nothing to do with the reader), trapped in its own image-repertoire, receives this fumbling as so many signs of weakness and offers him the image of a human, all too human master: a *liberal* one.

The choice is grim: conscientious functionary or free artist, the teacher escapes neither the theater of speech nor the Law staged within it: for the Law is produced, *not in what he says, but in the fact that he speaks at all.* In order to subvert the Law (and not simply to get around it), he would have to dismantle all vocal delivery, the speed and rhythm of words, until he achieved an *altogether different* intelligibility—or else not speak at all; but then he would be back in other roles: either that of the great silent mind, heavy with experience and reserve, or that of the militant who in the name of *praxis* dismisses all discourse as trivial. No help for it: language is always on the side of power; to speak is to exercise a will to power: in the space of speech, no innocence, no safety.

The summary

Statutorily, the teacher's discourse is marked by this characteristic: that it can (or may) be summarized (this is a privilege it shares with the discourse of politicians). In French schools, for example, there is an exercise known as *text reduction*; an expression which nicely expresses the ideology of the summary: on one side there is "thought," object of the message, element of action, of knowledge, a transitive or critical force, and on the other there is "style," an ornament associated with luxury, idleness, hence with the trivial; to separate thought from style is in a sense to rid discourse of its sacerdotal garments, to secularize the message (whence the bourgeois identification of teacher and politician); "form," it is assumed, is compressible, and such compression is not regarded as essentially detrimental: *from a distance,* i.e., from our Western promontory, is there really such a difference between the head of a living Jivaro and a shrunken Jivaro head?

It is difficult for a teacher to see the "notes" taken during his lectures; he has no desire to do so, either out of discretion (for nothing is more personal than "notes," despite the formal character of this practice) or else, more likely, out of fear of discovering himself in a reduced version, dead yet substantial, like a Jivaro "treated" by his fellow tribesmen; not knowing if what is taken (siphoned) out of the flow of speech is erratic statements (formulae, sentences) or the gist of an argument; in either case, what is lost is the *supplement,* just where the stake of the language is advanced: the summary is a disavowal of writing.

Conversely, therefore, we may call a "writer" (this word always designating a practice, not a social value) any sender whose "message" (thereby immediately destroying its nature as message) cannot be summarized: a condition which the writer shares with the madman, the compulsive talker, and the mathematician, but which it is precisely writing's task (i.e., the task of a certain practice of the signifier) to specify.

The teaching relationship

How can the teacher be identified with the psychoanalyst? It is precisely the contrary which occurs: it is the teacher who is psychoanalyzed.

Imagine that I am a teacher: I speak, endlessly, for and before someone who does not speak. I am the one who says *I* (the detours of *one* or *we,* of the impersonal sentence, are insignificant), I am the one who, under the cover of an *exposition* (of something known), *proposes* a discourse, *without ever knowing how it is received,* so that I can never have the reassurance of a definitive (even if damaging) image which might *constitute me*:

in the *exposé,* more aptly named than we assume, it is not knowledge which is *exposed,* it is the subject (who exposes himself to painful adventures). The mirror is empty: it reflects only the defection of my language as it emerges. Like the Marx Brothers disguised as Russian aviators (in *A Night at the Opera*—a work I regard as an allegory of many textual problems), I begin my *exposé* decked out in a big false beard; but, gradually flooded by the rising tide of my own speech (a substitute for the pitcher of water on the rostrum of the Mayor of New York from which the *mute* Harpo greedily drinks), I feel my beard peeling off in front of everyone: no sooner have I made the audience smile by some "clever" remark, no sooner have I reassured it by some "progressive" stereotype, than I feel the complacency of such provocations; I regret the hysterical pulsion, I'd like to retract it, preferring (too late) an austere discourse to a "smart" one (but, in the contrary case, it is the "severity" of the discourse which seems hysterical to me); should some smile answer my remarks, or some assent my intimidation, I am immediately convinced that such manifestations of complicity are produced by fools or flatterers (I am here describing an imaginary process); though it is I who want a response and take steps to provoke it, once the response comes, I am suspicious; and if the discourse I offer chills or postpones any response at all, I do not feel I am any more *on pitch* on that account, for then I must glory in the solitude of my speech, furnish it the alibi of missionary discourse (science, truth, etc.).

Hence, in accordance with psychoanalytic description (Lacan's, whose perspicacity here any speaker will confirm), when the teacher speaks to his audience, the Other is always there, *puncturing* his discourse; and his discourse, though sustained by an impeccable intelligence, armed with scientific "rigor" or political "radicality," would still be punctured: it suffices that I speak, that my speech flows, for it to flow away. Of course, though every professor is in the posture of an analysand, no student audience can claim the advantage of the converse situation; first, because there is nothing preeminent about psychoanalytic silence; second, because sometimes a subject, carried away, will irreversibly dash into the flame of discourse, mingle in the oratorical orgy (and if the subject stubbornly remains silent, he merely expresses the obstinacy of his mutism); but for the teacher, the student audience is still the exemplary Other because it *seems* not to be speaking—so that then, from deep in its apparent silence, it speaks all the louder *in you*: its implicit speech, which is your own, touches you all the more immediately because its discourse does not encumber you.

Such is the cross of all public speech: whether the teacher speaks or the listener claims the right to speak, in both cases we go straight to the couch; the teaching relation is nothing more than the transference it institutes; "science," "method," "knowledge," "ideas" come indirectly; they are given *in addition*; they are *leftovers*.

The contract

> *"Most of the time, relations between humans suffer, often to the point of destruction, from the fact that the contract established between them is not respected. Once two humans enter into a reciprocal relation, their usually tacit contract comes into force. It controls the form of their relations, etc."*
> —BRECHT

Although the demand articulated in the community space of a course is fundamentally intransitive, as is appropriate in any transferential situation, it is nonetheless overdetermined and takes shelter behind other apparently transitive demands; such demands form the conditions of an implicit contract between teacher and taught. This contract is "imaginary," it in no way contradicts the economic determination which impels the student to seek a career and the teacher to fulfill the requirements of a post.

Here, pell-mell (in the order of the image-repertoire there is no originating motive), is what the teacher asks of the taught: (1) to acknowledge him in whatever "role" it may be: of authority, of benevolence, of contestation, of knowledge, etc. (any visitor whom you cannot place with regard to the *image* he asks of you becomes disturbing); (2) to act as a relay, to extend him, to spread his ideas, his style, far afield; (3) to let himself be seduced, to assent to a loving relationship (granting all the sublimations, all the distances, all the forms of respect consonant with social reality and with the anticipated futility of this relationship); last, to permit him to honor the contract he himself has entered into with his employer, i.e., with society; the person taught is part of a (remunerated) practice, the object of a craft, the substance of a production (however delicate to define).

On his side, here, pell-mell, is what the person taught asks of the teacher; (1) to guide him to a favorable professional integration; (2) to fulfill the roles traditionally devolving upon the teacher (scientific authority, transmission of a body of knowledge, etc.); (3) to reveal the secrets of a technique (of research, of examinations, etc.); (4) under the banner of that secular saint Method, to be an initiator of ascesis, a guru; (5) to represent a "movement of ideas," a School, a Cause, to be its spokesman; (6) to admit him, the student, into the complicity of a private language; (7) for those obsessed by *the thesis* (a timid practice of writing, both disfigured and defended by its institutional finality), to guarantee the reality of this fantasy; (8) last, the teacher is asked to lend his services: to sign forms, recommendations, etc.

This is simply a Topic, a set of choices which are not all necessarily actualized at the same time in one individual. Yet it is at the level of contractual totality that the *comfort* of the teaching relation is worked out: the "good" teacher, the "good" student are those who philosophically accept the plurality of their determinations, perhaps because they know that the truth of a relationship of speech is *elsewhere*.

Research

What is a piece of "research"? To find out, we need some idea of what a "result" might be. What does one find? What does one want to find? *What is missing*? In which axiomatic field will the phenomenon be isolated, the meaning revealed, the statistical discovery placed? No doubt, in each case this depends on the particular science solicited. But once a piece of research concerns the text (and the text reaches much farther than the work), the research itself becomes text, production: any "result" is literally *im-pertinent.* "Research," then, is the discreet name which, under the constraint of certain social conditions, we give to the work of writing: research is on the side of writing, it is an adventure of the signifier, an excess of exchange; it is impossible to maintain the equation of a "result" *against* a piece of "research." This is why the discourse to which a piece of research must be submitted (in teaching it) has a purpose beyond its parenetic function ("Write!"): it is intended to recall "research" to its epistemological condition: whatever it seeks, it must not forget its nature as language—and it is this which ultimately makes an encounter with writing inevitable. In writing, the speech-act "deceives" the message by the effect of the language which produces it: this adequately defines the critical, "progressive," unsatisfied, productive element which even common usage grants to "research." Such is the historical role of research: to teach the scholar he *speaks* (but if he knew this, he would *write*—and the whole idea of science, *scientificity* itself, would be changed thereby).

The destruction of stereotypes

Someone writes me that "a group of revolutionary students is preparing a destruction of the structuralist myth." The expression delights me by its stereotypical consistency: the destruction of the myth begins, from the statement of its putative agents, with the finest myth of all: the "group of revolutionary students" is quite as good as "war widows" or "old soldiers."

Usually the stereotype is a sad business because it is constituted by a necrosis of language, a prosthesis used to plug a hole in writing; but at the same time it can only provoke a huge burst of laughter: it takes itself seriously; supposes itself closer to the truth because indifferent to its nature as language: it is both corny and solemn.

To distance the stereotype is not a political task, for political language itself is constituted by stereotypes; but a critical one, i.e., one seeking to put language in a state of crisis. Initially, this permits us to isolate that speck of ideology contained in all political discourse, and to attack it like an acid capable of dissolving the fats of "natural" language (i.e., of the language which pretends not to know it *is* language). Then, it is a way of breaking with the mechanistic conception which makes language the simple response to stimuli of situation or of action; it sets the production of language in opposition to its simple and fallacious utilization. Further, it disturbs the Other's discourse and constitutes, in short, a permanent operation of pre-analysis. Last of all: the stereotype is at bottom a form of opportunism: one conforms to the ruling language, or rather to what, in language, seems to *rule* (a situation, a privilege, a struggle, an institution, a movement, a science, a theory, etc.); to speak in stereotypes is to side with the power of language; it is this opportunism which must (today) be refused.

But can one not "transcend" stereotypes instead of "destroying" them? Such a solution is unrealistic; the operators of language have no power except to empty what is full; language is not dialectical: it allows only a two-stage movement.

The chain of discourses

It is because language is not dialectical (permitting the third term only as a formula, a rhetorical assertion, a pious hope) that discourse (discursivity), in its historical development, moves by fits and starts. Each new discourse can emerge only as the *paradox* which reverses (and often opposes) the surrounding or preceding *doxa*; it can be generated only as difference, distinction, standing out *against* what sticks to it. For instance, Chomskyan theory is built up *against* Bloomfieldian behaviorism; then, once linguistic behaviorism has been liquidated by Chomsky, it is *against* Chomskyan mentalism (or anthropologism) that a new semiotics is sought, while Chomsky himself, in order to find allies, must *skip* his immediate predecessors and hark back as far as the Port-Royal *Grammar*. But no doubt it is in one of the greatest dialectical thinkers, in Marx, that it would be most interesting to observe the undialectical nature of language: Marx's discourse is almost entirely *paradoxical*, the *doxa* being now Proudhon, now someone else . . . This double movement of detachment and revival results not in a circle but, according to Vico's great and beautiful image, in a spiral, and it is in this *offset* of circularity (of paradoxical form) that historical determinations are articulated. Hence, we must always try to find which *doxa* an author is opposing (it may be an extremely minority *doxa*, governing a limited group). Teaching can also be evaluated in terms of paradox, provided it is based on this conviction: that a system which calls for corrections, translations, openings, and denials is more useful than an unformulated absence of system; we may then avoid the immobility of prattle and join the historical chain of discourses, the progress (*progressus*) of discursivity.

Method

Some people speak of method greedily, demandingly; what they want in work is method; to them it never seems rigorous enough, formal enough. Method becomes a Law; but since this Law is devoid of any effect outside itself (no one can say what a "result" is in the "human sciences"), it is infinitely disappointed; proposing itself as a pure meta-language, it partakes of the vanity of all meta-language. Hence the invariable fact is that a work which constantly proclaims its will-to-method is ultimately sterile: everything has been put into the method, nothing remains for the writing; the researcher insists that his text will be methodological, but this text never comes: no surer way to kill a piece of research and send it to join the great scrap heap of abandoned projects than Method.

The danger of Method (of a fixation upon Method) comes from this: research work must satisfy two demands; the first is a demand for responsibility: the work must increase lucidity, expose the implications of a procedure, the alibis of a language—in short, must constitute a *critique* (let us recall once again that to *criticize* means to *call into crisis*); here Method is inevitable, irreplaceable, not for its "results" but precisely—or on the contrary—because it realizes the highest degree of consciousness of a language *which does not forget itself*; but the second demand is of a very different order: it is the demand for writing, for a space of desire's dispersion, where Law is dismissed; hence, it is necessary, *at a certain moment*, to turn against Method, or at least to regard it without any founding privilege, as one of the voices of plurality: as a *view*, in short, a spectacle, mounted within the text—the text which is, after all, the only "true" result of any research.

Questions

To question is to want to know something. Yet, in many intellectual discussions, the questions which follow the lecturer's remarks are in no way the expression of a "want," but the assertion of a plenitude. In the guise of questioning, I mount an aggression against the speaker; *to question* then takes on its police meaning: *to question* is to interpellate. Yet the interpellated subject must pretend to answer the letter of the question, not its "address." So a game is set up: although each side knows just what the other's intentions are, the game demands a response to the content, not to the way that content is framed. If I am asked, in a certain tone, "*What's the use of linguistics?*"—thereby signifying to me that it's of no use whatever—I must naïvely pretend to answer: "Linguistics is useful for this, for that," and not, in accordance with the truth of the dialogue: "*Why are you attacking me?*" What I receive is the connotation; what I must give back is the denotation. In the space of speech, science and logic, knowledge and argument, questions and answers, propositions and objections are the masks of the dialectical relation. Our intellectual discussions are as encoded as the old scholastic disputes; we still have the stock roles (the "sociologist," the "Goldmannian," the "Telquelian," etc.), but contrary to the *disputatio*, where these roles would have been ceremonial and have displayed the artifice of their function, our intellectual "intercourse" always gives itself "natural" airs: it claims to exchange only signifieds, not signifiers.

In the name of what?

I speak in the name of what? Of a function? Of a body of knowledge? Of an experience? What do I represent? A scientific capacity? An institution? A service? As a matter of fact, I speak only in the name of a language: it is because I have written that I speak; writing is represented by its contrary, speech. This distortion means that in writing *about* speech I am doomed to the following aporrhoea: denouncing speech's image-repertoire through writing's unreality; thus, at present, I am not describing any "authentic" experience, I am not photographing any "real" teaching, I am opening no "academic" dossier. For writing can tell the truth about language, but not the truth about reality (we are at present trying to learn what a reality without language might be).

The standing position

What could be a more dubious situation than speaking for (or before) people who are standing or uncomfortably seated? What is being exchanged here? What is such discomfort the price of? What is my speech *worth*? How could the hearer's discomfort fail to lead to questions about the validity of what he is hearing? Is not the standing position eminently *critical*? And is this not how, on another scale, political consciousness begins: in *discomfort*? Listening refers me to the vanity of my own speech, its *price,* for willy-nilly I am placed in a circuit of exchange; and listening is also the position of the person I address.

Familiarity

Occasionally—the wreckage of May '68—a student will speak to a teacher using the familiar *tu* form of address. This is a strong sign, a full sign, which refers to the most psychological of signifieds: the *will* to contestation or closeness—muscle. Since an ethic of the sign is here imposed, it can be contested in its turn and a subtler semantics preferred: signs are to be dealt with *against a neutral background,* and, in French, that background is the *vous* form of address. The *tu* form can escape the code only in cases where it constitutes a *simplification of grammar* (for example, in addressing a foreigner who speaks French poorly); in such cases, it is a matter of substituting a transitive practice for a symbolic behavior: instead of trying to signify *just who* I think the other is (and therefore just who I think I am), I simply try to make myself understood by him. But this recourse, too, is ultimately devious: the *tu* form becomes another form of escape behavior; when a sign displeases me, when the signification bothers me, I shift toward the operational: the operational becomes a censorship of the symbolic, and thus a symbol of asymbolism; many political and scientific discourses are marked by this shift (on which depends, notably, the entire linguistics of "communication").

An odor of speech

As soon as you have finished speaking, the vertigo of the image begins: you exalt or regret what you have said, the way you have said it, you *imagine yourself* (you consider yourself as an image); speech is subject to remanence, it *smells.*

Writing has no *smell*: produced (having accomplished its process of production), it *falls,* not like a collapsing soufflé but like a meteorite disappearing; it will *travel* far from my body and yet it is not a detached, narcissistically retained fragment, like speech; its disappearance is not disappointing; it passes, it traverses—no more. The time of speech exceeds the act of speech (only a jurist could make us believe that words vanish, *verba volant*). Writing, though, has no past (if society compels you to *administer* what you have written, you can do so only in the greatest tedium, the tedium of a false past). This is why the discourse in which your writing is discussed has a much less striking effect than the discourse in which your speech is discussed (though the stake is higher): I can *objectively* account for the former, for "I" am no longer in it; the latter, however laudatory, I can only try to get rid of, for it intensifies the impasse of my image-repertoire.

(How does it happen, then, that this particular text preoccupies me, that once finished, corrected, released, it remains or recurs in a state of doubt—in a state of fear, as a matter of fact? Is it not *written*, liberated by writing? Yet I see that I cannot *improve* it, I have arrived at just the form of what I wanted to say: it is no longer a question of *style*. Whereby I conclude that it is the text's very status which bothers me: what troubles me about it is precisely the fact that, dealing with speech, it cannot, *in the writing itself*, altogether liquidate speech. In order to write *about* speech, whatever the distances of writing, I am obliged to *refer* to illusions of experiences, memories, feelings occurring to me when I was speaking—occurring to me as a speaking subject; in such writing as that, *there is still a referent*, and it is what *smells* to my own nostrils.)

Our place

Just as psychoanalysis, with Lacan, is extending the Freudian topic into a topology of the subject (the unconscious here is never in *its* place), so we need to substitute for the old "magistral" space, which was actually a religious space (speech from the pulpit, up above; down below, the *flock*), a less Euclidian space where no one, neither the teacher nor students, would ever be *in his final place*. Then we should see that what must be made reversible are not the social "roles" (what is the point of quibbling over "authority," over the "right" to speak?) but the regions of speech. *Where* is speech? In locution? In listening? In the *returns* of each? The problem is not to abolish the distinction of functions (the *teacher*, the *student*: after all, as Sade has taught us, order is a guarantee of pleasure) but to protect the instability and, so to speak, the vertigo of the sites of speech. In the teaching space, no one should anywhere be in his place (I am reassured by this constant displacement: were I to *find my place*, I should not even go on pretending to teach, I should give up).

Yet does not the teacher have a fixed place—that of his *remuneration*, the place he has in the economy, in production? It is always the same problem we keep coming back to: the origin of a speech does not exhaust it; once the speech is spoken, a thousand adventures happen to it, its origin becomes confused, all its effects are not in its cause; it is this *redundancy* which we are exploring.

Two criticisms

The mistakes that can be made in typing a manuscript are so many meaningful incidents, and these incidents, by analogy, help shed light on the behavior we must adopt with regard to meaning when we discuss a text.

Either the word produced by the mistake (if a wrong letter disfigures it) signifies nothing, finds no textual contour; the code is simply interrupted: an asemic word is created, a pure signifier; for example, instead of writing "officer," I write "offiver," which is meaningless. Or else the erroneous (mistyped) word, without being the word I wanted to write, is a word which the lexicon permits identifying, which means something: if I write "ride" instead of "rude," the new word exists—the phrase keeps a meaning, however eccentric; this is the path (the pith?) of puns, anagrams, of signifying metathesis, of spoonerisms:

there is a skid *within the codes*: meaning subsists, but pluralized, faked, without law of content, of message, of truth.

Each of these two types of mistake figures (or prefigures) a type of criticism. The first type dismisses all meaning of the support text: the text must lend itself only to a signifying efflorescence; it is its phonism alone which is to be treated, but not interpreted: we associate, we do not decipher; reading *offiver* instead of *officer*, I gain access, by the mistake, to a *right of association* (I can make "offiver" explode in the direction of "offer," of "olive," etc.); not only does the ear of this first criticism hear the cracklings of the phono-pickup, but they are all it wants to hear—it will make them into a new music. In the second type of criticism, the "reading head" rejects nothing: it perceives both the meaning (s) and its cracklings. The (historical) stake of these two criticisms (I should like to be able to call the field of the first *signifiosis*, and that of the second, *signifiance*) is obviously different.

The first has in its favor the signifier's right to spread out where it likes (where it can?): what law and what meaning—from what source?—would be entitled to constrain it? Once the philological (monological) law has been relaxed and the text opened to plurality, why stop? Why refuse to take polysemy to the point of asemy? In the name of what? Like any radical right, this one supposes a utopian vision of freedom: we revoke the law *immediately*, outside of any history, in defiance of any dialectic (which is why this style of demand can seem ultimately petit-bourgeois). However, once it evades all tactical reason while nonetheless remaining implanted within a specific (and alienated) intellectual society, the signifier's disorder reverts to hysterical wandering: by liberating reading from all meaning, it is ultimately *my* reading which I impose, for in *this* moment of History the subject's economy is not yet transformed, and the rejection of meaning(s) is turned into subjectivity. At best, we can say that this radical criticism, defined by a foreclosure of the signifier (and not by its escape), *anticipates* History, anticipates a new, unprecedented state in which the signifier's efflorescence would be compensated for by no idealist counterpart, by no closure of the person. Yet, to *criticize* is to call into crisis, and it is not possible to do this without evaluating the conditions of the crisis (its limits), without taking account of its moment. Hence, the second type of criticism, the criticism attached to the division of meanings and to the "rigging" of interpretation, appears (at least to my eyes) truer historically: in a society subject to the war of meanings and thereby committed to rules of communication which determine its effectiveness, the liquidation of the old criticism can advance only *into* meaning (into the volume of meanings), and not outside it. Ideological criticism, as it happens, is today doomed to operations of theft: the signified, whose exemption is the materialist task par excellence, is more readily "pilfered" in the illusion of meaning than in its destruction.

Two discourses

Let us distinguish two types of discourse.

Terrorist discourse is not necessarily linked to the peremptory assertion (or to the opportunist defense) of a faith, a truth, a justice; it can simply seek to achieve the lucid adequation of the speech-act to the true violence of language, a native violence which is the consequence of the fact that no statement can directly express the truth yet has no other system at its disposal than the word's *coup de force*; hence, an apparently terrorist discourse will cease being so if, in reading it, we follow the clue it offers in and of itself: reestablishing in it the gap or the dispersion; i.e., the unconscious; such a reading is not always easy; certain minor terrorisms, functioning chiefly by stereotypes, themselves operate—like any discourse of good conscience—a foreclosure of the other scene; in short, such terrorisms *refuse to be written* (they can be detected by something inflexible in them: that odor of seriousness given off by the stereotype).

Repressive discourse is not linked to declared violence but to the Law. The Law then passes into language as equilibrium: an equilibrium is postulated between what is forbidden and what is permitted, between commendable meaning and unworthy meaning, between the constraint of common sense and the monitored freedom of interpretations; whence the preference shown by such discourse for vacillations, for verbal oppositions, for the thrust and parry of antitheses; to be *neither* for this *nor* for that (yet, if you add up *neithers* and *nors*, you will see that this *impartial, objective, human* speaker is *for* this, *against* that). Such repressive discourse is the discourse of good conscience, liberal discourse.

The axiomatic field

"All that is necessary," Brecht says, "is to establish which interpretations of the facts, appearing within the proletariat engaged in the class struggle (national or international), enable the proletariat to use them for its action. They must be synthesized in order to create an axiomatic field." Thus, each fact possesses several meanings (a plurality of "interpretations"), and among these meanings there is one which is proletarian (or at least which serves the proletariat in its action); by connecting these various proletarian meanings, we construct a (revolutionary) axiomatics. But who establishes meaning? The proletariat itself, Brecht thinks ("*appearing within the proletariat*"). This view implies that the division of classes has its inevitable counterpart in the division of meanings and that the class struggle corresponds no less inevitably to a war of meanings: so long as there is a class struggle (national or international), the division of the axiomatic field is inexpiable.

The difficulty (for all Brecht's verbal assurance: "*all that is necessary* . . .") comes from the fact that certain objects of discourse do not directly interest the proletariat (no interpretation of them appears within it) and that nonetheless the proletariat cannot remain indifferent to them, for they constitute—at least in the advanced states which have liquidated both poverty and folklore—the plenitude of the *other discourse*, within which the proletariat itself is compelled to live, seeking survival, diversion, etc.: this discourse is that of culture (it may be that, in Marx's day, culture's pressure on the proletariat was weaker than it is today: there was as yet no "mass culture" because there was no "mass communication"). How to attribute meaning for the struggle to what does not directly concern you? How could the proletariat determine, *within itself*, an interpretation of Zola, of Poussin, of pop art, of the Sunday sports supplement, or the latest news item? In order to "interpret" all these cultural relays, the proletariat requires *representatives*: those whom Brecht calls the "artists" or the "workers of the intellect" (the expression, at least in French, is a mischievous one, the intellect being so nearly off the top of the head), those who have at their command the language of the indirect, the indirect as language; in short, *oblates*, who dedicate themselves to the proletarian interpretation of cultural phenomena.

But then begins, for these procurators of proletarian meaning, a real headache, for their class situation is not that of the proletariat: they are not producers—a negative situation they share with (student) youth, an equally unproductive class with which they usually form an alliance of language. It follows from this that culture, from which it is their responsibility to derive a proletarian meaning, ultimately refers them to themselves and not to the proletariat: How to *evaluate* culture? According to its origin? It is bourgeois. According to its goal? Bourgeois again. According to dialectics? Although bourgeois, this does contain "progressive" elements; but what, *on the level of discourse*, distinguishes dialectics from compromise? And then, with what instruments? Historicism, sociologism, positivism, formalism, psychoanalysis? Every one of them *embourgeoisé*. Some people will ultimately prefer to skip the headache: to dismiss all "culture," which obliges them to destroy all discourse.

As it happens, even within an axiomatic field apparently clarified by the class struggle, the tasks are diverse, sometimes contradictory, and above all established according to different *tenses*. The axiomatic field consists of several individual axiomatics: cultural criticism develops *successively*, *diversely*, and *simultaneously* by opposing the New to the Old, sociologism to historicism, economism to formalism, logico-positivism to psychoanalysis, then again, *by another turn*, monumental history to empirical sociology, the alien to the New, formalism to historicism, psychoanalysis to scientism, etc. Applied to culture, critical discourse can only be a cross-hatching of tactics, a tissue of elements now past, now circumstantial (linked to contingencies of fashion), and now frankly utopian: to the tactical necessities of the war of meanings is added the strategic conception of the new conditions which will be applied to the signifier when this war is over: cultural criticism, as a matter of fact, must be *impatient*, because it cannot be carried on without desire. Hence, all the discourses of Marxism are present in its writing: apologetic (to exalt revolutionary science), apocalyptic (to destroy bourgeois culture), and eschatological (to desire, to call for the indivision of meaning, concomitant with the indivision of classes).

Our unconscious

The problem we set ourselves is this: how can the two great *epistemes* of modernity, i.e., materialist and Freudian dialectics, be made to converge, intersect, and produce a new human relation (nor is it to be excluded that a third term lurks in the inter-diction of the first two)? Which is to say: how to assist the inter-action of these two desires: to change the economy of the relations of production and to change the economy of the subject? (Psychoanalysis temporarily seems to us the power better suited to the second of these tasks; but other topics are imaginable, those of the East, for example.)

This generalized task comes up against the following question: What relation is there between class determination and the unconscious? By what displacement does this determination "slip" between subjects? Certainly not by "psychology" (as if there were mental contents: bourgeois / proletarian /intellectual, etc.), but obviously by language, by discourse: the Other—who speaks, who is all speech—is social. On one side, though the proletariat is *separated,* it is still bourgeois language, in its degraded, petit-bourgeois form, which unconsciously speaks in the proletariat's cultural discourse; and on the other side, though the proletariat is mute, it speaks in the discourse of the intellectual, not as a canonical, founding voice, but as an unconscious: it suffices to see how the proletariat *strikes* all our discourses (explicit reference of the intellectual to the proletariat in no way prevents the proletariat from occupying, in our discourses, the place of the unconscious: the unconscious is not "lack of consciousness"); only the bourgeois discourse of the bourgeoisie is tautological: the unconscious of bourgeois discourse is indeed the Other, but that Other is a different bourgeois discourse.

Writing as value

Evaluation precedes criticism. There is no calling into crisis without evaluating. Our value is writing. This stubborn reference, beyond the fact that it must often irritate, seems in some people's eyes to involve a risk: the risk of developing a certain *mystique.* The reproach is mischievous, for it inverts point by point the bearing we attribute to writing: that of being, in this little canton of our Western world, the *materialist field par excellence.* Though deriving from Marxism and from psychoanalysis, the theory of writing tries to shift—without breaking with—its place of origin; on one hand, it rejects the temptation of the signified, i.e., deafness to language, to the return and redundancy of its effects; on the other, it is opposed to speech in that speech is not transferential and escapes—partially at least, in very narrow, even particularist social limits—the traps of "dialogue"; in this theory of writing is the germ of a mass gesture; against all discourses (speeches, inauthentic writings, rituals, protocols, social symbolics), only the theory of writing, today, even in the form of a luxury, makes language into something *atopic*: without place: it is this dispersion, this non-situation, which is materialistic.

Peaceable speech

One of the things that can be expected from a regular meeting of speakers is simply this: *good will*; that such a meeting represent a space of speech divested of aggressiveness.

Such a divestiture cannot proceed without resistances. The first is of a cultural order: the rejection of violence passes for a humanist lie, courtesy (minor mode of this rejection) for a class value, and friendliness for a mystification related to the liberal idea of dialogue. The second resistance is of an imaginary order, an order of the image-repertoire: many people want a conflictual speech from motives of psychic liberation; the retreat from confrontation, they say, has something frustrating about it. The third resistance is of a political order: polemic is an essential weapon of the struggle; every space of speech must be splintered in order to reveal its contradictions—it must be subjected to scrutiny.

Yet what is preserved in these three resistances is finally the unity of the neurotic subject, which is *collected* in the forms of conflict. Yet we know that violence is always present (in language), and this very presence is why we may bracket its signs and thereby dispense with a rhetoric: violence must not be absorbed by the code of violence.

The first advantage would be to suspend, or at least to delay, the roles of speech: so that listening, speaking, answering, I am never the actor of a judgment, a subjection, an intimidation, the procurator of a Cause. No doubt, peaceable speech will ultimately secrete its own role, since, whatever I say, the Other always reads me as an image; but in the time I take to evade this role, in the work of language which the community will perform, week after week, in order to expel any stichomythia from its discourse, a certain expropriation of speech (from then on, close to writing) may be attained, or again *a certain generalization of the subject.*

Perhaps this is what is found in certain drug experiences (in the experience of certain drugs). Though not smoking oneself (if only because of a bronchial incapacity to inhale the smoke), one cannot be insensitive to the general *good will* which impregnates certain places, abroad, where *kif* is smoked. The gestures, the (infrequent) words, the whole relation of bodies (though a relation that is motionless and remote) is relaxed, disarmed (thus, nothing in common with alcoholic intoxication, the legal form of violence in the West): here space seems to be the product of a subtle ascesis (in which one can occasionally read a certain *irony*). The meeting of speakers, it seems to me, should aim at this *suspension* (no matter of what: it is a form that is desired), should try to connect with an *art of living*, greatest of all the arts, Brecht used to say (such a view is more dialectical than it appears, in that it compels us to distinguish and to evaluate the uses of violence). In short, within the very limits of the teaching space as given, the need is to attempt, quite patiently, to trace out a pure form, that of a *floating* (the very form of the signifier); such floating destroys nothing; it is content to disorient the Law: the necessities of promotion, professional obligations (which nothing henceforth keeps from being scrupulously fulfilled), imperatives of knowledge, prestige of method, ideological criticism—everything is there, but *floating*.

Tel Quel, 1971

To the Seminar

Is this a real site or an imaginary one? Neither. An institution is treated in the utopian mode: I outline a space and call it: *seminar*. It is quite true that the gathering in question is held weekly in Paris, i.e., *here and now*; but these adverbs are also those of fantasy. Thus, no guarantee of reality, but also nothing gratuitous about the anecdote. One might put things differently: that the (real) seminar is for me the object of a (minor) delirium, and that my relations with this object are, literally, *amorous*.

The three spaces

Our gathering is small, to safeguard not its intimacy but its complexity: it is necessary that the crude geometry of big public lectures give way to a subtle topology of corporeal relations, of which knowledge is only the *pre-text*. Thus, three spaces are present in our seminar.

The first is institutional. The institution determines a frequency, a schedule, a site, sometimes a *cursus*. Does it compel us to recognize levels, a hierarchy? Certainly not—at least here; elsewhere, knowledge is cumulative: one knows Hittite *more or less*, one knows demographic science *more or less*. But the text? Does one possess the language of the Text *more or less well*? The seminar—this seminar, ours—is not based on a community of science but on a complicity of language, i.e., of desire. It is a matter of desiring the Text, of putting in circulation a desire for the Text.

The second space is transferential (this word is given with no psychoanalytic rigor). Where is the transferential relation? Classically, it is established between the director (of the seminar) and its members. Even in this sense, however, this relation is not certain: I do not say what I know, I set forth what I am doing; I am not draped in the interminable discourse of absolute knowledge, I am not lurking in the terrifying silence of the Examiner (every teacher—and this is the vice of the system—is a potential examiner); I am neither a sacred (consecrated) subject nor a buddy, only a manager, an operator, a regulator: the one who gives rules, protocols, not laws. My role (if I have one) is to clear the stage on which horizontal transferences will be established: what matters, in such a seminar (the site of its success), is not the relation of the members to the director but the relation of the members to each other. That is what must be said (as I have learned by dint of discovering the discomfort of overcrowded groups, where each member complained of knowing nobody else): the famous "teaching relation" is not the relation of teacher to taught, but the relation of those taught to each other. The space of the seminar is not Oedipal but Phalansterial, i.e., in a sense, *novelistic* (an offshoot of the novel: in Fourier's work, *harmonian discourse* ends in *snatches* of a novel: this is the *amorous New World*); the novelistic is neither the false nor the sentimental; it is merely the circulatory space of subtle, flexible desires; within the very artifice of a "sociality" whose opacity is miraculously reduced, it is the web of amorous relations.

The third space is textual: either because the seminar assumes responsibility for producing a text, for writing a book (by a *montage* of writings); or because, on the contrary, it regards its own—non-functional—practice as already constituting a text: the rarest text, one which does not appear in writing. A certain way of being together can fulfill the inscription of significance: there are writers *sans* book (I know some), there are texts which are not products but practices; it might even be said that the "glorious" text will someday be a pure practice.

Of these three spaces, none is judged (disparaged, praised), none prevails over its neighbors. Each space is, in its turn, the supplement, the surprise of the other two, everything is *indirect.* (Orpheus does not turn back to look at his delight; when he turns back, he loses it; if we turn back to look at knowledge, or method, or friendship, or the very theater of our community, this whole plurality vanishes: nothing is left but the institution, or the task, or the psychodrama. *The indirect* is precisely what we walk ahead of without turning back to look back at it.)

As phalanstery, the seminar's work is the *production of differences.*

Difference is not conflict. In these small intellectual spaces, conflict is merely the realistic decor, the crude parody of difference, a phantasmagoria.

Difference means—what? That each relation, gradually (it takes time), is *made original*: discovers the originality of bodies taken one by one, breaks off the reproduction of roles, the repetition of discourses, counters any staging of prestige, of rivalry.

Disappointment

Since this gathering has some relation to gratification [*jouissance*], inevitably it will also be a space of disappointment.

Disappointment sets in at the end of two negations, the second of which does not destroy the first. If I observe that X . . . (teacher, manager, commentator) has not explained to me *why*, *how*, etc., this observation remains acceptable, more or less inconsequential: nothing is separated, because nothing has "set"; but if I intensify the negative moment, I produce the figure of the *climax*, I turn aggressively against an aggressive destiny; I then resort to the formula of disappointment par excellence, the "*not even*" which registers in a single phrase intellectual indignation and sexual fiasco: "X . . . has *not even* told us, explained, shown . . . gratified us." When disappointment is generalized, there is a *chaos* in the gathering.

Morality

Let us speak of *eroticism* wherever desire has an object. Here, the objects are many, flexible, or, better still, *passing*, caught up in a movement of appearance / disappearance: they are fragments of knowledge, dreams of method, snatches of sentences; they are the inflection of a voice, the look of a garment, in short whatever forms the *finery* of a community. This disperses, circulates. Similar perhaps to the mere scent of (say) marijuana, this minor erethism relaxes, releases knowledge, relieves it of its burden of utterances; makes it, precisely, a *speech-act* and functions as the textual guarantee of our work.

All of which is said only because it is usually never said. We start from so far back that it appears incongruous for a site of teaching to have as its function the *consideration* of the bodies represented here; nothing more transgressive than to insist on reading the *corporeal expression* of the group. Put the body back where it has been taken from, and a whole *slippage* of civilization may be perceived: "I consider Greek morality [*might we not say today: Eastern morality?*] as the highest that has ever existed; what proves this to me is that it has taken *corporeal* expression to its zenith. But the morality I am thinking of is the effective morality of the people, not that of the philosophers. With Socrates begins *the decline of morality* . . ." Hatred of all Socratism.

Conversation

Writing supervenes when a certain (contradictory) effect is produced: when the text is both an irrational expenditure and an inflexible reserve—as if, at the extreme term of loss, there still remained, inexhaustibly, something held back with regard to the text to come.

Perhaps Mallarmé suggested such a thing when he proposed that the Book be analogous to a *conversation*. For in conversation there is also a reserve, and this reserve is the body. The body is always the future of what is said "*entre nous*." A few tenths—

the beginning of a dislocation—separate discourse from the body: precisely those three-tenths whose fall defines style, according to the actor Zeami (Japan, fourteenth century): "Move your mind to the ten-tenths, move your body to the seven-tenths."

Giddiness

The etymology of *giddiness* is uncertain, but it seems to derive from the presence of the *god* in wine. We should not be surprised, then, if the seminar is somewhat "giddy," too: displaced beyond meaning, beyond the Law, abandoned to a certain minor euphoria, ideas being generated as though by chance, indirectly, from a flexible listening, from a sort of *swing* of the attention (they want to "speak up," but it is "listening up" which intoxicates, displaces, subverts; it is in listening that the Law's defect is to be found).

In the seminar, there is nothing to represent, to imitate; "grades," massive instrument of record, are out of place here; what is recorded, at an unpredictable rhythm, is only whatever traverses our listening, what is generated by a "giddy" listening. "Grades" are detached from knowledge as a model (a thing to copy); what is recorded is writing, not memory; grades are in production, not in representation (*showing the grade*).

Practices

Let us imagine—or remember—three educational practices.

The first is *teaching*. A (previous) knowledge is transmitted by oral or written discourse, swathed in the flux of statements (books, manuals, lectures).

The second is *apprenticeship*. The "master" (no connotation of authority: instead, the reference is Oriental) works *for himself* in the apprentice's presence; he does not speak, or at least he sustains no discourse; his remarks are purely deictic: "Here," he says, "I do *this* in order to avoid *that* . . ." A proficiency is transmitted in silence, a spectacle is put on (that of *praxis*), to which the apprentice, taking the stage, is gradually introduced.

The third is *mothering*. When the child learns to walk, the mother neither speaks nor demonstrates; she does not teach walking, she does not represent it (she does not walk before the child): she supports, encourages, calls (steps back and calls); she incites and surrounds: the child demands the mother and the mother desires the child's walking . . .

In the seminar (and this is its definition), all teaching is foreclosed: no knowledge is transmitted (but a knowledge can be created), no discourse is sustained (but a text is sought): teaching is *disappointed*. Either someone works, seeks, produces, gathers, writes in the others' presence; or else all incite each other, call to each other, put into circulation the object to be produced, the procedure to compose, which thus passes from hand to hand, suspended from the thread of desire like the ring in round games.

The chain

At either extremity of the metaphor, two images of the chain: one, abhorred, suggests the assembly line; the other, voluptuous, refers to the Sadean figure, the ring of pleasure. In the alienated chain, *objects are transformed* (an automobile motor), *subjects repeated*: the subject's repetition is the price of the merchandise produced. In the chain of gratification, of knowledge, the object is indifferent, but the subjects "pass."

Such would be, more or less, the movement of the seminar: to pass from one chain to the other. Along the first (classical, institutional) chain, knowledge is constituted, increased, assumes the form of a specialty, i.e., of merchandise, while the subjects persist, each in his place (in the place of his origin, of his capacity, of his labor); but along the other chain, the object (the theme, the question), being indirect or insignificant or abandoned, in any case severed from knowledge, is the stake of no pursuit, of no market: non-functional, perverse, it is never anything but *tossed out, thrown overboard, lost*; during its gradual dispersion, the subjects make desires circulate (in the same way, in round games, the object is to pass the ring, but the goal is to touch each other's hands).

The space of the seminar has its rules (a game always does) but is not regulated; no one in it is the "foreman" of the others, no one is there to supervise, keep accounts, amass; each member, in turn, can become the master of ceremonies; the only distinction is initial—there is only an initiating figure, whose role—it is only a gesture—is to put the ring into circulation. Then the metaphor of the round game ceases to apply; for henceforth it is no longer a chain we are concerned with but an order of ramifications, a tree of desires: an extended, broken chain which Freud has described: "The scenes . . . form, not simple strings as in a pearl necklace, but groups which ramify in the fashion of genealogical trees . . ."

Knowledge, death

In the seminar, what is involved are relations of knowledge and the body. When we say that knowledge must be shared, it is against death that this frontier is traced. *All for all*: let the seminar be that site where the demands of knowledge are geared down, where my body is not obliged each time to begin again the knowledge which has just died in another body (as a student, the only teacher I loved and admired was the Hellenist Paul Mazon; when he died, I never stopped regretting that so much knowledge of the Greek language would vanish with him, that another body should have to begin again the interminable trajectory of grammar, starting from the conjugation of *deiknumi*). Knowledge, like delight, dies with each body. Whence the vital idea of a knowledge which circulates, which "mounts up" through different bodies, outside of books; *learn this for me, I'll learn that for you*: economy of the *turn*, of requital, illustrated by Sade in the order of pleasure ("Now the victim of a particular moment, my lovely angel, and at the next moment my persecutrix . . .")

How to change hands?

When the "master" shows (or demonstrates) something, he cannot help manifesting a certain superiority (magister: one who is above). This superiority can derive from a status (that of "professor"), from a technical proficiency (for instance, that of a piano teacher), or from an exceptional mastery of the body (in the case of the guru). In any case, the occasion of superiority turns into a relation of superiority. How to stop (deflect) this movement? How to elude mastery?

This question depends on another: What is, in fact, my place in our seminar? Teacher? Technician? Guru? I am none of these. Yet (to deny it would be pure demagoguery) something, which I cannot control (and which is therefore anterior), establishes me as different. Or rather I am the one whose role is the first to *become original* (supposing, as has been said, that in the seminar, a space of differences, each relation tends toward originality). My difference comes from this (and from nothing else): *I have written.* Hence I have some chance of being situated in the field of gratification, not in that of authority.

However, the Law resists, mastery continues to weigh upon me, difference risks being perceived by fits and starts as vaguely repressive: I am the one who talks *more* than the others, I am the one who contains, measures, or retards the irrepressible rise of speech. The personal effort to *change hands* (in this case, speech) cannot overcome the structural situation which here establishes a plus-value of discourse and there, consequently, a ban on gratification. Each time I want to hand the seminar over to the others, it comes back to me: I cannot evade a kind of "presidence," under whose gaze speech is blocked, hampered, embarrassed . . . Therefore, let us risk more: let us write in the present, let us produce in the others' presence and sometimes with them a book *in process*; let us show ourselves *in the speech-act.*

The man of statements

The Father (let us continue to speculate a little upon this principle of intelligibility) is the Speaker: he who sustains discourse(s) outside of *praxis,* severed from all production; the Father is the Man of statements. Hence, nothing is more transgressive than to surprise the Father in the speech-act; this is to surprise him in intoxication, in gratification, in erection: an intolerable (perhaps *sacred,* in the sense Bataille gave this word) spectacle, which one of the sons attempts to conceal—for otherwise Noah would lose his paternity.

The one who shows, the one who states, the one who shows the statement, is no longer the Father.

To teach

To teach *what occurs only once*—what a contradiction in terms! Is not to teach, invariably, to repeat?

Yet this is what old Michelet believed he had done: "I have always been careful to teach only what I did not know . . . I have transmitted these things as they were then, in my passion—new, lively, blazing (and delightful for me), under love's first spell."

Guelf / Ghibelline

This same Michelet opposed Guelf to Ghibelline. The Guelf is the man of the Law, the man of the Code, the Legist, the Scribe, the Jacobin, the Frenchman (shall we add the Intellectual?). The Ghibelline is the man of the feudal link, of the oath sworn in blood, the man of affective devotion, the German (and also Dante). If we could extend this great symbolics to such minor phenomena, we might say that the seminar has a Ghibelline orientation, not a Guelf one—implying a superiority of body over law, of contract over code, of text over writing, of speech-act [*énonciation*] over statement [*énoncé*].

Or rather: we must get round this paradigm which Michelet experienced directly—we must rephrase it; we no longer set the dry intelligence in opposition to the warm heart; but we employ the formidable machinery of science, of method, of criticism, in order to express *gently*, *occasionally*, and *somewhere* (these intermittences being the seminar's very justification) what we might call, in antiquated style, the motions of desire. Or again: just as, for Brecht, Reason is never anything but the sum total of reasonable people, for us, seminary people, *research* is never anything but the sum total of people who, in fact, *search* (for themselves?) . . .

Hanging gardens

In the image of the hanging gardens (where in fact does this myth, this image come from?), it is suspension itself which attracts and pleases. A collectivity at peace in a world at war, our seminar is a suspended site; it is held each week, after a fashion, sustained by the world that surrounds it, but also resisting it, gently assuming the immorality of a fissure within the totality which presses in on all sides (rather say: the seminar has its own morality). Such a notion would be scarcely tolerable if one did not grant oneself a momentary right to the non-communication of behavior, of reasons, of responsibilities. In short, in its way, the seminar says *no* to the totality; it achieves, one might say, a *partial utopia* (whence the insistent reference to Fourier).

Yet this suspension is itself historical; it intervenes in a certain apocalypse of culture. The so-called human sciences no longer have much real relation to social *praxis*—except to be identified with and swallowed up by it (as in the case of sociology); and since culture, in its entirety, is no longer sustained by a humanist ideology (or is increasingly reluctant to sustain it), it returns to our lives only as comedy, farce, masquerade: culture is acceptable, one might say, only *in the second degree*—no longer as a direct value but as an inverted one: kitsch, plagiarism, game, pleasure, shimmer of a parody-language *in which we believe and do not believe* (the characteristic of farce), a fragment of pastiche; we are condemned to the anthology, short of rehearsing a moral philosophy of totality.

To the seminar

To the seminar: this expression must be understood as a locative, as an encomium (like the one the poet von Schober and the composer Schubert addressed "*An die Musik*"), and as a dedication.

L'Arc, 1974

The Indictment Periodically Lodged . . .

The indictment periodically lodged against *intellectuals* (since the Dreyfus Affair, which saw, I believe, the birth of the word and of the notion) is an indictment of magic: the intellectual is treated as a witch doctor might be by a tribe of dealers, businessmen, and jurists: he is the subject who upsets ideological interests. Anti-intellectualism is a historical myth, linked no doubt to the rise of the petite-bourgeoisie. Not long ago, Poujade gave this myth its crudest form ("the fish rots from the head down"). Such an indictment can periodically excite the gallery, like any witch trials; yet its *political* danger must not be overlooked: it is quite simply fascism, whose first objective always and everywhere is to liquidate the intellectual class.

The intellectual's tasks are defined by these very resistances, the site from which they emanate; Brecht formulated them on several occasions: to decompose bourgeois (and petit-bourgeois) ideology, to study the forces which change the world and advance theory. These formulas must of course include many practices of writing and language (since the intellectual is assumed as a being of language, and since language specifically jeopardizes the assurance of a world which arrogantly sets "realities" against "words," as if language were merely the futile decor of humanity's more substantial interests).

The intellectual's historical situation is anything but comfortable, not because of the absurd indictments lodged against him, but because it is a dialectical situation: the intellectual's function is to criticize bourgeois language within the bourgeoisie's very regnum; he must be both an analyst and a utopian, must represent both the world's difficulties and its mad desires: he seeks to be a philosophical and historical contemporary of the present: what would a society be worth—what would become of such a society?—which gave up seeing itself in perspective? And how to be seen except by being spoken?

Le Monde, 1974

Leaving the Movie Theater

There is something to confess: your speaker likes to *leave* a movie theater. Back out on the more or less empty, more or less brightly lit sidewalk (it is invariably at night, and during the week, that he *goes*), and heading uncertainly for some café or other, he walks in silence (he doesn't like discussing the film he's just seen), a little dazed, wrapped up in himself, feeling the cold—he's *sleepy*, that's what he's thinking, his body has become something *sopitive*, soft, limp, and he feels a little disjointed, even (for a moral organization, relief comes only from this quarter) irresponsible. In other words, obviously, he's coming out of hypnosis. And hypnosis (an old psychoanalytic device—one that psychoanalysis nowadays seems to treat quite condescendingly) means only one thing to him: the most venerable of powers: healing. And he thinks of music: isn't there such a thing as hypnotic music? The castrato Farinelli, whose *messa di voce* was "as incredible for its duration as for its emission," relieved the morbid melancholy of Philip V of Spain by singing him the same aria every night for fourteen years.

This is often how he leaves a movie theater. How does he go in? Except for the—increasingly frequent—case of a specific cultural quest (a selected, sought-for, *desired* film, object of a veritable preliminary alert), he goes to movies as a response to idleness, leisure, free time. It's as if, even before he went into the theater, the classic conditions of hypnosis were in force: vacancy, want of occupation, lethargy; it's not in front of the film and because of the film that he *dreams off*—it's without knowing it, even before he becomes a spectator. There is a "cinema situation," and this situation is pre-hypnotic. According to a true metonymy, the darkness of the theater is prefigured by the "twilight reverie" (a prerequisite for hypnosis, according to Breuer-Freud) which precedes it and leads him from street to street, from poster to poster, finally burying himself in a dim, anonymous, indifferent cube where that festival of affects known as a film will be presented.

What does the "darkness" of the cinema mean? (Whenever I hear the word *cinema,* I can't help thinking *hall,* rather than *film.*) Not only is the dark the very substance of reverie (in the pre-hypnoid meaning of the term); it is also the "color" of a diffused eroticism; by its human condensation, by its absence of worldliness (contrary to the cultural *appearance* that has to be put in at any "legitimate theater"), by the relaxation of postures (how many members of the cinema audience slide down into their seats as if into a bed, coats or feet thrown over the row in front!), the movie house (ordinary model) is a site of availability (even more than cruising), the inoccupation of bodies, which best defines modern eroticism—not that of advertising or strip-tease, but that of the big city. It is in this urban dark that the body's freedom is generated; this invisible work of possible affects emerges from a veritable cinematographic cocoon; the movie spectator could easily appropriate the silkworm's motto: *Inclusum labor illustrat*; it is because I am enclosed that I work and glow with all my desire.

In this darkness of the cinema (anonymous, populated, numerous—oh, the boredom, the frustration of so-called private showings!) lies the very fascination of the film (any film). Think of the contrary experience: on television, where films are also shown, no fascination; here darkness is erased, anonymity repressed; space is familiar, articulated (by furniture, known objects), tamed: the eroticism—no, to put it better, to get across the particular kind of lightness, of unfulfillment we mean: the *eroticization* of the place is foreclosed: television *doomed* us to the Family, whose household instrument it has become—what the hearth used to be, flanked by its communal kettle.

* * *

In that opaque cube, one light: the film, the screen? Yes, of course. But also (especially?), visible and unperceived, that dancing cone which pierces the darkness like a laser beam. This beam is minted, according to the rotation of its particles, into changing figures; we turn our face toward the *currency* of a gleaming vibration whose imperious jet brushes our skull, glancing off someone's hair, someone's face. As in the old hypnotic experiments, we are fascinated—without seeing it head-on—by this shining site, motionless and dancing.

It's exactly as if a long stem of light had outlined a keyhole, and then we all peered, flabbergasted, through that hole. And nothing in this ecstasy is provided by sound, music, words? Usually—in current productions—the audio protocol can produce no *fascinated* listening; conceived to reinforce the *lifelikeness* of the anecdote, sound is merely a supplementary instrument of representation; it is meant to integrate itself unobtrusively into the object shown, it is in no way detached from this object; yet it would take very little in order to separate this sound track: one displaced or magnified sound, the grain of a voice milled in our eardrums, and the fascination begins again; for it never comes except from artifice, or better still: from the *artifact*—like the dancing beam of the projector—which comes from overhead or to the side, blurring the scene shown by the screen *yet without distorting its image* (its *gestalt*, its meaning).

For such is the narrow range—at least for me—in which can function the fascination of film, the cinematographic hypnosis: I must be in the story (there must be verisimilitude), but I must also be *elsewhere*: a slightly disengaged image-repertoire, that is what I must have—like a scrupulous, conscientious, organized, in a word *difficult* fetishist, that is what I require of the film and of the situation in which I go looking for it.

The film image (including the sound) is what? A *lure*. I am confined with the image as if I were held in that famous dual relation which establishes the image-repertoire. The image is there, in front of me, for me: coalescent (its signified and its signifier melted together), analogical, total, pregnant; it is a perfect lure: I fling myself upon it like an animal upon the scrap of "lifelike" rag held out to him; and, of course, it sustains in me the misreading attached to Ego and to image-repertoire. In the movie theater, however far away I am sitting, I press my nose against the screen's mirror, against that "other" image-repertoire with which I narcissistically identify myself (it is said that the spectators who choose to sit as close to the screen as possible are children and movie buffs); the image captivates me, captures me: I am *glued* to the representation, and it is this glue which established the *naturalness* (the pseudo-nature) of the filmed scene (a glue prepared with all the ingredients of "technique"); the Real knows only distances, the Symbolic knows only masks; the image alone (the image-repertoire) is *close*, only the image is "*true*" (can produce the resonance of truth). Actually, has not the image, statutorily, all the characteristics of the *ideological*? The historical subject, like the cinema spectator I am imagining, is also *glued* to ideological discourse: he experiences its coalescence, its analogical security, its naturalness, its "truth": it is a lure (*our* lure, for who escapes it?); the Ideological would actually be the image-repertoire of a period of history, the Cinema of a society; like the film which lures its clientele, it even has its photograms; is not the stereotype a fixed image, a quotation to which our language is glued? And in the commonplace have we not a dual relation: narcissistic and maternal?

How to come unglued from the mirror? I'll risk a pun to answer: by *taking off* (in the aeronautical and narcotic sense of the term). Of course, it is still possible to conceive of an art which will break the dual circle, the fascination of film, and loosen the glue, the hypnosis of the lifelike (of the analogical), by some recourse to the spectator's critical vision (or listening); is this not what the Brechtian alienation-effect involves? Many things can help us to "come out of" (imaginary and/or ideological) hypnosis: the very methods of an epic art, the spectator's culture or his ideological vigilance; contrary to classical hysteria, the image-repertoire vanishes once one observes that it exists. But there is another way of going to the movies (besides being armed by the discourse of counter-ideology); by letting oneself be fascinated *twice over*, by the image and by its surroundings—as if I had two bodies at the same time: a narcissistic body which gazes, lost, into the engulfing mirror, and a perverse body, ready to fetishize not the image but precisely what exceeds it: the texture of the sound, the hall, the darkness, the obscure mass of the other bodies, the rays of light, entering the theater, leaving the hall; in short, in order to distance, in order to "take off," I complicate a "relation" by a "situation." What I use to distance myself from the image—that, ultimately, is what fascinates me: I am hypnotized by a distance; and this distance is not critical (intellectual); it is, one might say, an amorous distance: would there be, in the cinema itself (and taking the word at its etymological suggestion) a possible bliss of *discretion*?

Communications, 1975

The Image

It so happens that this text, prepared in haste a few days ago, will seem to *copy* what has been said subsequently and what you may recognize in passing. It is a review of persistent themes, put in a certain perspective: the perspective of my reality insofar as it is unreal.

At the origin of everything, Fear. (Of what? Of blows, of humiliations?) Parody of the *Cogito* as the fictive moment when, everything having been "razed," this *tabula rasa* will be reoccupied: "I'm afraid, therefore I'm alive." An observation: According to today's *mores* (we need an ethology of intellectuals), one never speaks of fear: it is foreclosed from discourse, and even from writing (could there be a writing of fear?). Posited at the origin, it has a value as *method*; from it leads an initiatic path.

In Greek, *Mache* means: combat, battle—single combat, duel, struggle in a contest. "Ludism" of the conflict, of the joust: I loathe this. The French seem to like it: rugby, "face to face," round tables, bets, always stupid, etc. There used to be a more penetrating meaning: "contradiction in terms"; i.e., logical trap, double bind, origin of psychoses. The logical antonym of *Mache* is *Acolouthia*, natural succession, consequence, exclusive of conflict; this word also has another meaning, to which we shall return.

Language is the field of *Mache*: *pugna verborum*. There is a whole dossier to be collected—a book to be written: that of the governed contestations of language; they are always regulated: in language, nothing is ever wild, primitive, everything is coded, even and especially trials of strength: Sophistics, *Disputatio*, *Hain-*

Tenys, political confrontations, today's intellectual debates. The model—or the assumption—for all this is the "scene," in the domestic sense of the term.

In the arena of language, constructed like a football field, there are two extreme sites, two goals that can never be avoided: Stupidity at one end, the Unreadable at the other. These are two "jewels": untarnishable transparency of Stupidity; unbreakable opacity of the Unreadable.

Stupidity is not linked to error. Always triumphant (impossible to overcome), it derives its victory from an enigmatic power: it is *Dasein* in all its naked splendor. Whence a terror and a fascination, that of the corpse. (Corpse of what? Perhaps of truth: truth as dead.) Stupidity does not suffer (Bouvard and Pécuchet: more intelligent, they will suffer more). Hence, it *is there*, obtuse as Death. Exorcism can only be a formal operation, which confronts it *en bloc*, from outside: "Stupidity is not my strong point" (M. Teste). This remark is sufficent *for the first encounter*. But there is an infinite series of remarks: "it" becomes stupid all over again.

This mechanism of different "times," in relation to language, is important. Consider the "complete" systems (Marxism, Psychoanalysis), *initially* they have an (effective) function of counter-Stupidity: to pass through them is to educate oneself; those who entirely reject one or the other (those who say no, on account of temperament, blindness, stubbornness, to Marxism, to psychoanalysis) nurse, in their den of rejection, a kind of stupidity, of grim opacity. But subsequently these systems themselves become stupid. Once they "take," there is stupidity. That is why it is inescapable. One feels like going elsewhere: *Ciao! No, thanks!*

A certain text is said to be "unreadable." I have an intense relation to unreadability: I suffer when a text seems unreadable to me, and I have often been accused of being unreadable. Here I am back at the same panic that Stupidity inspires: Is it me? Is it the other? Is it the other who is unreadable (or stupid)? Am

I the one who is limited, inept, am I the one who doesn't understand?

Confronted with a text I cannot read, I am, literally, "bewildered"; a vertigo occurs, a disturbance of the semicircular canals: all the "otoliths" fall on just one side; in my hearing (my reading), the signifying mass of the text collapses, is no longer ventilated, balanced by a cultural action.

The status of "unreadability" is "scientifically" (linguistically) inapprehensible, unless we can refer to certain norms, but these norms are variable and vague. Which inexorably brings us back to a *situation of language (language in use)*; linguistics is well aware that it must now deal with this, otherwise it will perish; but this means dealing with the whole surface of the world, of the subject. Unreadability is a kind of Trojan horse in the fortress of the human sciences.

Yet little by little I recognize in myself a growing desire for readability. I want the texts I receive to be "readable," I want the texts I write to be "readable," too. How? By work on the Sentence, on Syntax; I accept the "thetic" (linked to the Sentence by Julia Kristeva, apropos of the *Olophrase*), or else I fake it by means other than syntax. A "well-made" sentence (according to a classical mode) is clear; it can *tend* toward a certain obscurity by a certain use of *ellipsis*: ellipses must be restrained; metaphors, too; a continuously metaphorical writing exhausts me.

A preposterous notion occurs to me (preposterous by dint of humanism): "We shall never be able to say how much love (for the other, the reader) there is in *work on the sentence*." Charity of the Thetic, Agape of the syntax? In negative theology, *Agape* is steeped in *Eros*; hence, eroticism of the "readable" Sentence?

I return to the intimidations of language—to language as Combat, as *Mache*. A metaphor occurs to me: that of the *leech*. I am thinking of complete, systematic languages, the language of the subjects who have a faith, a certainty, a conviction, and for me this is a permanent enigma: How can a body *stick* to an idea—or an idea to a body? There are leech-languages, whose enigma is doubled when a language-system of demystification, of criticism, which in principle aims at *de-leeching* language, itself becomes a "stickiness" by which the militant subject becomes the (happy) parasite of a specific type of discourse.

I have several times suggested (actually, I should do it myself) making a list, a code of "figures of system"; analogous to "figures of rhetoric," these would be turns of thought, "arguments," if you like, which would have the same function, from one system to the next (thus, we would be dealing with a "form"): to assure the system in advance as to the *answer* one could make to its propositions; in other words, to integrate into its own code, into its own language, the resistances to that code, to that language: *to explain* these resistances, according to one's own system of explanation; for example, when François Wahl tells us that Psychoanalysis is today the only reservoir of Metaphor (thereby distinguished from today's general decadence), he produces, it seems to me, a figure of system: Psychoanalysis claims that it alone honors a function which it alone has postulated and described; in the same way, more crudely, when Psychoanalysis makes the venality of the psychoanalytic act into a procedure which issues not from a mercantile economy but from obligations immanent to cure; or again, when Marxism—at least, its vulgate—"reduces" all opposition to Marxism to a class dispute; or finally—to take an instance from Christianity, a language system once "complete"—when Pascal drapes in Christian discourse the very resistance to that discourse ("You would not seek me, if you had not already found me").

These figures of system have great power (that is their interest) and it is difficult to escape them—since we do not seek to contradict one system in the name of another, but only to "suspend," to escape the will-to-domination which such languages imply. How to endure, limit, postpone the powers of language? How to escape the "fanaticisms" (the "racisms") of language?

To an old question, no answer that is still new, it seems to me. History has produced no way of *skipping* Discourse: where the Revolution has occurred, it has not been able to "change language," The rejection of language's intimidations therefore consists, modestly, in *drifting* within familiar words (without too much concern if they are outdated); for example: Tolerance, Democracy, Contract.

Tolerance: we must rework the notion, define a new Tolerance, since there is a new Intolerance (it would be instructive to make a map of today's world in terms of these new Intolerances). *Democracy*: a word saturated with disillusions, to the point of disgust, sometimes of violence; the lures of bourgeois democracy have been abundantly demystified. Perhaps we must, nonetheless, not throw out the baby with the bathwater. I'd like a theory of History's "layers of experience": the bourgeoisie is like the earth, made up of several layers, some good, others bad; we must sort out—establish a differential geology. Then, too, we can have a *difficult* notion of Democracy: can define it, not as the realization of a stifling "gregarity," but as "what should produce aristocratic souls" (says one commentator on Spinoza). *Contract*: this word has gathered a whole socio-political dossier, and a psychoanalytic one as well; let us leave it aside, defining Contract *a minimo*, as a casual apparatus which keeps the other (and therefore, conversely, myself) from imprisoning me in the pincers of a double term: to be either a swine (if I must answer his blows, his will-to-power) or else a saint (if I must answer his generosity); actually, the Contract has this virtue: to dispense anyone from being a Devil or a Hero (Brecht: "Woe to the country which needs heroes").

All this implies that in my eyes there is a cowardice, a triviality in conflicts, and even, I often feel, a kind of "Gallic asininity" in these wills-to-conflict, the puerile craving to "start something." This impression of mediocrity takes the form of an aphorism: Who wants to be violent has a paltry notion of violence. For me, the real violence is that of "Everything passes," of ruin, of oblivion. The violence of effacement is stronger than that of fracture; death is violent; not so much the death one inflicts, that one wants to inflict, as the death that *comes all by itself* (a violence which perhaps cannot be understood before middle age).

Combat of language-systems: metaphor of the leech. Now let us return to the combat of Images ("image": what I believe the other thinks of me); how does an image of myself "take," to the point where I am wounded by it? Here is a new metaphor: "In the skillet, the oil spreads, smooth, flat, matte (barely any smoke): a kind of *materia prima*. Drop a slice of potato into it: it is like a morsel tossed to wild beasts only half asleep, waiting. They all fling themselves upon it, attack it noisily: a voracious banquet. The slice of potato is surrounded—not destroyed, but hardened, caramelized, made crisp; it becomes an object: a French-fried potato." This is how, on any object, a good language-system *functions*, attacks, surrounds, sizzles, hardens, and browns. All languages are micro-systems of ebullition, of frying. That is the stake of linguistic *Mache*. The language (of others) transforms me into an image, as the raw slice of potato is transformed into a *pomme frite*.

Here is how I become an image (a "French fried") under the offensive of a quite minor language-system: the dandiacal and "impertinent" Parisianism apropos of *A Lover's Discourse*: "Delicious essayist, favorite of intelligent adolescents, collector of avant-gardes, Roland Barthes offers us memories which are anything but, in the tone of the most brilliant salon conversation, but with a touch of narrow pedantry apropos of 'ravishment.' Recognizable, among others: Nietzsche, Freud, Flaubert." Nothing for it, I must pass through the Image; the image is a kind of social military service: I cannot get myself exempted from it; I cannot get myself discharged, cannot desert, etc. I see man sick of Images, man sick of his Image. To know one's Image becomes a desperate, exhausting search (one never achieves it), analogous to the insistence of a man who wants to know if he's entitled to be jealous ("Misery of my life," Golaud says, vainly interrogating the dying Mélisande).

In order to be immortal (for the body to be immortal, not

the soul, with which it was unconcerned), the Tao recommended Abstinence from Cereals. I crave, I long for Abstinence from Images, for every Image is bad. The "good" Image is surreptitiously bad, poisoned: either false, or debatable, or incredible, or unstable, or reversible (even compliments wound me). For instance: each "honor" awarded institutes an image; hence, I should refuse it; but in doing so, I institute another, that of "the kind of person who refuses honors" (a moralistic, Stoical image). Hence, the point is not to destroy Images but to unstick them, to distance them. In Taoist "Meditation," there is an initiatic operation, *Wang-Ming*: to lose consciousness of the Name (which I call: the Image). Abstinence from the Name is the only real problem of this Colloquium. I conceive *Wang-Ming* in the form of two possible paths, to which I give Greek names: *Epoche*, Suspension, *Acolouthia*, Retinue.

Epoche, a skeptic notion, is the suspension of judgment. I say: suspension of Images. Suspension is not negation. This difference was well known to negative theology: "If the ineffable is what cannot be said, it ceases to be ineffable by the fact that something is said of it by calling it so." If I reject the Image, I produce the image of the kind of person who rejects Images: St. Augustine recommended avoiding this aporrhoea by silence. One must obtain from oneself a silence of the Images. This does not mean that such a silence would be a superior indifference, serenity, mastery: *Epoche*, suspension, remains a *pathos*: I would continue to be *moved* (by Images) but no longer *tormented*.

Here is a spontaneous form of that *Epoche*: I feel incapable of turning against "ideas." Doubtless, I can be irritated, annoyed—or perhaps even frightened—by "stupid" ideas; "stupid" ideas form a *doxa*, a public opinion, not a doctrine. In the intelligentsia, by definition, there are no "stupid" ideas; the intellectual makes a profession of intelligence (it is his conduct which may sometimes be unintelligent). Such equanimity with regard to "ideas" is offset by an intense sensibility, positive or negative, to people, to personalities: Michelet used to oppose the Guelf spirit (passion for the Law, for the Code, for the Idea, the world of legists, Scribes, Jesuits, Jacobins—I should add: of Militants) to the Ghibelline spirit, resulting from an attention to the body, to ties of blood based on a devotion of man for man, according to a Feudal pact. I feel myself to be more Ghibelline than Guelf.

Perhaps a way of thwarting the Image is to corrupt languages, vocabularies; the proof that one has succeeded is the indignation, the reprobation of purists, of specialists. I cite the Others, even as I distort them; I shift the meaning of words. For example, in the case of Semiology, which I helped constitute, I have been my own corrupter, I have gone over to the side of the Corrupters. It could be said that the field of this Corruption is aesthetics, literature: "catastrophe" is a technical term in mathematics, in the work of R. Thom; I can misuse "Catastrophe," which then becomes something "beautiful." History exists only because words are corrupted.

I have spoken of the combat of languages, of the Combat of Images (*Mache*). I have said that the main drift away from such combats was suspension: *Epoche*. There is another prospect of liberation: *Acolouthia*. In Greek, *Mache* designates combat in general, but also, in a technical sense that has to do with logic, means *a contradiction in terms* (the trap in which, through language, I attempt to catch the other); in this sense, *Mache* has an antonym, *Acolouthia*: the transcendence of contradiction (I interpret: the opening of the trap). Now, *Acolouthia* has another meaning: the retinue of friends who accompany me, guide me, to whom I entrust myself. I should like to designate by this word that rare field where ideas are steeped in affectivity, in which friends, by that retinue which accompanies your life, permit you to think, to write, to speak. These friends: I think for them, they think inside my head. In that *color* of intellectual work (or of writing), there is something Socratic: Socrates sustained the discourse of the Idea, but his *method*, the step-by-step of his discourse, was erotic; in order to speak, he required the guarantee of inspired love, the assent of a beloved whose responses marked the progression of reasoning. Socrates knew *Acolouthia*; but (and this I resist) he maintained in it the snare of contradictions, the arrogance of truth (so we are not surprised that he ultimately "sublimated"—rejected Alcibiades).

Colloquium at Cerisy-la-Salle, 1978

Deliberation

I've never kept a journal—or, rather, I've never known if I should keep one. Sometimes I begin, and then, right away, I leave off—and yet, later on, I begin again. The impulse is faint, intermittent, without seriousness, and of no doctrinal standing whatever. I guess I could diagnose this *diary disease*: an insoluble doubt as to the value of what one writes in it.

Such doubt is insidious: it functions by a kind of delayed action. Initially, when I write the (daily) entry, I experience a certain pleasure: this is simple, this is easy. Don't worry about finding *something to say*: the raw material is right here, right now; a kind of surface mine; all I have to do is bend over—I don't need to transform anything: the crude ore has its own value, etc. Then comes the second phase, very soon after the first (for instance, if I reread today what I wrote yesterday), and it makes a bad impression: the text doesn't hold up, like some sort of delicate foodstuff which "turns," spoils, becomes unappetizing from one day to the next; I note with discouragement the artifice of "sincerity," the artistic mediocrity of the "spontaneous"; worse still: I am disgusted and irritated to find a "pose" I certainly hadn't intended: in a journal situation, and precisely because it doesn't "work"—doesn't get transformed by the action of work—*I* is a *poseur*: a matter of effect, not of intention, the whole difficulty of literature is here. Very soon, continuing my reperusal, I get tired of these verbless sentences ("Sleepless night. and the third in a row," etc.) or sentences whose verb is carelessly condensed ("Passed two girls in the Place St.-S.")—and try as I will to reestablish the propriety of a complete form ("I passed . . ." "I spent a sleepless night"), the matrix of any journal, i.e., the reduction of the verb, persists in my ear and exasperates me like a refrain. In a third phase, if I reread my journal pages several months, several years after having written them, though my doubt hasn't dissipated, I experience a certain pleasure in rediscovering, thanks to these lines, the events they relate, and even more, the inflections (of light, of atmosphere, of mood) they bring back. In short, at this point, no literary interest (save for problems of formulation, i.e., of phrasing), but a kind of narcissistic attachment (faintly narcissistic—let's not exaggerate) to *my* doings (whose recall is inevitably ambiguous, since to remember is also to acknowledge and to lose once again what will not recur). But still, does this final indulgence, achieved after having traversed a phase of rejection, justify (systematically) keeping a journal? Is it *worth the trouble*?

I am not attempting any kind of analysis of the "Journal" genre (there are books on the subject), but only a personal deliberation, intended to afford a practical decision: Should I keep a journal *with a view to publication*? Can I make the journal into a "work"? Hence, I refer only to the functions which immediately come to mind. For instance, Kafka kept a diary in order to "extirpate his anxiety," or if you prefer, "to find salvation." This motive would not be a natural one for me, or at least not a constant one. Nor would the aims traditionally attributed to the Intimate Journal; they no longer seem pertinent to me. They are all connected to the advantages and the prestige of "sincerity" (to express yourself, to explain yourself, to judge yourself); but psychoanalysis, the Sartrean critique of bad faith, and the Marxist critique of ideologies have made "confession" futile: sincerity is merely a second-degree image-repertoire. No, the journal's justification (as a work) can only be *literary* in the absolute, even if nostalgic, sense of the word. I discern here four motives.

The first is to present a text tinged with an individuality of writing, with a "style" (as we used to say), with an idiolect proper to the author (as we said more recently); let us call this motive: poetic. The second is to scatter like dust, from day to day, the traces of a period, mixing all dimensions and proportions, from important information to details of behavior: don't I take great pleasure, when I read Tolstoy's Journal, in discovering the life of a Russian nobleman in the nineteenth century? Let us call this motive: historical. The third is to constitute the author as an object of desire: if an author interests me, I may want to know the intimacy, the *small change* of his times, his tastes, his moods, his scruples; I may even go so far as to prefer his person to his work, eagerly snatching up his Journal and neglecting his books. Hence, I can attempt—making myself the author of the pleasure others have been able to afford me—I can attempt in my turn to seduce, by that swivel which shifts from writer to person, and vice versa; or, more seriously, I can attempt to prove that "I am worth more than what I write" (in my books): the writing in my journal then appears as a *plus-power* (Nietzsche: *Plus von Macht*), which it is supposed will compensate for the inadequacies of public writing; let us call this motive: utopian, since it is true that we are never done with the image-repertoire. The fourth motive is to constitute the Journal as a workshop of sentences: not of "fine phrases," but of correct ones, exact language: constantly to refine the exactitude of the speech-act (and not of the speech), according to an enthusiasm and an application, a fidelity of intention which greatly resembles passion: "Yea, my reins shall rejoice, when thy lips speak right things" (Proverbs 23:16). Let us call this motive: amorous (perhaps even: idolatrous—I idolize the Sentence).

For all my sorry impressions, then, the desire to keep a journal is conceivable. I can admit that it is possible, in the actual context of the Journal, to shift from what at first seemed to me improper in literature to a form which in fact rallies its qualities: individuation, spoor, seduction, fetishism of language. In recent years, I have made three attempts; the first and most serious one—because it occurred during my mother's last illness—is the longest, perhaps because it corresponded in some degree to the Kafkaesque goal of extirpating anxiety by writing; each of the other two concerned only one day: they are more experimental, though I can't reread them without a certain nostalgia for the day that has passed (I can give only one of these, the second one involving others besides myself).

1

U——, July 13, 1977

Mme ——, the new cleaning woman, has a diabetic grandson she takes care of, we are told, with devotion and expertise. Her view of this disease is confused: on the one hand, she does not admit that diabetes is hereditary (which would be a sign of inferior stock), and on the other, she insists that it is fatal, absolving any responsibility of origin. She posits disease as a social image, and this image is beset with pitfalls. The Mark certainly appears as a source of pride and of pain: what it was for Jacob-Israel, dislocated, disconnected by the Angel: delight and shame of being remarked.

Depression, fear, anxiety: I see the death of a loved one, I panic, etc. Such an imagination is the very opposite of faith. For constantly to imagine the inevitability of disaster is constantly to accept it: to utter it is to assert it (again, the fascism of language). By imagining death, I discourage the miracle. In Ordet *the madman did not speak, refused the garrulous and peremptory language of inwardness. Then what is this incapacity for faith? Perhaps a very human love? Love, then, excludes faith? And vice versa?*

Gide's old age and death (which I read about in Mme van Rysselberghe's Cahiers de la Petite Dame*) were surrounded by witnesses. But I do not know what has become of these witnesses: no doubt, in most cases, dead in their turn: there is a time when the witnesses themselves die without witnesses. Thus, History consists of tiny explosions of life, of deaths without relays. Our human impotence with regard to transition, to any science of degrees. Conversely, we can attribute to the classical God the capacity to see an infinity of degrees: "God" as the absolute Exponential.*

(Death, real death, is when the witness himself dies. Chateaubriand says of his grandmother and his great-aunt: "I may be the only man in the world who knows that such persons have existed": yes, but since he

has written this, and written it well, we know it too, insofar, at least, as we still read Chateaubriand.)

July 14, 1977

A little boy—nervous, excited, like any number of French kids, who so quickly pretend to be grown up—is dressed up as a musical-comedy grenadier (red and white); doubtless, he will march ahead of the band.

Why is Worry harder to bear here than in Paris? —This Village is a world so natural, so exempt from any extravagance, that the impulses of sensibility seem entirely out of place. I am excessive, hence excluded.

It seems to me I learn more about France during a walk through the village than in whole weeks in Paris. Perhaps an illusion? The realist illusion? The rural, village, provincial world constitutes the traditional raw material of realism. To be a writer meant, in the nineteenth century, to write from Paris about the provinces. The distance makes everything signify. In Paris, in the street, I am bombarded with information—not with signification.

July 15, 1977

At five in the afternoon, how calm the house is, here in the country. Flies. My legs ache a little, the way they did when I was a child and had what was called growing pains—or when I was getting the grippe. Everything is still, peaceful, asleep. And as always, the sharp awareness, the vivacity of my own "seediness" (a contradiction in terms).

X visits: in the next room, he talks endlessly. I don't dare close the door. What disturbs me is not the noise but the banality of the conversation (if at least he talked in some language unknown to me, and a musical one!). I'm always amazed, even flabbergasted, by the resistance of others: for me, the Other is the Indefatigable. Energy—and especially verbal energy—stupefies me: this is perhaps the only time (aside from violence) when I believe in madness.

July 16, 1977

Again, after overcast days, a fine morning: luster and subtlety of the atmosphere: a cool, luminous silk. This blank moment (no meaning) *produces the plenitude of an evidence: that it is worthwhile being alive. The morning errands (to the grocer, the baker, while the village is still almost deserted) are something I wouldn't miss for anything in the world.*

Mother feeling better today. She is sitting in the garden, wearing a big straw hat. As soon as she feels a little better, she is drawn by the house, filled with the desire to participate; she puts things away, turns off the furnace during the day (which I never do).

This afternoon, a sunny, windy day, the sun already setting, I burned garbage at the bottom of the garden. A complete course of physics to follow; armed with a long bamboo pole, I stir the heaps of paper, which slowly burn; it takes patience—who would have guessed how long paper can resist the fire? On the other hand, the emerald-green plastic bag (the garbage bag itself) burns very fast, leaving no trace*: it literally vanishes. This phenomenon might serve, on many an occasion, as a metaphor.*

Incredible incidents (read in the Sud-Ouest *or heard on the radio? I don't remember): in Egypt it has been decided to execute those Moslems who convert to another religion. In the U.S.S.R., a French agent was expelled because she gave a present of underwear to a Soviet friend. Compile a* contemporary *dictionary of intolerance (literature, in this case Voltaire, cannot be abandoned, so long as the evils subsist to which it bears witness).*

July 17, 1977

As if Sunday morning intensifies the good weather. Two heteroclite intensities reinforce each other.

I never mind doing the cooking. I like the operations *involved. I take pleasure in observing the changing forms of the food as they occur (colorations, thickenings, contractions, crystallizations, polarizations, etc.). There is something a little perverse about this observation. On the other hand, what I can't do, and what I always do badly, are proportions and schedules: I put in too much oil, afraid everything will burn; I leave things on* the fire too long, afraid they won't be cooked through. In short, I'm afraid because I don't know (how much, how long). Whence the security of a code (a kind of guaranteed knowledge): I'd rather cook rice than potatoes because I know it takes seventeen minutes. This figure delights me, insofar as it's precise (to the point of being preposterous); a round number would seem contrived, and just to be certain, I'd add to it.

July 18, 1977

Mother's birthday. All I can offer her is a rosebud from the garden; at least it's the only one, and the first one since we're here. Tonight, M. is coming for dinner and will do the cooking: soup and a pimento omelette; she brings champagne and almond cookies from Peyrehorade. Mme L. has sent flowers from her garden, delivered by one of her daughters.

Moods, in the strong, Schumannian sense: a broken series of contradictory impulses: waves of anxiety, imaginations of the worst, and unseasonable euphorias. This morning, at the core of Worry, a crystal of happiness: the weather (very fine, very light and dry), the music (Haydn), coffee, a cigar, a good pen, the household noises (the human subject as caprice: such discontinuity alarms, exhausts).

July 19, 1977

Early in the morning, coming back with the milk, I stop in the church to have a look around. It's been remodeled according to the prescribed New Look: now it resembles nothing so much as a Protestant establishment (only the wooden galleries indicate a Basque tradition); no image, the altar has become a simple table, no candle, of course. Too bad, isn't it?

Around six in the evening, I doze on my bed. The window is wide open, the gray day has lifted now. I experience a certain floating euphoria: everything is liquid, aerated, potable (I drink the air, the moment, the garden). And since I happen to be reading Suzuki, it seems to me that I'm quite close to the state Zen calls sabi; or again (since I'm also reading Blanchot), to the "fluid heaviness" he speaks of apropos of Proust.

* * *

July 21, 1977

Some bacon, onions, thyme, etc.: simmering, the smell is wonderful. Now this fragrance is not that of food as it will be served at table. There is an odor of what is eaten and an odor of what is prepared (observation for the "Science of Motley," or "diaphorology").

July 22, 1977

For some years, a unique project, apparently: to explore my own stupidity, or better still: to utter *it, to make it the object of my books. In this way I have already* uttered *my "egoist" stupidity and my "lover's" stupidity. There remains a third kind, which I'll someday have to get down on paper: political stupidity. What I think of events politically (and I never fail to think something), from day to day, is stupid. This is a stupidity which I should now* utter *in the third book of this little trilogy, a kind of* Political Diary. *It would take enormous courage, but maybe this would exorcise that mixture of boredom, fear, and indignation which the Politician (or rather Politics) constitutes for me.*

"I" is harder to write than to read.

Last night, at Casino, the Anglet supermarket, with E.M., we were fascinated by this Babylonian Temple of Merchandise. It really is the Golden Calf: piles of (cheap) "wealth," mustering of the species (classified by types), Noah's ark of things *(Swedish clogs to eggplants), predatory stacking of carts. We're suddenly convinced that people will buy anything (as I do myself): each cart, while parked in front of the cash register, is the shameless chariot of manias, impulses, perversions, and cravings: obvious, confronting a cart proudly passing before us, that there was no* need *to buy the cellophane-wrapped pizza ensconced there.*

I'd like to read (if such a thing exists) a History of Stores. What happened before Zola and Au Bonheur des dames?

August 5, 1977

Continuing War and Peace, *I have a violent emotion, reading the death of old Prince Bolkonsky, his last words of tenderness to his daughter*

("My darling, my friend"), the Princess's scruples about not disturbing him the night before, whereas he was calling to her; Maria's feeling of guilt because for a moment she wanted her father to die, anticipating that she would thereby gain her freedom. And all this, so much tenderness, so much poignance, in the midst of the crudest scuffles, the threatened arrival of the French, the necessity of leaving, etc.

Literature has an effect of truth much more violent for me than that of religion. By which I mean, quite simply, that literature is like *religion. And yet, in this week's* Quinzaine, *Lacassin declares peremptorily: "Literature no longer exists except in textbooks." Whereby I am dismissed, in the name of . . . comic strips.*

August 13, 1977

This morning, around eight, the weather was splendid. I had an impulse to try M's bicycle, to go to the baker's. I haven't ridden a bike since I was a kid. My body found this operation very odd, difficult, and I was afraid (of getting on, of getting off). I told all this to the baker—and as I left the shop, trying to get back on the bike, of course I fell off. Now by instinct I let myself fall excessively, *legs in the air, in the silliest posture imaginable. And then I understood that it was this silliness which saved me (from hurting myself too much): I* accompanied *my fall and thereby turned myself into a spectacle, I made myself ridiculous; but thereby, too, I diminished its effect.*

All of a sudden, it has become a matter of indifference to me whether or not I'm modern.

(. . . And like a blind man whose finger gropes along the text of life, here and there recognizing "what has already been said.")

2

Paris, April 25, 1979

Futile evening.

Yesterday, around seven in the evening, under a cold rain in a bad spring, I ran to catch the no. 58 bus. Oddly, there were only old people on the bus. One couple was talking very loudly about some History of the War (which war? you can't tell anymore): "No distance, no perspective," the man was saying admiringly, "only details." I got off at the Pont-Neuf. Since I was early, I lingered a little along the Quai de la Mégisserie. Workmen in blue smocks (I could smell how badly paid they were) were brutally stacking big cages on dollies where ducks and pigeons (all fowls are so stupid) were fluttering hysterically, sliding in heaps from one side to the other. The shops were closing. Through the door, I saw two puppies: one was teasing the other, which kept rebuffing it in a very human manner. Once again, I had a longing for a dog: I might have bought this one (a sort of fox terrier), which was irritated and showed it in a way that was indifferent and yet not haughty. There were also plants and pots of kitchen herbs for sale. I envisioned myself (both longingly and with horror) stocking up on the lot before going back to U., where I would be living for good, coming to Paris only for "business" and shopping. Then I walked down the deserted and sinister rue des Bourdonnais. A driver asked me where the BHV was: oddly enough, he seemed to know only the abbreviation, and had no idea where or even what the Hôtel de Ville was. At the (crumbling) Galerie de l'Impasse, I was disappointed: not by D.B.'s photographs (of windows and blue curtains, taken with a Polaroid camera), but by the chilly atmosphere of the opening: W. wasn't there (probably still in America), nor R. (I was forgetting: they've quarreled). D.S., beautiful and daunting, said to me: "Lovely, aren't they?" "Yes, very lovely" (but it's thin, there's not enough here, I added under my breath). All of which was pathetic enough. And since, as I've grown older, I have more and more courage to do what I like, after a second quick tour of the room (staring any longer wouldn't have done any more for me), I took French leave and indulged in a futile spree, from bus to bus and movie house to movie house. I was frozen, I was afraid I had caught bronchitis (I've thought of this several times). Finally I warmed up a little at the Flore, ordering some eggs and a glass of Bordeaux, though this was a very bad day: an insipid and arrogant audience: no face to be interested in or about which to fantasize or at least to speculate. The evening's pathetic failure has impelled me to begin, at last, the reformation of my life that's been in my mind for so long. Of which this first note is the trace.

(Rereading: this bit gave me a distinct pleasure, so vividly did it revive the sensations of that evening; but curiously, in reading it over, what I remembered best was what was not written, *the interstices of notation: for instance, the gray of the rue de Rivoli while I was waiting for the bus; no use trying to describe it now, anyway, or I'll lose it again instead of some other silenced sensation, and so on, as if resurrection always occurred* alongside *the thing expressed: role of the Phantom, of the Shadow.)*

However often I reread these two fragments, nothing tells me they are publishable; on the other hand, nothing tells me that they are not. Which raises a problem that is beyond me—the problem of "publishability"; not: "is it good or is it bad?" (a form every author gives to his question), but "is it publishable or isn't it?" This is not only a publisher's question. The doubt has shifted, slides from the text's quality to its image. I raise for myself the question of the text from the Other's point of view; the Other is not the public, here, or any particular public (that is the publisher's question); the Other, caught up in a dual and somehow personal relation, is *anyone who will read me.* In short, I imagine that my Journal pages are put in front of "whom I am looking at," or under the silence of "whom I am speaking to." —Is this not the situation of any text? —No. The text is anonymous, or at least produced by a kind of *nom de guerre,* that of the author. This is not at all true of the Journal (even if its "I" is a false name): the Journal is a "discourse" (a kind of *written record* according to a special code), not a text. The question I raise for myself: *"Should I keep a journal?"* is immediately supplied, in my mind, with a nasty answer: *"Who cares?"* or, more psychoanalytically: *"It's your problem."*

All I have left to do is analyze the reasons for my doubt. Why do I suspect, *from the point of view of the image,* Journal writing? I believe it is because this writing is stricken, in my eyes, with a kind of insidious disease, negative characteristics—deceptive and disappointing, as I shall try to say.

The Journal corresponds to no *mission.* Nor is this word

laughable. The works of literature, from Dante to Mallarmé, Proust, and Sartre, have always had, for those who wrote them, a kind of social, theological, mythic, aesthetic, moral end. The book, "architectural and premeditated," is supposed to reproduce an order of the world; it always implies, I believe, a monist philosophy. The Journal cannot achieve the status of the Book (of the Work); it is only an Album, to adopt Mallarmé's distinction (it is Gide's life which is a "work," not his Journal). The Album is a collection of leaflets not only interchangeable (even this would be nothing) but above all *infinitely suppressible*: rereading my Journal, I can cross out one entry after the next, to the complete annihilation of the Album, with the excuse that "I don't like this one": this is the method of Groucho and Chico Marx reading aloud and tearing up each clause of the contract meant to bind them. —But can't the Journal, in fact, be considered and practiced as that form which essentially expresses the inessentials of the world, the world as inessential? —For that, the Journal's subject would have to be the word, and not me; otherwise, what is uttered is a kind of egotism which constitutes a screen between the world and the writing; whatever I do, I become consistent, confronting the world which is not so. How to keep a Journal without egotism? That is precisely the question which keeps me from writing one (for I have had just about enough egotism).

Inessential, the Journal is unnecessary as well. I cannot invest in a Journal as I would in a unique and monumental work which would be dictated to me by an incontrovertible desire. The regular writing of the Journal, a function as daily as any other physiological one, no doubt implies a pleasure, a comfort, but not a passion. It is a minor mania of writing, whose necessity vanishes in the trajectory leading from the entry produced to the entry reread: "I haven't found that what I've written so far is particularly valuable, nor that it obviously deserves to be thrown away" (Kafka). Like any subject of perversion (I am told), subjected to the "yes, but . . ."—I know that my text is futile, but at the same time (by the same impulse) I cannot wrest myself from the belief that it exists.

Inessential, uncertain, the Journal is also inauthentic. I don't mean by this that someone who expresses himself in one is not sincere. I mean that its very form can only be borrowed from an antecedent and motionless Form (that, precisely, of the Intimate Journal), which cannot be subverted. Writing my Journal, I am, by status, doomed to simulation. A double simulation, in fact: for since every emotion is a copy of the same emotion one has read somewhere, to report a mood in the coded language of the Collection of Moods is to copy a copy: even if the text was "original," it would already be a copy; all the more so if it is familiar, worn, threadbare: "The writer, by his pains, those dragons he has fondled, or by a certain vivacity, must set himself up, in the text, as a witty histrion" (Mallarmé). What a paradox! By choosing the most "direct," the most "spontaneous" form of writing, I find myself to be the clumsiest of ham actors. (And why not? Are there not "historic" moments when one must be a ham actor? By practicing an antiquated form of literature to the bitter end, am I not saying that I love literature, that I love it in a harrowing fashion, at the very moment when it's dying? I love it, therefore I imitate it—but precisely: not without complexes.)

All of which says more or less the same thing: that the worst torment, when I try to keep a Journal, is the instability of my judgment. Instability? Rather, its inexorably descending curve. In the Journal, as Kafka pointed out, the absence of a notation's value is always recognized too late. How to transform what is written at white heat (and take pride in the fact) into a nice cold dish? It is this waste, this dwindling which constitute's the Journal's uneasiness. Again, Mallarmé (who, moreover, didn't keep one): "Or other verbiage become just that, provided it is exposed, persuasive, pensive, and true when one confides it in a whisper": as in that fairy tale, under the effect of a curse and an evil power, the flowers that fall from my lips are changed into toads. "When I say something, this thing immediately and definitively loses its importance. When I write it here, it also loses it, but sometimes gains another importance" (Kafka). The difficulty proper to the Journal is that this secondary importance, liberated by writing, is not certain: it is not certain that the Journal recuperates the word and gives it the resistance of a new metal. Of course, writing is indeed that strange activity (over which, hitherto, psychoanalysis has had little hold, understanding it with difficulty) which miraculously arrests the hemorrhaging of the image-repertoire, of which speech is the powerful and pathetic stream. But precisely: however "well written," is the Journal "writing"? It struggles, swells, and stiffens: am I as big as the text? Never! you aren't even close. Whence the depressive effect: acceptable when I write, disappointing when I reread.

At bottom, all these failures and weaknesses designate quite clearly a certain defect of the subject. This defect is existential. What the Journal posits is not the tragic question, the Madman's question: "Who am I?", but the comic question, the Bewildered Man's question: "Am I?" A comic—a comedian, that's what the Journal keeper is.

In other words, I never get away from myself. And if I never get away from myself, if I cannot manage to determine what the Journal is "worth," it is because its literary status slips through my fingers: on the one hand, I experience it, through its facility and its desuetude, as being nothing more than the Text's limbo, its unconstituted, unevolved, and immature form; but on the other hand, it is all the same a true scrap of that Text, for it includes its essential torment. This torment, I believe, consists in this: that literature is *without proofs*. By which it must be understood that it cannot prove not only *what* it says but even *that* it is worth the trouble of saying it. This harsh condition (Play and Despair, Kafka says) achieves its very paroxysm in the Journal. But also, at this point, everything turns around, for out of its impotence to prove, which excludes it from the serene heaven of Logic, the Text draws a *flexibility* which is in a sense its essence, which it possesses as something all its own. Kafka—whose Journal is perhaps the only one that can be read without irritation—expresses this double postulation of literature to perfection: Accuracy and Inanity: ". . . I was considering the hopes I had formed for life. The one which appeared the most important, or the most affecting, was the desire to acquire a way of seeing life (and, what was related, of being able, by writing, to convince others) in which life would keep its heavy movement of rise and fall, but would at the same time be recognized, and with a no less admirable clarity, as a nothing, a dream, a drifting state." Yes, that is just what the ideal Journal is: at once a rhythm (rise and fall, elasticity) and a trap (I cannot join my image): a writing, in short, which tells the truth of the trap and guarantees this truth by the most formal of operations, rhythm. On which we must doubtless conclude that I can rescue the Journal on the one condition that I labor it *to death*, to the end of an extreme exhaustion, like a *virtually* impossible Text: a labor at whose end it is indeed possible that the Journal thus kept no longer resembles a Journal at all.

Tel Quel, 1979